Working in Jamie's Kitchen

# Working in Jamie's Kitchen

## Salvation, Passion and Young Workers

Peter Kelly
and
Lyn Harrison

palgrave
macmillan

First published 2009 by
PALGRAVE MACMILLAN

Palgrave Macmillan in the UK is an imprint of Macmillan Publishers Limited, registered in England, company number 785998, of Houndmills, Basingstoke, Hampshire RG21 6XS.

Palgrave Macmillan in the US is a division of St Martin's Press LLC, 175 Fifth Avenue, New York, NY 10010.

Palgrave Macmillan is the global academic imprint of the above companies and has companies and representatives throughout the world.

Palgrave® and Macmillan® are registered trademarks in the United States, the United Kingdom, Europe and other countries.

ISBN 978–0–230–51554–3

This book is printed on paper suitable for recycling and made from fully managed and sustained forest sources. Logging, pulping and manufacturing processes are expected to conform to the environmental regulations of the country of origin.

A catalogue record for this book is available from the British Library.

A catalog record for this book is available from the Library of Congress.

10  9  8  7  6  5  4  3  2  1
18  17  16  15  14  13  12  11  10  09

Printed and bound in Great Britain by
CPI Antony Rowe, Chippenham and Eastbourne

*For Noreen and Georgia, Mum and Dad – Peter*

*For Kate – Lyn*

# Contents

# Acknowledgements

Extracts from *Jamie's Kitchen* courtesy of Jamie Oliver and Fresh One Productions.

Extracts from *Jamie's Kitchen Australia* courtesy of FremantleMedia Australia.

In Chapter 2 parts of the section 'The problem of youth' first appeared, in a different form, in P. Kelly, 'Youth as an artefact of expertise: problematising the practise of youth studies', *Journal of Youth Studies* 3, 3 (2000), pp. 301–15.

In Chapter 2 parts of the section 'The problem of the youth labour market' first appeared, in a different form, in A. Furlong and P. Kelly, 'The Brazilianisation of youth transitions in Australia and the UK?', *Australian Journal of Social Issues*, 40, 2 (2005), pp. 207–25.

In Chapter 3 parts of the section 'The DIY self: risk, reflexivity and individualization', first appeared, in a different form, in P. Kelly, 'Youth at Risk: Processes of Responsibilization and Individualization in the Risk Society', *Discourse*, 22, 1 (2001), pp. 23–34.

In Chapter 3 parts of the section 'The care of the self: power and the subject', first appeared, in a different form, in P. Kelly, 'Youth as an artefact of expertise: problematising the practise of youth studies', *Journal of Youth Studies*, 3, 3 (2000), pp.301–15.

In Chapter 6 parts of the section '(Neo)liberal governmentalities: the emergence of the entrepreneurial self', first appeared, in a different form, in P. Kelly, 'The entrepreneurial self and youth at-risk: exploring the horizons of identity in the 21st century', *Journal of Youth Studies*, 9, 1 (2006), pp. 17–32.

# Introduction: Wasted Lives

*'Keep ancient lands, your storied pomp!' cries she*
*With silent lips. 'Give me your tired, your poor,*
*Your huddled masses yearning to breathe free,*
*The wretched refuse of your teeming shore.*
*Send these, the homeless, tempest-tost to me,*
*I lift my lamp beside the golden door!'*
(Emma Lazarus, 'The New Colossus',
Statue of Liberty, New York, NY)

Jamie Oliver will open a branch of his successful Fifteen restaurant in Cornwall next week, in the full glare of the world's media. Out of the spotlight will be Liam Black, the quietly charismatic social entrepreneur who runs the Fifteen Foundation – a registered charity that receives all profits from the eponymous restaurant in east London – and whose job it is to turn Oliver's social enterprise into a global brand.

This means establishing a string of franchise restaurants that combine Oliver's trademark cooking with stylish locations, and that guarantee to train and support 20 disadvantaged young people each year to become professional chefs.

The foundation's mission is to inspire unemployed, undereducated and low-skilled young people and to provide them with the know-how necessary to forge a career in the restaurant and hospitality industry. It pays trainees £50 a week to attend college full time, rising to £100 as a Fifteen apprentice, plus travel costs...

Yet its initial failure to offer the aspiring chefs help with issues such as drug taking, or finding accommodation, drew criticism. One of

> Black's first moves was to employ youth support worker Claire O'Neill. She identified cannabis use, housing difficulties and an inability to change their often chaotic lifestyles as major obstacles preventing some of the young people from graduating. She hopes that drugs counselling and life skills coaching, together with extra educational help for those who need it, will improve Fifteen's 73% success rate.
>
> (Alison Benjamin, 2006, 'Recipe for Success', *Guardian*)

Zygmunt Bauman, the influential sociologist of *liquid modernity*, argues that at the start of the twenty-first century large numbers of people around the globe – hundreds of millions, in fact – are surplus to requirements, are, indeed, redundant. In *Wasted Lives: Modernity and its Outcasts*, Bauman (2004, pp. 5–6) argues that this redundancy is a consequence of the global spread and triumph of modernisation processes: 'The production of "human waste" ... (the "excessive" and "redundant", that is the population of those who either could not or were not wished to be recognized or allowed to stay), is an inevitable outcome of modernization'. These modernization processes can, largely, be understood in terms of the colonization of all aspects of life, of all spaces and places by market forces, practices and processes under regimes of capital accumulation. As processes of modernization have become truly globalized, as the 'totality of human production and consumption has become money and market mediated, and the processes of the commodification, commercialization and monetarization of human livelihoods have penetrated every nook and cranny of the globe', then the *'crisis of the human waste disposal industry'* (emphasis in original) has become more acute.

A key element to Bauman's (2004, pp. 5–7) argument is that the history of European colonization is a history characterized by exporting 'redundant humans' to the *pre-modern, under-developed* spaces of the New World, Africa, Asia and the Pacific. The triumphant globalization of modernization has resulted not only in the continued (over)production of wasted lives in the *overdeveloped* West, but also the disappearance of a colonial solution to *waste disposal*. Moreover, the figures of the *immigrant*, the *asylum seeker* and the *refugee* represent the reversal of the flows of waste disposal: a reversal that provokes fear and anxiety in the imaginations of the twenty-first-century inhabitants of the affluent, but increasingly insecure, West.

Being surplus to requirements, being redundant means that individuals (and who among us can be sure that we will not *become* redundant) are confronted with a life that does not provide the means to secure a livelihood. The idea of redundancy, the reality that you, or I, or we might be *in-excess*, is a powerful and disturbing concept and reality. In the first instance the concept of redundancy says something, means something, different to the concept of *un*employment. Importantly, for Bauman (2004, pp. 11–12), this concept says something different in a particular time and space (the affluent West at the turn of a millennium); and speaks powerfully to a particular generation (although it could be argued that the very idea of redundancy also echoes powerfully in the imagination of the Baby Boomer generation as it confronts a working life nearly over): 'How different is the idea of "redundancy" that has shot into prominence during the lifetime of Generation X! Where the prefix "un" in "unemployment" used to suggest a departure from the norm – as in "unhealthy" or "unwell" – there is no such suggestion in the notion of "redundancy"'. Rather, as Bauman indicates, redundancy 'whispers permanence and hints at the ordinariness of the condition'. In this sense redundant 'names a condition without offering a ready-to-use antonym'. Can you be *un-redundant*?

Redundancy, the sense that you, or I, or we are of limited or no use – particularly in social, cultural and commercial environments in which *usefulness* not only brings material rewards, but also gives purpose and meaning to a life – can have profound consequences for a sense of self. As Bauman (2004, p. 12) suggests: 'To be "redundant" means to be supernumerary, unneeded, of no use – whatever the needs and uses are that set the standard of usefulness and indispensability. The others do not need you; they can do as well, and better, without you.' What is more, to be redundant suggests that there is no 'self evident reason for your being around and no obvious justification for your claim to have the right to stay around. To be declared redundant means to have been disposed of *because of being disposable* – just like the empty and non-refundable plastic bottle or once-used syringe, an unattractive commodity with no buyers...'

For Bauman (2004, p. 12) redundancy, as a concept (but also, significantly, as a state of *being*) shares its 'semantic space with "rejects", "wastrels", "garbage", "refuse" – with *waste*'. To be redundant or surplus to requirements holds out different possibilities or prospects to being unemployed: 'The destination of the *un*employed, of the "reserve army of labour", was to be called back into active service. The destination of waste is the waste yard, the rubbish heap.'

And it is on the rubbish heaps, in the spaces of *wasted lives*, that we locate our introduction to a discussion and analysis of *Jamie's Kitchen*, of young workers, and of an ethic of enterprise in a globalized risk society. For it is here, in these places and spaces, that we witness the Fifteen Foundation, as a global social enterprise brand, intervening to produce, to make up, a form of entrepreneurial selfhood in young people who are destined to live wasted lives without some sort of intervention.

## Jamie's Kitchen and the master's apprentices

About seven years ago when I'd just started working at The River Cafe I was having a cup of tea with a friend, Kirsty. At the time she was working with problem children – aggressive and bad tempered, they weren't fitting into their school or home environments very well – and she was explaining to me that the main thing was to inspire and empower them, and to give them some hands-on responsibility. She said that cooking classes had been going really well with her because they could feel, smell and create things, and above all it was fun. Plus they could eat what they'd made! I realised that my biggest weapon in life was the determination, enthusiasm, hands-on and 'actions speak louder than words' approach my father taught me, and I wanted to get this across to others, especially those interested in food. Having had five really great years, I felt it was about time to give a little back and help inspire others.

(Jamie Oliver, 2002, *Jamie's Kitchen*, p. 8)

In the UK in 2002 the high-profile celebrity chef Jamie Oliver set out to transform a group of unemployed young Londoners into the enterprising, *ideal* workers of twenty-first-century, flexible capitalism. This process of transformation was captured, even manipulated and managed, in the hugely successful Channel 4 TV series *Jamie's Kitchen*. As Jamie Oliver's biographer Gilly Smith (2006) points out, the series was one of Channel 4's top two shows in 2002 with an average weekly audience over five million. It would go on to be televised in a further 34 countries. In Australia, where we viewed it, the series was screened on Channel 10 over five weeks during July and August 2003. This series, and its figure of the entrepreneurial, passionate, risk-taking, small businessman (who in this instance is also a global celebrity brand) seeking to develop similar dispositions and behaviours in a workforce that initially does not display such character features, might be dismissed as an ephemeral, lightweight, *reality* TV series: a series that has little to offer by way of serious commentary on the new worlds of work, and the new forms of work ethic required to be successful under these regimes.

And this may, in all honesty, have been our initial reaction to what was just another instalment in the TV-based life of a somewhat/sometimes engaging, 30 something, celebrity TV chef. At the time the show went to air we may have even asked each other if we'd seen the new show called *Jamie's Kitchen*. Later, however, in conversations and seminars about young people, work and training, references to *Jamie's Kitchen* started to pop up as a means to talk about and illustrate some of the points that we – individually and collectively – were interested in exploring. It was from these conversations – and from associated discussions about the new worlds of work, about new generations of workers, and problems of transition, education and training, and the place of work in the lives of these new generations – that we developed a sense that *Jamie's Kitchen* could actually provide a vehicle to explore some of these issues. *Jamie's Kitchen* could, in effect, be seen as both a metaphor, and an exemplar of the forms of work-related identity (work ethics) that are expected within an enterprise culture, and the possible education, training, management and policy implications related to young people's transitions into work.

Many readers may have an awareness of the original *Jamie's Kitchen* TV series. This awareness may be more or less developed, and may be situated in some sort of relation to an awareness of Jamie Oliver as a celebrity/brand who appears at regular intervals on TV. In some contexts, such as the UK and Australia, Oliver may be better known for his campaign for healthier school dinners in English schools – a successful, ongoing campaign that again entered the public consciousness via the medium of reality TV. This identity – of Jamie Oliver, social entrepreneur – is itself a phenomenon that will be examined in more detail in a later chapter. A flavour of what is of interest here can be found in a Channel 4 news poll that named Oliver as the most inspiring political figure in the UK in 2005 on the back of his School Dinners campaign: a ranking that placed him ahead of, in order: Shami Chakrabati (a civil rights campaigner), George Galloway (an outspoken UK parliamentarian), Bob Geldof (activist against world poverty), David Cameron (at that time, newly elected Conservative party leader), and Tony Blair (British Prime Minister). This public affirmation followed a number of industry and social enterprise awards, and an MBE in the New Year's Honours list of 2003 for his work with Fifteen.

What many readers may not be aware of is that since the initial TV series was screened in 2002 there have been larger, yearly, cohorts of trainees, and in 2004 the Fifteen Foundation was established as a charitable organisation to carry on the work of Cheeky Chops, the umbrella organization for the initial training and restaurant venture. The Fifteen Foundation has since opened restaurants in Watergate Bay, Cornwall (UK), Amsterdam (Holland), and, in 2006, Melbourne (Australia).

> The Foundation exists to inspire disadvantaged young people – homeless, unemployed, overcoming drug or alcohol problems – to believe that they can create for themselves great careers in the restaurant industry ... We want to provide skills and experience in food preparation and service at the same time as helping our people to believe in themselves, to know that they can achieve anything they want in their lives despite what setbacks they may already have experienced.
>
> (Fifteen Foundation, 2007)

At the outset it is appropriate to set some guidelines for how we will use the televised content of *Jamie's Kitchen*. Some may argue that such a show provides a fairly limited source on which to base an examination of the issues we have outlined. Yet, in many respects, the televised content presents only part of the picture that we will develop. A closer examination of the TV show, the background to its development and the commentary associated with it, and the training and employment programmes that continue under the auspices of the Fifteen Foundation, together with community, policy, commercial and academic data and debates comprise a platform from which we can build our discussion.

Throughout this book we will also refer to a second reality TV series that adds further dimensions to the story of Jamie Oliver and the Fifteen Foundation. *Jamie's Kitchen Australia* was a successful, high-rating 13-part series that was screened on Channel 10 (Australia) during September to November 2006. This series tracked the opening of the Fifteen franchise in Melbourne, and followed a similar format to the original 2002 series – indeed it paid *homage* to that series and structured much of its content and format via references to similar incidents, issues and problems that gave form, and drama, to the original. While the Australian version followed a similar format to the UK series, there were a number of key differences and developments. These will be referred to in more detail in the following chapters. However, these differences, and the research and discussions about *Jamie's Kitchen* that we have been involved in since 2003, have had a number of outcomes that are important to highlight at this time. These thoughts give some clues as to the direction that our discussion will take.

First, in *Jamie's Kitchen Australia* there was a greater emphasis on the detail and character of the *wasted lives* led by many of the young people who became trainees. These dramatic, televisual techniques – which can be understood and critiqued as elements of the reality TV genre – are problematic in a voyeuristic sense. However, this exposure of wasted lives reflects a change in emphasis by the Fifteen Foundation to explicitly target, identify, recruit, train and support those young people most marginalized in a globalized risk society. In one scene from *Jamie's Kitchen Australia* an articulate, capable, skilled applicant was rejected because Fifteen Foundation recruiters judged that she did not need the intervention and support of the Foundation to succeed.

Second, the activities of the Fifteen Foundation have developed in ways that enable us to think explicitly about the Foundation as a social enterprise franchise: a hybrid commercial, for-profit enterprise that has a professed commitment to recruit, train, support and employ young people whom others see as surplus to requirements, as redundant: 'The Foundation is also driving forward our dream of building Fifteen into a global social enterprise brand inspiring young people all over the world' (Fifteen Foundation, 2007; Lethlean, 2006). This entity, the social enterprise brand, raises questions about the roles of other enterprises in *waste production*, and in the subsequent need for *waste management*. In *Jamie's Kitchen Australia* a number of iconic Australian brands – including the National Australia Bank (NAB) and food processor Leggo's – figured prominently as *proud sponsors* of *Jamie's Kitchen*. Yet these same organizations would not themselves take on the risks of recruiting, training and supporting this *type* of young person. Indeed, these and other businesses are the profit-driven organizations that energize the processes of waste production and redundancy which Bauman so powerfully highlights.

Third, the figures of Jamie Oliver (global brand, celebrity, social entrepreneur) and the Fifteen Foundation (global social enterprise brand) raise issues related to corporate social responsibility, and the role of these social enterprises in taking on tasks that were once the responsibility of state agencies. One aspect of the development of this franchise, and in the changing practices associated with annual intakes of unemployed young people, is that the brand has become married to the social enterprise, social entrepreneur phenomenon that is integral to much of the policy development and practice associated with the Third Way political project in many Anglo-European democracies. Our discussion of these issues in later parts of the book will be informed by Foucauldian-inspired critiques of the neo-Liberal governmentalities that provide the context for the emergence of the social entrepreneur/enterprise.

Finally, food and passion loom large in the narrative structure of these shows. What becomes clear over these two series are the roles that food assumes in transforming the lives, and the sense of self of these young people/trainees. In the analysis that we will develop throughout this book we will argue that in *Jamie's Kitchen*, food – or a particular understanding of food – becomes a *technology of the self*. For Foucault (2000b, p. 87) technologies of the self comprise the practices, processes and ways of knowing that are 'suggested or prescribed to individuals in order to determine their identity, maintain it, or transform it in terms of a certain number of ends, through relations of mastery or self knowledge'. As a technology of the self, food provides a series of techniques, skills, capacities, knowledges, and understandings that offer the possibility of provoking certain ways of being, certain ways of thinking about the self and others, certain ways of thinking about a life and the possibilities that are opened up, and closed off throughout a life. In *Jamie's Kitchen* food is something that you should be passionate about. In thinking of food, in being passionate about food, the trainees (the audience) should shift their thinking about food from the processed, the industrial, the convenient, the take-away, the fast – to food as slow, as something that can be grown and produced with passion and with care, as something that can be understood, thought about, worked with, transformed, presented and consumed, as having taste, texture, smell, colour. As a technology of the self, food also provides a powerful metaphor for exploring waste, consumption, work, excess, redundancy and risk (scraps, eating, cooking, butter mountains/wine lakes, famine): particularly in a world where many businesses are both *proud to sponsor* and committed to *trimming the fat*.

Many organizations work with at-risk, marginalized, redundant young people to transform their lives. In Australia, for example, the Salvation Army runs furniture making/carpentry workshops to skill and motivate young people to turn their lives around. These hands on, creative activities and skills provide the vehicle for producing new behaviours and dispositions, a new, more productive sense of self for these 'targeted populations' (Dean, 1995). In *Jamie's Kitchen*, food, as an elemental necessity of life, provides a powerful technology for producing a passionate, entrepreneurial form of selfhood. This is, however, a technology that is principally, solely, work based. Work, in this context, with these young people, in terms of wasted lives and redundancy, is a means of salvation. As Max Weber noted one hundred years ago, work promises to give meaning and purpose to lives that have other, less productive purposes. Work provides a reason to get out of bed in the morning and submit to the disciplines of rationalized, clock time (something that many of the trainees in *Jamie's Kitchen* have great difficulty with). Work, in the globalized, rationalized, market-dominated spaces of the twenty-first century, can provide the only worthwhile purpose or meaning in many people's lives. It can be *better than sex* (Trinca and Fox, 2005). At the same time it provides the *ontology of redundancy*. Indeed, wasted lives and redundancy only mean what they mean because work is what matters. Work is what we do. Work time, work discipline, the work ethic – these are the key markers of a life governed by the demands and expectations of rationalized progress and modernization.

Work is also, increasingly, understood as an individualized means of salvation in a world which offers fewer life options and choices outside the paid world of work. An individual's skills, capacities, behaviours and dispositions, effort and enterprise are what secure participation in the world of work. A personal lack of these characteristics results in redundancy, in being surplus to requirements. Waste management then is not about changing processes that lead to the production of waste. Rather, waste management is about intervening in wasted lives, to produce a self capable of securing its own salvation – for now. The two series of *Jamie's Kitchen*, and the changed practices of the Fifteen Foundation, indicate that trainers, employers, franchisees, social entrepreneurs and celebrity brands have developed an awareness that the production of a self that can conform to the disciplines of paid work is not an easy task for many young people who have lived a life on the rubbish heap – and the difficulties of producing this self are not necessarily indicative of individual skills, capacities, ethics. Indeed, these difficulties may be more about processes, systems, rationalities, technologies that are geared to waste production more than to salvation.

## Situating our discussion: critical management studies and social enterprise

This task of making up the entrepreneurial self: of devising, developing, deploying, managing and reviewing a variety of systems, processes and practices that promise to facilitate the emergence and continuing practice of an enterprising and self-regulating form of selfhood, is one faced to varying degrees by many work organizations at the start of the twenty-first century. In many respects, then, an analysis of how Jamie Oliver and the Fifteen Foundation conceive of, and implement and review, the processes and practices they develop could be of the sort to be found in many management case studies or texts. However, our purpose is not to develop an analysis that would reveal a variety of tips or techniques or suggestions for how these management tasks might be imagined more effectively, implemented more efficiently, delivered more productively. Rather, our purpose – hinted at by our use of Zygmunt Bauman's (1997) critical, sociologically flavoured, analyses of our times, our predicaments, our *discontents* – is to develop an analysis that sits more comfortably, more provocatively in the domain marked out by critical management studies (CMS).

At this point our intent is not to do a genealogy of CMS or examine the contexts or conditions of possibility that enable the field or domain of CMS to emerge. Useful references for those interested in these issues can be found in a number of spaces (for example, Alvesson and Deetz, 2000; Grey and Willmott, 2005a – especially Paul Thompson's (2005) contribution in that collection: 'Brands, Boundaries, and Bandwagons: A Critical Reflection on Critical Management Studies'). Rather, we want to briefly sketch some of the theoretical, epistemological and methodo-logical considerations that help to mark out the limits and possibilities of the field of CMS.

Chris Grey and Hugh Willmott (2005b, pp. 5–6), in their Introduction to *Critical Management Studies: A Reader*, identify three central, related, concerns of CMS. Drawing on Fournier and Grey's (2000) formula-tions they suggest that CMS can be conceived as being shaped by three moments, or movements of critique. In the first instance they refer to the intent in CMS to *de-naturalize* the taken-for-granted dimensions of organizational life, of labour, management and associated processes and practices. These naturalized, often unexamined ways of rendering reality knowable are made problematic, in CMS, in relation to any number of purposes, consequences, costs, benefits, aims and outcomes. A second concern is with what Grey and Willmott refer to as *anti-performativity*. Here the concern is with a critique of the dominance – in mainstream organizational and management practices, processes and studies – of technical, means–ends rationalities, of an instrumental logic that val-ues knowledge, and ways of knowing, in terms of inputs/outputs and efficiency; all in relation to purposes and ends (profits, performance, productivity) that are largely naturalized and unexamined. The final thread in Grey and Willmott's account of what characterizes CMS is the idea and practice of *reflexivity*. Reflexivity acknowledges that positions within a field (owner/manager, trainee, researcher) produce particular views and understandings of knowledges, processes and practices. This understanding of reflexivity qualifies or critiques the value or possibility of objectivity; science as ideology; or value-neutral knowledge – especially as they too privilege particular accounts of organizational life.

In this characterization CMS bears a striking resemblance to many other critical social sciences – including critical education studies, critical sociology, critical political science, feminist post-structuralism. This becomes apparent as Grey and Willmott trace the emergence and influence of CMS, particularly in the UK, to the migration of critical social scientists into emerging Business Schools during the last half of the twentieth century – and the subsequent translation of various Marxist, Frankfurt School Critical Theory, postmodernist and post-structuralist systems of thought into these institutional contexts. These discourses have certainly been influential in the development of our ways of problematizing and critiquing various institutions, practices and knowledges.

So, the form of CMS we are thinking of here has interests in work identities and processes, and management practices, technologies, and rationalities – and in the relationships between these ways of being, actions and rationalities as they emerge from, and give shape to, organizational life. The critical dimensions of these studies are varied and, for our purposes, can be characterized in the following ways:

1. These studies make problematic *official*, often technical (*how to*), versions of the *realities* of organizational life – cultures, structures, labour processes, productivity, efficiency and effectiveness, motivations, purposes;
2. These studies examine organizational life from a variety of positions – positions that contribute in diverse ways to the constitution and the dynamism of organizational structures, cultures, life. In CMS there will often be an explicit privileging of particular positions – a privileging that has as its purpose an attempt to give voice, via a research process, to individuals, groups and teams who experience, and contribute to, organizational life in ways that are shaped by their location in the organization;
3. CMS often work with a sense that an organization needs to be located in social, economic, political, cultural and technological time/space/place. Here there is a need to examine the myriad and complex ways that organizations exist in time/space/place and in some form of relationship to events, happenings, ideas, processes, and other organizations. Some of the most interesting work in this area has emerged with the understanding that organizations are *complex adaptive systems* (see, for example, Cilliers, 1999, Lichtenstein, 2000);

4. With these interests shaping critical analyses and descriptions of diverse aspects of organizational life, CMS is, variously, concerned with understanding the roles played by gender, social class, ethnic background, sexuality, disability/ability and age in structuring relations and interactions in organizational life;

5. Many of these issues come together in a concern within CMS with power – and different ways of understanding the nature, workings, consequences, and relationships of power in giving form and shape to organizational culture, structures, processes, life.

In the work that we want to do in analysing the purposes, practices and outcomes of what Jamie Oliver and the Fifteen Foundation undertake in trying to train unemployed young people as chefs, the figures of the *social entrepreneur* and the *social enterprise* will be important at a number of levels. These, we trust, will become evident as the story we tell unfolds. At this point, though, we want to be explicit that for-profit, franchised, social enterprises create dilemmas in terms of analysis and critique. This is particularly so for forms of analysis and critique that locate themselves, as we have already done in the first few pages of this book, in positions which want to make problematic the globalized, rationalized modernization processes that result in many millions of human lives being reduced to waste, to having little or limited meaning or purpose beyond their productive capacity or value to profit-driven enterprises.

Put simply, do the Fifteen Foundation's training, employment and commercial activities do anything (*enough*) to alter the processes of waste production Bauman identifies? What forms of salvation does Fifteen offer its trainees? Is a form of salvation that facilitates young people's incorporation into the very processes, environments and relations that produce wasted lives a limited, contradictory, paradoxical form of salvation (*welcome to the world of wage slavery, consumer and housing debt!*)?

In an article in *Society Guardian* in April 2007 Alison Benjamin (2007, p. 5) profiles Nigel Kershaw the CEO of Big Invest, a specialist finance company owned by The Big Issue Company. Big Invest's mission is to use market-based mechanisms such as the leveraged buyout to buy out existing enterprises that seek various forms of *social transformation*. Kershaw, a former union official and one of the key figures in the establishment and success of the Big Issue brand, identifies the roles to be played by seeking business solutions to social problems. In this model, social enterprises exist, and will be financed by the likes of Big Invest, for the parts that they promise to play in transforming, in necessarily limited ways, the practices, processes and relations that, historically and characteristically, have driven globalized, rationalized modernization and its ceaseless production of human waste. Big Invest has, indeed, played a role in funding the Fifteen Foundation (see also, Reynolds, 2007; Pati, 2007). In this model Kershaw indicates a dislike for the term *not-for-profit* to describe emerging models of social enterprise. In Kershaw's model: 'We're for loads of profit. The issue is what you do with it'. Kershaw, however, cautions against the possibilities of governments and businesses *outsourcing* their social responsibilities onto an expanding Third sector (*At NAB we're proud to sponsor Jamie's Kitchen!*). The possibility of this so-called *socialwashing*, argues Kershaw, needs to be engaged at the level of a debate about social transformation versus privatization: 'If we're just privatising the NHS and not creating social transformation, what is the point?'

Rob Paton (2005, pp. 32–4), in a text that provides both a description and analysis of various managerial, performance and audit processes that are reshaping – with a variety of consequences – what might once have been called the charity or not-for-profit sector, presents a definition of social enterprise that is useful at this point in our discussion. Part of his discussion around definition points to the reality that domains/sectors such as *private enterprise* and, in this case, *social enterprise* are marked by such diversity – in terms of activities, practices, ends, organizational forms – that any definition is, or should be seen as, provisional and open to review. Given the difficulties associated with defining the term he, nevertheless, suggests that what he calls a *regulated social enterprise* has the following characteristics.

1. The pursuit of social outcomes in relation to either individuals or communities (and hence considerable goal ambiguity is commonplace);
2. Governance that involves a substantial lay or non-executive element, and often quite diverse stakeholder representation (multiple accountabilities are usual);
3. Key staff who are human service professionals or bring other strong and distinct value commitments to their roles: the integration of these with managerial rationalities is often problematic;
4. Funding obtained from a mix of voluntary, public and commercial sources, increasingly through quasi-market or other competitive processes...
5. Close public scrutiny ... through some combination of supervision regarding professional standards, managerial arrangements, client or citizen involvement...
6. Working in or through partnerships, whether for financial reasons, statutory requirement or because of the nature of the task (these

partnerships may involve firms, governmental bodies or other social enterprises).

While this is a useful framework for locating the Fifteen Foundation as a social enterprise, it leaves one key element in need of further clarification at this point. What exactly is the social in social enterprise? An answer at this stage can be found in Jacques Defourny's (2001, pp. 15–18) 'Introduction: From Third Sector to Social Enterprise'. Defourny's discussion covers similar ground to Paton (with some differences not relevant to our present discussion), but attempts to give form to what the *social* might mean in *social* enterprise.

In the first instance he suggests that the purposes of the core – not just peripheral – activities of an organization define it as a social enterprise. Embedded in this characterization are ideas that the profits or surpluses of any activities undertaken by the enterprise are to be *socialized* – not solely/largely to be retained by, or returned to *owners*, but rather reinvested or used for the benefits of other people beside owners.

In the second instance Defourny identifies the role played by what he calls *non-commercial resources* in shaping the activities of a social enterprise. Here there is a sense that resources (financial, in-kind, human, material) necessary for the generation of social activities can not always be found in the market, and that subsidies, sponsorships, and support schemes are often essential in order for these activities to be developed, deployed and sustained. (*At NAB we're proud to sponsor Jamie's Kitchen!*)

Finally, Defourny suggests that particular organizational methods give a distinct character to social enterprises. Here there is a sense that independence and autonomy are important, particularly in contexts where resourcing and purpose require that a social enterprise often has to work in partnership or collaboration with other enterprises and organizations from government, non-government and private sectors. Often, also, these characteristics of social enterprise result in multiple stakeholders having some claim to voice, representation, presence in decision-making processes and structures.

It would seem, and we will develop this observation throughout the book, that managing a for-profit social enterprise presents a range of different issues and challenges to managing other forms of organization. Managing the Fifteen trainees – as individuals, teams, or groups – in a social enterprise context is different to managing and training and inducting individuals/teams in a work organization where employees who do not display, or are unable to develop, appropriate work-related behaviours and dispositions can be sacked. In a social enterprise such as the one that the Fifteen Foundation operates, the core business of the franchise is to train, work with, support and encourage those young people that other organizations wouldn't employ – for any number of reasons. Yet, as the drama of *Jamie's Kitchen* can demonstrate, in this social enterprise context a whole range of issues that exist in organizations take on a starker, *more in-your-face* character. Here issues associated with gender relations in organizations; differences in thinking, understanding and values based in social class, ethnic background, sexuality; differing models, modes and means of teaching, training and learning where the development and exercise of certain skills, behaviours and dispositions are the desired outcomes, are rendered more explicit. Indeed, this clarity – which is still a representation energized by the conventions of the reality TV genre – can enable us to discuss these issues beyond the spaces of *Jamie's Kitchen*.

But this doesn't mean that our analysis is a celebration of the Fifteen Foundation, or of Jamie Oliver. But neither is it analysis that sees in Jamie Oliver a middle-class Essex boy made good, or a global celebrity brand and a social enterprise doing good (*do-gooders*). What we are witness to, though, are initiatives and programmes that should be located in broader political, cultural, economic and technological shifts. For our purposes many of the significant elements of these shifts can be understood, following Foucault (1991) and the governmentality literature, in terms of the widespread emergence of advanced Liberal, or (Neo)Liberal governmentalities that have reconfigured both the relations between the State, Civil Society, the Economy, the Self, on one hand, and, on the other, the nature of the rights, roles, responsibilities of these entities in relation to a range of problems: including, in this instance, the problems of marginalization, of individual preparedness for entry to labour markets, the role of the State in regulating the economy, labour and unemployment, and of enterprise (broadly understood at this point as private, social, self) in shaping responses to these problems (see, for example, Barry *et al.*, 1996).

We want to suggest, then, that the narratives about work and an ethic of enterprise that underpin the entertainment value of this pop culture product, and the ways in which this entertainment value is enhanced by focusing on the drama and conflict, and possible failures as these young people negotiate their very public entry into a workplace structured by this ethic of enterprise, provides a means to explore key features of what has been called a *brave new world of work* (Beck, 2000). In other words, the marginalized young people who appear as trainees in *Jamie's Kitchen* illuminate the *positive*, the ideal worker of this brave new world of work, via the *negative* that is their lack of education and training, workplace experience and skills, and appropriate entrepreneurial disposition.

## Young people, new worlds of work and an ethic of enterprise

Over the last three decades or so the rationalized, globalized modernization of the kind discussed by Bauman has transformed paid work in the labour markets of the highly developed West. This transformation has been material – in terms of production and labour processes and practices. It has also been discursive, in terms of the ways in which governments, employers, trade unions and individuals conceive of work and workers. Increasingly, the idea and practice of 'flexibility', 'casualization', 'upskilling', 'multi-skilling', 'life-long learning' 'core' and 'peripheral' workforces energize the globalized labour markets of 'fast capitalism' (Gee *et al.*, 1996). The ways in which these transformations have been identified and analysed are diverse, and in Chapter 2 of this book we will discuss these changes, their impacts on young workers, and on the ways we *know* young people from the perspectives of contemporary critical sociologies of work. A key element of that discussion, and of the analysis we will develop throughout the book, relates to the ways in which rationalized, globalized, twenty-first-century capitalism provokes a concern with the ethical dispositions to work that individuals or groups, or generations exhibit or lack. In a world of work that is characterized by risk, uncertainty and redundancy an entrepreneurial disposition to work, opportunity and responsibility is seen to hold out the promise of securing participation in labour markets. In a recent policy speech to sell new forms of workplace relations regulation, Australia's then Prime Minister John Howard described the rise of a new type of worker in this context of 'flexible capitalism', a type of worker with a more entrepreneurial disposition to work:

What unites our enterprise workers ... is an attitude of mind. They recognise the economic logic and fairness of workplaces where initiative, performance and reward are linked together ... They have a long-term focus, knowing that short-term gains without regard to productivity are illusory if the result is inflation and jobs at risk.

(Howard, 2005)

This focus on individual behaviours and dispositions, and of the capacity of individuals to develop and perform an appropriate work-self, is a recurring and powerful motif in discussing the transition of young people into work. It is, as we shall see, a powerful motif in the drama of *Jamie's Kitchen*. In a general sense the theme recurs as a consequence of attempts to analyse the distinct characteristics of the youth labour markets in many of the Anglo-European democracies. These youth labour markets tend to have markedly higher levels of unemployment, different occupational profiles, lower rates of pay, and higher degrees of casualization than other, older, labour market segments (Australian Bureau of Statistics (ABS), 2004). These characteristics have provoked community, academic and policy discussions to consider the concept of youth transitions in new ways. Youth as a time in the lifecourse, as a concept in many policy and academic discussions, is most often imagined in terms of transition. Transition, which is itself a metaphor signifying movement from *somewhere*, to *somewhere else*, takes on new meanings if the labour market – as a space of arrival – is increasingly a space marked by uncertainty and risk. Much of this contemporary debate suggests that present-day transitions are less linear, more fragmented, and longer than for previous generations of young people. Indeed, terms such as *post-adolescence, over-aged young adults, generation on hold, extended transitions,* and even *parasitic youth* figure prominently in discussions about the nature of the transitions for Generations X and Y (Furlong and Kelly, 2005; Freeland, 1996).

The problem of young people's transition into, and participation in, various labour markets is understood differently from different points of view. The community, policy and academic debates about these issues are significant influences on the ways in which employers, trade unions and government and non-government agencies respond to, and manage young workers. From the perspective that we will develop the question of individual behaviours and dispositions, of a work-related identity or sense of self, is one that can be explored and analysed via the variety of behaviours and dispositions which young people are encouraged to develop – by employers, trainers, trades unions, governments – in order to be identified as a 'good' worker, a 'teamplayer', a 'crew member', 'entrepreneurial'. In 1997 an Australian Parliamentary Committee addressed these kinds of concerns and argued that: '*Expectations of young people and employers do not always match each other closely ... employers place paramount importance on attitudinal factors when making employment decisions*' (HRSCEET, 1997, p. xv; emphasis added). This concern we have with the self will be elaborated more fully in Chapter 3 where we will tease out the characteristics of, and mechanisms for, developing the passionate, entrepreneurial self that attracts so much attention in discussions about how one can secure individual salvation in contemporary labour markets.

Employers, management, and their consultants often simplify the complexity and heterogeneity of demographic sectors such as the 15–29-year age group. This simplification tends to produce generalizations of generations. So in many management, organizational behaviour and development texts and contexts we witness the identification and discussion of the behaviours, dispositions and values that 'pre-Boomers', 'Boomers', 'Cuspers', 'Generation X' and 'Generation Y' apparently exhibit (for example, Berta, 2001). These claims are often contradictory and generalized. *Generation X* (25–35 years of age) have apparently, and willingly, come to see work as *'better than sex'* as a culture of 70-hours plus working weeks has emerged for white collar professionals (Trinca and Fox, 2005; Bunting, 2004). This is an interesting development as a decade ago this generation was identified as a cynical, disengaged, *slacker* generation. *Generation Y* (under 25 years of age), or that part of it identified by Sheahan (2005) as *talent*, not *labour*, has a disposition to work that is characterized as being *street smart, lifestyle centred, independently dependent, informal, tech savvy, stimulus junkies, sceptical, impatient*.

Organizations and their representatives (managers, trainers, HR managers, etc.) draw on these representations as they seek to manage the identities of their young workers. Citing a Bank of South Australia survey of 600 small businesses in South Australia, HRSCEET (1997) points out that 25 per cent of these employers agreed that young workers are 'excellent employees' – the same number disagreed with this statement, while 57 per cent agreed that young workers required 'constant supervision'. Management consultants Real World Training and Consulting (2002) suggest that young workers are 'not like us' ... They don't have the same work ethic. They don't respect tradition'. Tricia Robinson (a marketing executive for a software developer) argues that young workers are 'smart', 'ambitious', 'collaborate well' and 'aren't afraid to stand up to an idea'. However, she questions their work ethic, arguing that, 'My parents gave me a very, very strong work ethic – that the person you blame is yourself when things don't go right at work ... I don't know whether they've necessarily got that' (cited in Neusner *et al.*, 2001, p. 28).

Trade Unions too mobilize particular understandings of young people to help understand and explain why contemporary populations of young workers (along with increasing numbers of older workers) are not 'joiners'. Some explanations of this non-collective sense of identity suggest that employment contracts, casualization and part-time work in the labour market sectors where young people work 'effectively exclude' many young workers from union membership/representation (Lowe and Rastin, 2000, p. 205; see also Marles, 2002 ). Positions in these discussions range from Trade Union officials who think the problem lies not with Trade Unions but with young people's 'ignorance' of what unions do; to the view that young workers today have a profoundly 'different experience of working life to that of previous generations'. For these young people work is largely an 'individualistic experience' which works against them imagining collective solutions to the risks and uncertainties that characterize contemporary workplaces (Gallagher, 1996; see also Palmer, 1991; Wood, 1991).

Throughout the advanced Anglo-European, North American and Australasian economies many government initiatives to make young people 'more employable' operate within rationalities that place the burden of employability onto young people – citing a range of deficiencies in relation to young people's education, experience, knowledge of the job market and motivation. In Australia, Federal Government 'Work for the Dole' programmes imagine young people in these terms: 'Skills are important but attitude is everything. Work for the dole is about inculcating the right attitude. It is about creating that work culture. That's the most important thing' (Tony Abbott, then Federal Minister for Employment Services, on ABC TV's *7.30 Report* on 7 May 1999). Governments also construct young people's workplace identities in distinct ways in relation to education, training and apprenticeship policies, wage rates, and human resource management/industrial relations issues such as harassment and unfair dismissal.

The purpose of this brief discussion at this stage is to highlight the ways in which young peoples' transitions into work appear as particular problems for a variety of agencies, organizations and individuals. These processes of transition, the periods of education, training, care and development that precede, facilitate and/or hinder transition, can profoundly shape the course of young peoples' future life choices and chances. These issues, the debates around them, the systems of thoughts that make them knowable and promise to make them governable and manageable, have been the focus of much of our work over the last decade. The discussions we will develop in what follows (which are informed by this history) are given a particular shape via our focus on the work of the Fifteen Foundation and *Jamie's Kitchen*. Jamie Oliver and the Fifteen Foundation do not set out to transform the lives of redundant, in-excess Baby Boomers: men and women over 50 with few options for re-training and re-skilling in the twilight years of a productive life. And this is certainly a generational cluster, across a variety of industries and occupational categories, that faces the *phantom* and reality of redundancy in ways that are different to those of Generations X and Y.

Rather, the interventions by Oliver and the Fifteen Foundation in the lives of young people who face the prospect and reality of life on the rubbish heap of rationalized, globalized twenty-first-century capitalism direct our focus to the *start* of a working life, and to beginnings that can be difficult for certain individuals and groups to initiate and sustain. This focus also illuminates the powerful individualizing processes that suggest individual behaviours and dispositions, and ethical orientations to the disciplines of the world of work are what secure participation in work – not processes that are geared to human resource use and human waste production in the pursuit of competitive efficiencies and performance. In addition, the nature of production and labour processes in *Jamie's Kitchen* – the core business of food preparation, presentation and consumption in a high-pressure, present-centred environment (*Get a good product on the table now and see the fruits of your labour in that instant*) – bring the particular demands on the working self into sharp relief. A relief that is sharpened because the young trainees recruited by the Fifteen Foundation generally do not exhibit the characteristics of the self that work environments in the twenty-first century demand.

## Structure of the book

In Chapter 1 we will also introduce and detail the life of Jamie Oliver: celebrity chef, global brand, author and social entrepreneur. Drawing on a number of sources we will build a picture of Jamie Oliver the social entrepreneur and global brand as being very much a product of a particular moment in history. The argument we will develop here is that Oliver's (sex) appeal, success and social entrepreneurship are intimately connected to particular ways of being an English *lad* in Tony Blair's *cool Britannia*. This *laddishness* is given a pronounced flavour in the context of significant transformations in the ways in which large numbers of producers and consumers understand, think about, talk about, produce, prepare and consume food. We will suggest that Oliver's story is a complex tale of success and celebrity involving issues of entertainment and education that are food centred, overexposure, consumer backlash, reinvention, social enterprise in a global context, and scepticism, even cynicism, about his motives.

We will also in Chapter 1 present narratives of some the apprentices drawing on the original *Jamie's Kitchen, Jamie's Kitchen Australia*, and a variety of online resources. These *case histories* will examine the ways in which individual young workers embrace, or struggle with, the demands to develop an ethic of enterprise. These narratives, and the dilemmas, dramas, events, and attitudes that make *Jamie's Kitchen* work as *good* reality TV make explicit the dramas confronting many young people as they encounter the demands of the adult world of work – demands that often *break* many young people, or condemn them to marginal participation in labour markets because they fail to measure up. These biographical sketches also serve to illustrate these students' skills, abilities, personalities and behavioural characteristics as a counterpoint to what is expected of those who wish to work in *Jamie's Kitchen*.

The Fifteen Foundation targets its training, education, work placement and employment programmes to a particular population: a population that can be characterized as marginalized, unemployed (even unemployable) young people, aged 16–24 who have little or no employment history, or marketable employment (life) skills and capacities. Often, these labour market-related deficits are further complicated by drug- and alcohol-use issues, criminal activity, homelessness, and histories of abuse and violence. In Chapter 2 we will present an initial discussion of the work that the Fifteen Foundation undertakes with marginalized young people, and the ways in which the discipline and self-regulation of paid work is seen to offer the possibility of salvation to these young people. The Chapter will also discuss recent sociologies of work that have pointed to the emergence of widespread anxieties and uncertainties as individuals work away at their own Do-It-Yourself (DIY) biographical projects in increasingly globalized settings. In this discussion the emphasis will be on establishing a sense that youth labour markets are risky and uncertain spaces of transition. In these transitional spaces relationships between gender, social class, ethnicity, ability and geographical location shape young people's engagements with paid work, employers, governments and trade unions.

In the chapter that follows we will develop an argument that food, understood in the way it is in *Jamie's Kitchen*, promises to provide the means to provoke passion in the young people targeted by the Fifteen Foundation. This idea that certain understandings of food can provoke and give focus to a passion that is not readily apparent and that this passion, once provoked and disciplined, can actually transform the self, emerges from particular understandings of the self. Our analysis and discussion of the ways of knowing the self will draw on two influential conceptualizations of the self that have made uneven contributions to the critical study of management, of work, of youth, of identity. These ways of thinking about the self will be important elements of the discussion in this book. The first of these stories is sociological and understands the self as reflexive. This reflexive, Do-It-Yourself (DIY), individualised self is the central character in the reflexive modernization literatures shaped by the work of Ulrich Beck, Anthony Giddens and Scott Lash. The second of these orientations to the self owes much to the later focus by Michel Foucault (1986) on *the care of the self*, and to the governmentality literature that has emerged under the influence of Foucault's legacy. In this story the self is the product of diverse undertakings/projects that seek to guide or direct the self to know itself in certain ways, to act in certain ways, to govern and regulate itself in certain ways. In this story there is a focus on the techniques/technologies and rationalities that promise to produce certain forms of selfhood. This story of the self as an ongoing, regulated, ethical achievement provides a powerful tool for understanding the ways in which the Fifteen Foundation seeks to provoke in young people a passion that is focused on particular understandings of food: a passion that holds out the promise that an entrepreneurial self can emerge from the training facilitated by the Fifteen Foundation.

Chapter 4 picks up, and discusses in more detail, a central theme in this book: that of passion. As we have already indicated, passion is something that is integral to the story of the ways in which Jamie Oliver and the Fifteen Foundation engage marginalized young people in the project of the development of an entrepreneurial selfhood. As we will discuss in that chapter many of the young trainees initially fail to display passion – for much at all, let alone an intense period of structured training and work-placement. This lack of passion confounds and confuses Oliver and the other adults whose task it is to train these young people. The chapter will discuss the ways in which this apparent lack of passion is tackled and the central role that food plays in providing something that can become the *object* of a young person's passion. This recurring, central concern with passion, and the ways in which it is provoked, developed and regulated/managed provides a means to think about the nature and role of passion in education, training and development contexts beyond the confines of *Jamie's Kitchen*.

Jamie's *laddishness* – contrived, manufactured, authentic or otherwise – is, by definition, gendered. *He's a lad*! His apparent (to some) boyish charms, his appeal, his brand is gendered. The trainees we see in both series of *Jamie's Kitchen* are also gendered, as are the trainees in additional, ongoing intakes. In many stories from the restaurant and hospitality industries the largely, male celebrity chefs provide accounts of an industry that is also gendered and intensely hierarchical. Often this results in female employees occupying lower ranks in the *food chain*, and in bullying and harassment by macho, male chefs further up the food chain. In Chapter 5 we will discuss the complexity of gender relations, young workers, training and this industry. This discussion has its origins in the following exchange from the very first episode of the original *Jamie's Kitchen*.

> *Jamie:* I was a bit upset about Elisa [Roche]. I think she's quite sharp and I think she loves food. And I had a good time with her when we were doing the recipe cooking.
>
> *Ruth:* Because she's pretty?
>
> *Gennaro:* They're all pretty.
>
> *Ruth:* She was asking far too many questions. Because they were questions you had already answered. I think it's great to ask questions if you don't know about something or whatever. But actually it was as if she had no instruction from you whatever at any stage. I feel for myself that in a kitchen situation she would be very flaky. She's too distracted.
>
> [Jamie Oliver and colleagues/mentors discussing the merits of particular trainees in the midst of the selection process.]
>
> (*Jamie's Kitchen*, Episode One, Broadcast in Australia on Channel 10, 21 July 2003)

This chapter will identify and discuss the dynamic of gender and attraction/flirtation that comes through in the different approaches to male and female apprentices that are evident from the first episode of *Jamie's Kitchen*. This is not to deny that flirtation/attraction is not/should not be part of workplace relations. But, what do these relations say about the different experiences of young men and women in the workplace, particularly as certain labour markets, certain industries, certain occupations are segmented along gender lines? Young men and women also have different experiences and structured locations in different forms of employment – full-time, part-time, casual, precarious. The discussion here, while provoked by the drama of *Jamie's Kitchen*, extends beyond this example – without suggesting that what we see in *Jamie's Kitchen*, or what we know of the Fifteen Foundation's programme, is characterized by harassment or bullying. Indeed, as we will discuss, a key dramatic episode in *Jamie's Kitchen Australia* revolved around the consequences of ongoing harassing behaviour by a *boys' group* among the trainees. This behaviour resulted in one of the boys being suspended from the programme.

Chapter 6 explores the demands for certain, preferred behaviours and dispositions in the world of work, and the difficulties that some trainees have in conforming to these demands. In a similar vein to the preceeding chapter the discussion here emerges from an incident in the early stages of the original *Jamie's Kitchen*. In that incident – detailed below – the demands for conformity, for behaving and thinking in certain ways, for knowing the self in appropriate ways, are starkly illustrated.

> *Peter Richards:* Don't be a smart arse. Because I know my work. I know my work because I know it's good. You know your work because at the moment it's crap. You're going to be doing this for real. You're going to be sending this out to somebody to eat and pay for and I wouldn't be prepared to pay for that.
>
> [Peter Richards, chef/lecturer, disciplining a trainee in Jamie's Kitchen who tried to substitute Peter's work example for his own, inferior, example.]
>
> (*Jamie's Kitchen*, Episode Two, Broadcast in Australia on Channel 10, 29 July 2003)

In this chapter we will further discuss the question/problem of young people in ways that connect to the contemporary *fetishization* of young people under 24 as belonging to Generation Y. Our concerns in the discussion are with the consequences that emerge when we fetishize age in our characterizations of population. We will review characterizations of Generation Y, and explore suggestions that Generation Y's orientations to paid work, its purposes, the roles it plays in a lifecourse, the meanings that attach to it, mark this generation as being significantly different to prior generations. Our intent is to locate Generation Y in particular historical, cultural and social settings. Drawing on Foucault's understandings of power/knowledge/subjects and government we will suggest that across a range of settings/spaces particular understandings of the *individual as enterprise* shape a variety of programmes, practices, processes that seek to regulate and provoke a variety of human behaviours and dispositions.

As we will argue throughout this discussion, the twenty-first-century self is expected to be passionate, to be entrepreneurial, and to be willing to do what is required to secure individual salvation via the construction of a working life. Contemporary work practices, the management of these, and general and vocational education and training programmes place responsibility onto young workers (indeed all workers) to manage themselves and their career paths in ways that will minimize the risks of globalized labour markets. Working in *Jamie's Kitchen* places young workers under the microscope – under the surveillance of trainers, and more senior chefs, who create expectations and demand certain behaviours and approaches to work. Deviations from these demands and expectations are not tolerated. The world of work demands certain forms of compliance, and increasingly the opportunities and costs associated with these demands are carried by the individual. In *Jamie's Kitchen* the tensions associated with meeting these demands are explicit and provide a means to make broader comments about contemporary workplaces, the young workers who work in them and the forms of personhood that they must cultivate if they want to participate in the labour market. From our perspective the manufactured, dramatic, and in some senses, manipulative *hyperreality* of *Jamie's Kitchen* provides a powerful vehicle for exploring the issues we have sketched here.

# 1
# The Naked Chef and the Master's Apprentices

## Introduction

> 'I've got two questions ...' Roger said. We were watching the telly together in his house. There was nothing else to do. 'Firstly, why the fuck is Jamie Oliver on my fucking telly screen? And secondly, why is it that whenever that little ... shit ... rears his ugly head, the bastard remote control disappears?' He always got like this when he saw celebrity chefs.
>
> (*Lifeofbob* weblog, 2007)

We confess to having differing, and changing, attachments to Jamie Oliver the celebrity chef – sufficient to provoke us to watch or be aware of his presence on the programming schedules of various TV stations in the city where we live. However, as the LifeofBob blog indicates, this is an attachment that is not shared by everyone – celebrity attachments are not universal and a backlash (overexposure) can dim a celebrity's appeal quickly. Oliver first came to our notice in Australia through his series *The Naked Chef* (renamed *Oliver's Twist* in America). In this series the then young, boisterous, boyishly handsome, foodaphile jumped around the set (not accidentally in his own kitchen) at frenetic speed, talked to someone off-camera, lisped and pranced around, pulled earnest faces, introduced us to a vast array of *mates*, and seemingly threw together food that looked great and we could imagine tasted great as well. For one of us this interest was/is an extension of a long-held passion for the *art* of food as produced by a range of media for our consumption – both metaphorically and literally.

Alongside our interest in food as entertainment, as nourishment, as art, we also have a long-term academic interest in young people and the myriad ways that they are represented in a range of media texts and discourses. Our focus on *Jamie's Kitchen* then is no accident.

This chapter, presented in two sections, has a number of purposes that are central to the structure of the discussion that we will develop through this book. In Section One we will sketch some details of Jamie Oliver, the celebrity chef and social entrepreneur, and the two reality TV series, *Jamie's Kitchen* and *Jamie's Kitchen Australia*, so as to provide the reader with a sense of a number of elements central to the narrative we intend to develop. Included here will be detail on the Fifteen Foundation, the for-profit social enterprise that manages and promotes the Fifteen franchise. These two shows and material from the Fifteen Foundation will provide much of the data that we will draw on in the following chapters.

We will also discuss the possibilities and problems associated with suggesting that these reality TV shows represent something that is worthy of sustained and serious discussion in relation to young people and work in the globalizing economies of the twenty-first century. That is, what, if anything, is *real* about reality TV, and in particular, about *Jamie's Kitchen*? In the same vein we will approach a discussion about Jamie Oliver the celebrity chef, and the Master's Apprentices (the trainees), with a number of similar provocations: what is *real* about celebrity chefs? What or who is the *real* Jamie Oliver? What is the restaurant industry *really* like? Who is Kerryann Dunlop or Dwayne Montford – or any of the other trainees who appear in the TV shows – and can we say who they *really* are, or what they are *really* like? Should we burden ourselves with a quest for the truth of these matters or can we argue that these figures, these mediated representations, do, indeed, point to various important issues, ideas and concepts in the realities that exist outside media representations? We spend the remainder of this first section introducing and discussing Jamie Oliver in his various guises as the figure of the modern entrepreneurial self.

In Section Two we introduce a number of Oliver's apprentices and sketch out, albeit briefly, some of their biographical details. Not all of the trainees appear in this section: some appear here and only briefly elsewhere in the book, if at all. Others have a much greater role to play. This section serves to introduce readers to a variety of trainees from *Jamie's Kitchen* and *Jamie's Kitchen Australia* as a way of exploring their life-worlds, their motivations and dispositions and their training experiences. We of course only come to know these young people through their media portrayals. Nonetheless the dilemmas they face are firmly connected and illustrative of the lives of other young people living in precarious circumstances.

Much is made of the fact that these young people come from marginalized backgrounds. Indeed, in the Melbourne series some young people were rejected because they weren't disadvantaged enough. The dangers and risks that these young people face – often coping with educational failure, drug and alcohol abuse and marginalized family situations – exemplify the possibilities for a life on the *rubbish heaps* of a rationalized, globalized modernity (Bauman, 2004). Again in the Melbourne series, Oliver often argued that he had very little connection to, and understanding of, their life-worlds; something he was only beginning to acknowledge and understand in the first series in the UK. Here Jamie's *habitus* becomes an important factor as he tries to make his trainees into likenesses of himself, drawing on his own model of an entrepreneurial selfhood with the capacities, the behaviours and dispositions necessary for success in globalized markets – labour and entertainment.

These biographical sketches also serve to illustrate these students' skills, abilities, personalities and behavioural characteristics as a counterpoint to what is expected of those who wish to work in *Jamie's Kitchen*. Our argument, to be developed in later chapters, is that the making of the *passionate* and *entrepreneurial* self requires particular disciplinary and governmental practices; and the development of particular knowledges of the self, particular types of self-understanding. *Jamie's Kitchen* and *Jamie's Kitchen Australia* illustrate the ways in which these processes of self-transformation are promised and delivered (for some) via a range of techniques and spaces, including:

- particular forms of training and discipline – conforming to dress codes, the mechanics of food preparation, the drudgery of kitchen cleaning, arriving on time (or early), having a go, working quickly and as part of a team;
- in various sites – training colleges, farm visits to local food producers, commercial kitchens;
- and by particular people with appropriate dispositions to training and work – Jamie himself, Jamie's mentors, college trainers, other chefs during work experience, psychologists, social workers.

What becomes clear from an examination of the students' dispositions and of those who train them is that those who are able to conform to particular disciplinary practices, and develop forms of self-government are those more likely to succeed. This is, as the drama of reality TV shows us, problematic for a number of these trainees.

## Section One

### Jamie Oliver, celebrity chef: who/what is the real Naked Chef?
*Jamie the lad*

From a number of perspectives Jamie Oliver appears as the amiable, likeable, energetic, cool country boy made good through hard work, determination and a prodigious talent. He was born in Essex, England in 1975 and arrived in London in 1991 at the beginning of a 'new exciting food scene' and the advent of a 'new breed of superstar chef' (Smith, 2006, p. 55). We have come to know him through his numerous television series in the UK, USA and Australia: *The Naked Chef* (renamed *Oliver's Twist* in the US), *Jamie's Italy*, *Jamie's Kitchen*, *Jamie's School Dinners*, *Jamie's Kitchen Australia*, and in 2007 *Jamie at Home*. In her biography of Oliver, Gilly Smith (2006) cites friends of Jamie seeking to explain dimensions of his appeal as a *lad*:

> 'A lot of the stuff we did at Sainsbury's was about the food of love', said a friend who shared the late-night shoots. 'It was about what to cook for your girlfriend; it was about entertaining your best mates. There were a lot of TV chefs around then, so when he burst through he was the one for the lads. Before Jamie blokes in their late 20s lived in a tip and relied on their mothers to do their cooking and laundry. But here was a guy who looked cool – his hair and his clothes, the whole lifestyle was cool. Suddenly it was about energetic guys doing something. And he was so into food, that's what was making him high. It was inspirational for young men who wanted to pull women.'
>
> (2006, p. 107)

At one point Oliver was appearing on our television screens here in Australia every night of the week with first releases and re-runs of earlier series on different channels. His cookery books, with titles that mirrored his television series, are extremely popular with, for example, his second book *Return of the Naked Chef* knocking his first book off the British best-seller list in October 1991 (Smith, 2006). There are often questions raised about the influence so-called celebrities have on their (actual and accidental) audiences, particularly the younger members of these audiences.

Indeed, a number of these celebrities are often accused of being negative role models. Oliver himself has come in for his fair share of criticism at various times. However, he currently appears to be enjoying resurgence as Britain's golden boy: a persona, a representation, that is embraced enthusiastically here in Australia, and in the US, as a celebrity exemplar of what is sometimes called 'cool Britannia'.

In the way of the modern entrepreneur and media personality, Oliver has a proliferation of websites devoted *to* him and *sometimes* against him, and an unauthorized biography, *Turning up the Heat*, written by journalist Gilly Smith (2006). Smith charts Jamie's career from growing up in the village of Clavering in Essex and learning to love food and food preparation in The Cricketers, his parents' pub, through to his television series *Jamie's School Dinners* and then *Jamie's Italy*.

In a profile that accompanied a segment on CBS's (2006) *60 Minutes* in the US we are told that: 'In spite of his Cockney streetwise image, Jamie Oliver's upbringing was very different from that of his trainees. He had a comfortable childhood, growing up in Essex in a 16th century inn, which belonged to his father who serves food that is well above the usual English pub fare.' Yet, he may have a number of things in common with those of his trainees who experienced learning difficulties in the institutionalized settings of compulsory schooling:

> As a child, Oliver was happier working with his father in the pub's kitchen than he was at school. He was dyslexic and was teased by the other kids when he was taken out of class for special instruction. 'They used to sing songs as I left, 'cause they used to come every Wednesday to pick me up right in the middle of English class,' Oliver recalls. ' "Yes, please, we've come to pick up Jamie and Richard Saunders for special needs." And everyone used to turn round ... and then they sort of, like, you know, (would sing) "special needs, special needs, special needs, special needs." They'd be singing it ... but you know, I kind of managed to handle myself.'
>
> (CBS, 2006)

As we write we are watching his current incarnation as the 'slow food' revolutionary in his new television series *Jamie at Home* – where in the first episode he exhorted us in that laddish, earnest voice-to-camera way – that can cause you to love or hate him depending on how your day has been – to grow your own; be organic; save animals and 'good' insects; grow and cook seasonally, and save the environment all in 50 minutes. Although his popularity has waxed and waned over the years, his ability to reinvent himself has kept him in the media spotlight and in our lounge rooms.

After his initial period of significant success in the UK, US and Australia sections of the British press began to suspect that he 'was becoming too big for his boots'. In response he was quoted as saying: 'I have done more for English food throughout the world in the past two years than anyone else has done in the past 100. I have put it on the map, for Chris-sakes' (Connolly, 2003; see also Lyall, 2003). These are hardly comments designed to endear him to a press that delights in tearing down tall pop-pies. Capitalizing on his success he took up a reported £1/4 (quarter) million deal to be the pin-up boy for the UK supermarket giant Sains-bury's (Smith, 2006). The advertisements he produced for Sainsbury's capitalized on *The Naked Chef* format, and involved him cooking super-market ingredients for his family and friends. This move by Jamie was a deliberate attempt on his part to promote home cooking with seasonal produce and he was able to effect considerable change in the types of produce offered and how these were presented to the public. However, and building on the idea that he had become too big for his boots, not everyone was as enthusiastic about this move as Oliver. He was criticized for 'sleeping with the enemy': and what was Oliver's response to the criticism about his Sainsbury's affiliation?

'My relationship with Sainsbury's is really honest,' he said. 'I tell them the way it is – no prisoners. I want those pre-packed aisles to get smaller and smaller, but they are getting bigger and bigger. But I have re-launched their herb range and sales are up 40 per cent. We have introduced five new herbs around the whole country, for crying out loud! Summer savory, golden marjoram, lemon thyme, lemon basil and purple basil. Right? Don't tell me that is not an amazing thing!'
(Smith, 2006, p. 108)

Around about this time his long-time collaborator and producer Pat Llewellyn was reportedly upset to see *The Naked Chef* format that she had co-created with Oliver translated into Sainsbury's commercials with-out consultation (Smith, 2006, p. 108). As well, both she and Optomen Television, who had been jointly credited in Jamie's first book *The Naked Chef*, were completely missing from the credits of the third book, *Happy Days with the Naked Chef*. Llewellyn was quoted as saying: 'I feel that the whole thing about the books was unbelievably unfair … And I think personally I gave him a lot. But what can I say?' (Smith, 2006, p. 109).

All of which raises the questions: who or what is the *real* Jamie Oliver? Is he the celebrity chef? The transformative and/or charismatic leader? The social entrepreneur? The food revolutionary? The lad? The respectful son? The husband? The father? All of these figures are representations produced in a range of media texts. In one sense they are all fictions (can we know the *real* Jamie Oliver?) but they all have effects in the everyday (Couldry, 2006a, 2006b; Hage, 2003). What is important for our argument is not whether the representations of Jamie Oliver and his trainees that we see across a range of media are *real*, but that these representations come to signify certain aspects of contemporary forms of the self.

*Jamie the transformative/charismatic leader?*

> Q: How would you describe Jamie Oliver?
>
> A very funny guy and very caring towards those he works with. He always gives 110% [Michael Pizzey].
>
> He's inspirational to me. He's completely down to earth, which is incredible considering he's only 28. He's got a filthy mind though and he's always joking [Tim Siadatan].
>
> Very passionate about food; a determined, nice person, He's much less OTT than he seems on the telly [Nicola Andronicou].
>
> He's become a friend; it's more than a boss and trainee thing now. I think he wanted to keep a distance but he's got involved with us all now [Elisa Roche].
>
> What you see is what you get [Kevin Boyle].
>
> He's bloody lovely and marvellous to put himself in this situation for us [Kerryann Dunlop].
>
> (*Return to Jamie's Kitchen: Meet the Trainees*, Channel 4, 2007)

The management literature devotes some space to the idea of the transformative/charismatic leader. There is no shortage of *how to* guides and role models for this form of leadership – Donald Trump and Richard Branson spring to mind as examples who also have a certain celebrity status and media profile in various market segments in a globalized media environment. It is not our intention here to evaluate this literature with a view to position an analysis of Jamie Oliver the leader. As Mats Alvesson and Stanley Deetz (2000, p. 51) argue in a review of the *sorry state* of leadership research, even some mainstream, neo-positivist/normative leadership researchers are sceptical of the direction, outcomes and prognoses that flow from the plethora of leadership studies: 'Most of the theories are beset with conceptual weaknesses and lack strong empirical support. Several thousand empirical studies have been conducted on leadership effectiveness, but most of the results are contradictory and inconclusive.' Another study on leadership is not really the task we set ourselves here.

However, Jamie Oliver is interesting because not only do his trainees/apprentices see him as a charismatic leader, but also he is young, able to appeal to a wide age and demographic range, and espouses and evidences a strong social change agenda. Over time he has morphed into a charismatic, influential, celebrity social entrepreneur. These qualities have been identified as marketable in a crowded marketplace of leadership tips, techniques and training strategies. The first TV series of *Jamie's Kitchen* was the impetus for the production of a set of leadership training videos and DVDs which are accompanied by various teaching aids such as slide presentations and worksheets. On the website that advertises these training packages (The Richardson Company, 2006) the stated aim of these resources is 'To show how to become a better leader', and the makers assert that:

> Jamie is a natural and instinctive leader. And anyone who takes on a leadership role can learn a lot from watching him in action. Part of the new two-part Jamie's Kitchen training series, Fifteen Lessons on Leadership demonstrates that leadership is an activity and not a position. Leaders and potential leaders will identify with Jamie's honesty and openness.

The advertising and promotional material on this site goes on to state that: 'The program covers five key learning points' [Lead the way, Show them how, Believe in them, Deal with it, Learn and Adapt] 'backed up by *real* examples from Jamie's journey' (emphasis added). The perceived benefits of paying US$1640 for this package (which includes the companion series *Fifteen Lessons on Teamwork*) are listed as:

- Real-life example of classic team development in action
- Positive role model to inspire your audience
- Will improve skills of both new and existing leaders
- Pressurized role reflects real life for today's leaders
- Energetic style will keep audience engaged.

*Jamie the social entrepreneur, food revolutionary?*

Oliver's social change agenda is evidenced, in part, by his focus on fresh, locally sourced ingredients; a celebration and promotion of what has become known as *slow food*; and an associated campaign against processed, industrialized, *fast food*. In addition he has a certain renown for his mission to change the eating patterns of UK schoolchildren, This particular, ongoing campaign, was promoted and popularized in yet another television series, *Jamie's School Dinners*. *School Dinners* documented his attempts to change the eating habits of schoolchildren in schools in the UK, and was perhaps the most controversial of his initiatives. As *60 Minutes* reported in the US:

> Oliver has practically become a national hero in Britain for exposing the unhealthy diet of junk food that is served in schools at lunchtime. To prove that good food can be produced as cheaply, he took over the school catering in one London borough and cooked a range of fresh and healthy dishes. Oliver is proposing to carry out the same experiment in American schools but he says that we shouldn't expect an overnight transformation. Cooking good food is one thing – getting the kids to eat it is quite another.
>
> (CBS, 2006)

The parents of the targeted children resisted being told what to feed their children; school dinner ladies rebelled against the extra work involved in *preparing* meals rather than *opening* packets of pre-prepared and processed food; and the children themselves were resistant to change. Some commentators likened the battle to class wars as the *darling of the middle classes* attempted to tell mainly working-class women what they should be doing. His actions also included petitioning British Prime Minister Tony Blair to increase budget allocations for school dinners.

> **My manifesto by Jamie Oliver**
> For the past couple of years I've been campaigning to ban the junk in schools and get kids eating fresh, tasty, nutritious food instead. Without your support for the Feed Me Better campaign we wouldn't have got the commitment from Tony Blair for new school meal standards and £280 million to start sorting out the problem.
>
> In my new programme, we show that parents are key and without cooking skills, kitchen facilities and political support on the ground it's going to be very hard to make lasting improvements.

> During the course of filming I spoke to the Prime Minister and he committed more longer term funding for school food. I don't want to sound ungrateful, but the amounts are tiny when you divide it up between all the schools in the country – Nora only gets £2,000. Local and national government need to come up with a ten-year strategy and some real money to re-educate people about proper eating habits.
> Big love, Jamie O, Xxx
> > (Channel 4, 2006, *Jamie's School Dinners: The Campaign*)

Oliver's focus on changing the lives of a select group of marginalized young people through his *Jamie's Kitchen* television series, facilitated through the philanthropic Fifteen Foundation, is another example of his social entrepreneurship. In many respects Oliver is a man of his time, reflecting as he does the focus on corporate social responsibility that is a significant element of New Labour's Third Way political agenda/manifesto in the UK. Then Prime Minister Tony Blair's (2006) *Our Nation's Future* series of speeches gives a flavour of the emphasis on social entrepreneurship and corporate social responsibility characteristic of the enabling state/social enterprise discourse central to the Third Way project (we will return to a critique of these positions in Chapter 6):

> We have tried to develop a concept of the State as enabling, its task to empower the individual to be able to make the choices and decisions about their life that they want ... An enabling state should be supporting the public service risk-takers, the social and public entrepreneurs who make the changes that make the difference ... Today across a range of areas, we are opening up provision to the independent and voluntary sectors and making the public sector the commissioner of services: in welfare, in health, even in areas like the management of offenders ... Business, if no longer subject to a misguided ideological attack on profit, must recognise a corporate and social responsibility as the price of the new consensus in support of their role in wealth creation.
> > (Blair, 2006)

Oliver himself argues that he is forced to develop his approach to training marginalized young people because governments (in the UK,

Europe, Australia and the US) are increasingly withdrawing from such social responsibilities or else are insisting that the responsibility should be shared with the private sector. All of this social entrepreneurship on Oliver's part is underpinned by contemporary preoccupations with food: food is too fast, too processed, it is making us fat, or unhealthy or ill, we are eating too much of it, some of us are not eating enough, it causes cancer, it prevents cancer ... In the case of the Fifteen trainees, food, understood in the way Jamie wants it to be understood, provides a vehicle for transforming the self – from disadvantaged to advantaged in terms of employment.

So, is Jamie Oliver a middle-class 'tosser' telling the working classes what they should be eating? Possibly. But, we would argue, this sort of characterization is, in many respects, unsophisticated and not one that sits well with the analysis we want to develop. It is more interesting, and possibly provocative, to think about a range of issues to do with the *Naked Chef* phenomenon, Oliver's social entrepreneurship, and the meanings associated with food the way that Jamie (and others) think about it, by briefly exploring the following:

**A: The industrialization and rationalization of food**
**B: Globalization and the aestheticization of food ('food porn')**
**C: Celebrity culture and social enterprise**

*A The industrialization and rationalization of food.*   Food used to be something that people grew, hunted, caught, fished for. Many around the world still do. We should not romanticize this past with this statement. Pre-industrialized food supplies, quantity and quality were heavily dependent on climate, luck (good and bad) and skills as hunter/gatherer, farmer, hunter, trader. Industrialization in this sense is also rationalization. The industrialization and rationalization of food removes, largely, the matter/question of fate from food production, processing, distribution. We need no longer learn, develop or pass on a variety of skills, knowledges related to food production, preparation, cooking, and presentation in order to feed ourselves. In many respects we have been de-skilled in terms of food.

This is one of the key elements or features of much of what Jamie Oliver has done throughout the various phases and manifestations of his TV career as celebrity chef. He has sought to educate people about alternative ways of understanding food to those that emerge with the industrialization and rationalization of food production, processing and consumption.

These matters of education, skilling, training are key points because all of these, in different ways, involve processes that seek transformations of the self, the development of different sorts of self-understandings that are primarily located in the physical, visceral, embodied process of eating food; and the myriad processes that can be involved in the production, processing, preparation and presentation of the food we consume.

The positions of critique that are available here are also many and varied and located in different intellectual histories, traditions and domains (sociology, psychology, media/cultural studies, education, management, etc.). The point to stress here, and one that we will develop throughout the book, is that discourses of education and training have the capacity for limited translation into management/work contexts, spaces and discourses. In these spaces human resource management, human capital development, culture change, training and development processes all involve an educational element. Just as Jamie Oliver's educational practices take place in spaces other than classrooms (kitchens, gardens, farms, the media), so too in various workplaces education occurs in a variety of spaces, practices and processes; some more or less structured than others.

*B Globalization and the aestheticization of food (food porn).*   Of interest here is the circulation, translation and transformation of foodstuffs on a global scale (New Zealand lamb in the UK, Californian oranges in Australia, etc.). This element has much to do with industrialization and rationalization of food. But alongside these processes we witness the circulation, translation and transformation of the understandings and meanings associated with food within increasingly mediated and globalized settings.

There are paradoxical, contradictory and complex processes to explore and disentangle here. At one level seasonal, regional, localized patterns of food production, processing, preparation and consumption – that might have pre-dated the industrialization and rationalization of food – are transformed. We can eat bananas, strawberries, lamb, salmon … *out of season*, year round, because of rationalized, industrialized, globalized production and supply chains of foodstuffs that are controlled and managed by massive transnational organizations. Moreover, as consumers, we have come to understand this to be appropriate, and something that large numbers of us expect, want, and demand.

Recently these globalized, rationalized food production networks and supply chains have been questioned on grounds such as the impact on the environment of food production and transportation on this globalized scale (here the idea of *food miles* enters various discourses).

These production networks and supply chains, and the rationalization processes that energize, regulate and manage them have also been questioned in terms of impacts on local food production and consumption practices in different localities around the globe. Are local food cultures – with their fundamental relation to other elements of our lives – under threat of unplanned, unwanted transformation by the globalized industrialization and rationalization processes we are discussing here?

At another level globalization has reinforced regional food identities, as these regional cultures, cuisines, diets, styles of life are examined at any number of levels. For example, longevity, obesity, various forms of disease (vascular, diabetes, cancer, etc.) are understood and made known in terms of diet and lifestyles associated with particular ways of producing, preparing and consuming food (for instance, the so-called Mediterranean diet and lifestyle supposedly impacts in beneficial ways on health and longevity).

Globalization has also resulted in the emergence of food styles that are labelled *fusion*. Here various national, ethnic, regional styles are transformed, translated, indeed *fused*, to produce hybridized dishes, styles of preparation and presentation, and different combinations of ingredients.

In addition a globalized slow food movement has emerged and spread in response to the globalized industrialization and rationalization of food. Jamie Oliver is a key figure in this movement in global media and celebrity spaces – but he is by no means the only or most important figure in this context.

Against this complex, contradictory background Jamie Oliver has appropriated, translated and transformed elements of these processes in his version of what food production, preparation, presentation and consumption should involve. For example, his exploration of regional food variations in his journey through Italy (see Oliver, 2005) presents a picture of food production, preparation, presentation, consumption that is largely based in peasant or working-class, rural and urban contexts: contexts in which knowledge about these elements is fiercely, proudly, and loudly articulated and defended. This knowledge locates food – understood in these ways – at the centre of collective, social, familial, village, and neighbourhood life. These understandings of food are applauded, respected, honoured, sometimes romanticized by Oliver as expressions of what ought to be in terms of food. Yet, in these spaces the middle-class Essex boy – in the paradoxical globalized/regionalized/localized spaces of twenty-first-century food – is often represented as being out of his depth, and seen by many of the people he encounters as unskilled in the ways that they understand food.

In a classic scene in this series a very young (pre-school age) girl is shown displaying her pasta-making skills on the doorstep of her (great) grandmother's house. The child's skills make Oliver appear as amateurish. Indeed, in this context/space the food tables are reversed and Jamie Oliver appears as unskilled as many of Fifteen's trainees as they start their process of self-transformation. However, Oliver's skills base, and his cultural capital as a global media celebrity/brand give him a platform of ability and confidence from which he can respond to the challenges posed to his self-understanding.

In this context, to claim that Oliver's understandings of food are *middle-class* misses their location in complex, often contradictory globalized/regionalized networks of meaning and material processes.

*C Celebrity culture and social enterprise.* Celebrity Culture and Social Entrepreneurship is also a complex space for understanding Oliver as a brand, as someone involved in trying to (re)educate large populations about food, and as an individual who provokes diverse, often passionate, forms and levels of attachment and antagonism.

Celebrity culture is a powerful influence in many settings, contexts and relationships in the globalized, mass-mediated spaces that characterize the start of the twenty-first century. Movie and music performers, sports people, chefs, politicians, can all be, or aspire to be, celebrities. The literature on sports celebrities (see, for example, Ellis Cashmore's (2004) *Beckham*: also Toby Miller's (2001) *Sportsex*, and Barry Smart's (2005) *The Sport Star*) points to the ways that we *consume* celebrity, and develop relationships and attachments to celebrities – both in the process of consumption and in the desire to consume.

One element of these analyses of the ways in which audiences consume celebrity (particularly in Cashmore) is the concept of a *para-social* interaction or relationship. The concept highlights the ways in which we, as consumers, locate ourselves in what is, essentially, a one-way relationship with a celebrity. To illustrate: we know that Jamie Oliver exists. We form a sense of who he is. As a consequence of his media presence, profile, personae, we develop an orientation to him. *He annoys us. We like him. We admire what he does with food. We are sceptical about his motivations.* The possibilities for this orientation, attachment, or relationship are many – not only for us, but for the many millions of other consumers of celebrity who also *know* Jamie Oliver. Yet, importantly, he does not need to know that we exist for him to continue to be a celebrity, or to involve himself in media, educational, and political processes. We can be/are completely irrelevant to him, even though his public manifestations can have significant impact on us. He has the capacity to educate us (and millions of others) about his understandings of food, yet he need never know that we exist.

Again, this educative capacity can be understood and critiqued in various ways. But the power of this capacity is enhanced within a context which is also shaped by the idea, practice and products of social entrepreneurship. It can also be read as a middle-class, celebrity 'tosser' telling working-class *victims* how and what they should eat, and how this orientation to food is central to all aspects of their lives, their styles of life, their capacities for making choices and exercising their freedom in particular ways. But, as we have suggested this is not necessarily a useful, satisfactory reading of a complex phenomenon.

*Jamie the celebrity chef*

> Today, celebrities have little choice: their status is entirely dependent on their preparedness to become a commodity. Think of [English footballer, global celebrity brand, David Beckham] the creator: his actions on the field of play have moved many to compare his work with that of an artist. Think of him as a creation: near-identical images of him adorn too many items to mention, each helping to shift products from shelves in the same way that logos and familiar labels shift soup and soft drinks. Yet, he remains studiously absent, only a public persona breaking through every so often. Everyone can desire, though no one can have the real Beckham, if indeed there is such a being. Still, as Warhol himself argued, the famous are there not to be admired or cherished and certainly not to be analysed, but to be bought and sold like anything else on the market.
>
> (Ellis Cashmore, 2004, *Beckham*, p. 213)

Jamie Oliver is only one in a long line of celebrity chefs to hit our TV screens, not all of them young but almost always male. There are, of course, exceptions to the rule: Margaret Fulton and Stephanie Alexander in Australia, Delia Smith and Nigella Lawson in the UK, and Alice Waters in the United States are some examples. The phenomenon of the celebrity chef is not a new one. Elizabeth David, for example, who published numerous cookery books that are still prized today, is considered responsible for bringing French and Italian cooking into the British home post-Second World War. Her celebration of regional foods echoes

Jamie Oliver's current concerns with slow, regional, and seasonal foods. Global telecommunications technologies have energized a widespread interest in watching food being prepared by others, and in sharing vicariously in its preparation and consumption – a phenomenon identified by some as *food porn* (Probyn, 2003; Lumby and Probyn, 2003a). Paradoxically – but perhaps not coincidentally – this has occurred at the same time as our consumption of over-processed and convenience food has increased, and the art of cooking has become lost, or a novelty for many of us.

Recently, tell-all exposés of the restaurant industry, such as Anthony Bourdain's (2000) *Kitchen Confidential*, Bill Buford's (2006) *Heat* and Marco Pierre White's (2006) *White Slave*, have painted a colourful, frenetic, even debauched picture of life in the restaurant kitchen for most of those who work there. Anthony Bourdain (2000, p. 61), an American celebrity chef, quotes respected chef Scott Bryan as suggesting that the business attracts *fringe elements*: 'people for whom something in their lives has gone terribly wrong'. In Bourdain's account, and in others, working life in a commercial kitchen is overwhelmingly macho and sexist in culture, marked by long hours, poor pay, casual labour, drug and alcohol abuse, sexual promiscuity, bad behaviour, exploitation and endless ritual and repetition. In this account *kitchen slaves* are part of the *culinary underbelly* in the subtitle to his book. In one anecdote, Bourdain tells of his time as a mature-age student at a famous American cookery institute; he describes his relationship with the younger trainees thus: 'I felt no shame or guilt taking their money, selling them beat drugs or cheating at cards. They were about to enter the restaurant industry; I figured they might as well learn sooner rather than later' (2000, p. 370).

These, and other, anecdotes highlight the sometimes brutish elements of life in these kitchens. They also point to the rigidly hierarchical nature of the profession. Bill Buford, in his book *Heat* (2006), illustrates this hierarchy well via his fine-grained descriptions of learning how to chop vegetables properly under the judgemental, critical gaze of his line supervisors: a disciplined/disciplining activity that he was required to do all day, every day until he mastered the art of vegetable slicing and dicing. Only then could he progress to other tasks such as dicing meat for stocks and stews, all of it painstaking and all of it repetitious. Once these basics were mastered he was then able to move up the ladder to the position of line cook. In this position you are responsible for one aspect of the daily menu. Buford's account of his time at the 'Grill Station' gives some idea of the difficult conditions he, and others like him, are required to work under:

> The grill station is hell. You stand at it for five minutes and you think: so this is what Dante had in mind. It is in a dark, hot corner – hotter than any other spot in the kitchen; hotter than anywhere else in your life. Recently air-conditioning was installed in the kitchen, but there is none over the grill during service; how else can it maintain its consistent hot temperature? The light is bad, for no sensible reason except that there isn't enough of it, reinforcing a feeling of a place where no one wants to be – too greasy, too unpleasant. What light there is seems to come from the flames themselves; they are lit about an hour before the service starts and remain burning for the next eight hours.
>
> (Buford, 2006, p. 81).

Bourdain's (2000, p. 3) chaotic and earthy picture of the underbelly of the restaurant business – often marked by cruel treatment towards newcomers – also highlights the hierarchical, almost dictatorial culture of the commercial kitchen: 'a subculture whose centuries-old militaristic hierarchy and ethos of "rum, buggery and the lash" make for a mix of unwavering order and nerve-shattering chaos'. The hierarchical nature of the business is writ large in his exposé and he describes the strict order of progression from kitchen sweeper and grease-trap cleaner to specialized line cook. Addressing would-be chefs in his final chapter he argues that 'at least in the beginning, you *have no rights*, are not entitled to an opinion or a personality, and can fully expect to be treated as cattle – only less useful' (2000, p. 293).

This is of course a different world to the representations of most of the celebrity chefs who inhabit our screens (picture Delia Smith in her pristine kitchen, her beautiful garden framed by very clean picture windows) and, in particular, the life we are led to imagine that Jamie Oliver inhabits and the life his trainees imagine for themselves. Indeed, the cover notes for *Kitchen Confidential* include a quote from a newspaper review of the book that claims that Bourdain is a 'man whose innate debauchery exposes Jamie Oliver for the choirboy that he is'. Which, for some, may raise the question: *what's real about the representations we see of Jamie's Kitchen as a workplace, training environment and space in which lives might be transformed?*

*What's real about Jamie's Kitchen?*

The original *Jamie's Kitchen* screened on the UK's Channel 4 in 2002 – it was broadcast a year later on free to air television (Channel 10) in Australia over five weeks. As we indicated in the introduction to this book, the series was enormously popular and attracted an average weekly audience of over five million in the UK alone (Smith, 2006). In the series Jamie took 15 unemployed young Londoners and tried to turn them into trainee chefs who had the capacity to work in his new London restaurant called, appropriately, Fifteen. The original series was followed by *Jamie's Kitchen Australia* – a successful, high-rating 13-part series that was screened on Channel 10 (Australia) during September–November 2006. This series tracked the opening of the Fifteen franchise in Melbourne, and followed a similar format to the original 2002 series – indeed it paid *homage* to that series and structured much of its content and format via references to similar incidents, issues and problems that gave form, and drama, to the original. Westminster Kingsway College (WKC), London, Jamie's old catering school, was the training site in the first series. Box Hill TAFE (Institute of Tertiary and Further Education) in Melbourne's North East was the training site for *Jamie's Kitchen Australia*.

In the first series the candidates were chosen from a pool of thousands of hopefuls who turned up for interviews in response to advertisements. The first couple of episodes introduced us to the young people who had been gradually whittled down to the final fifteen candidates. In Episode One each candidate sat in front of a camera and talked about what food they liked, and why they wanted to become chefs.

---

*Jamie Oliver (in a radio station studio discussing his training proposal with DJs):* I want to see these kids kind of be instinctive about cooking, feeling it, smelling it and really getting into it and talking about food like they know what they're talking about and enjoy it.

[At various times during discussion camera cuts to footage of different young men and women talking to camera about the food they like.]

*White Girl #1:* I ain't really got a favourite food. I like all food. I don't mind what's put in front of me. I'll have a try. I'd taste it. I wouldn't mind a roast dinner though or pie and mash. I like things like that. I ain't too picky on my food.

*White Boy #2 (pimply with hat):* Mashed potato.

> *Black Girl #1:* My favourite food has to be my mum's cooking. I'm sorry probably everyone's saying my mum but it definitely is my mum. My favourite dish has to be on a Sunday when I go over there she cooks boiled rice with stewed chicken, plantain, red kidney beans with pig's tail. Pig's tail is absolutely gorgeous.
>
> *White Boy #4:* I like to cook best is stuff like pasta tagliatelle and spaghetti bolognaise. All stuff like that.
>
> *Voice Over:* and how do you cook it?
>
> *White Boy #4:* In a pan.
>
> *White Boy #5:* My favourite food is pasta. I first learned I liked it when I tried to lose some weight. Cook the pasta properly, cook some broccoli, make a cheese sauce, sprinkle some cheese on top. Put it in the oven until it's nice and golden brown.
>
> *Black Boy #3:* Chips and scrambled egg.
>
> (*Jamie's Kitchen*, Episode One, Broadcast in
> Australia on Channel 10, 21 July 2003)

After the selection team watched these videos the applicants were whittled down to 60. Follow-up interviews, which incorporated a taste test – in which they were marked out of 10 for their responses to food they had not eaten before – reduced the number to 30. Most of the young people seen in this video footage were nervous and/or inarticulate and this voice-to-camera technique made most of them look stupid. One young woman gave a detailed explanation of how to make mashed potatoes. Although some appeared more passionate, articulate and convincing than others, it was clear from the beginning that their food repertoires were limited in terms of the variety of food available to them, their food preferences and their previous cooking experience. This device made it clear that Jamie and his crew had a big job ahead of them if they were to turn these young people into chefs.

The format was similar to other reality TV shows such as the *Idol* franchise. In both *Idol* and *Jamie's Kitchen* the audience watched the selection process, which involved mass interviews over some weeks in order to reduce thousands of applicants down to a chosen few. Again, using a format similar to *Idol*, the audience was privy to the deliberations of Jamie and his team as they tried to sort out the wheat from the chaff. We witnessed the pain and disappointment of those who did not make the cut, as well as the excitement of those who did. The series was described as having 'all the ingredients of a soap opera' by *60 Minutes* in the USA (CBS America, 2006): providing, as it did, the kind of fly-on-the-wall, almost larger-than-life, insight into the lives of Jamie and his trainees, accompanied by all the drama and pathos we have come to expect from the soap opera genre. There was a parallel story-line in both series as Jamie – in partnership with his Australian friend/fellow chef Toby Puttock in *Jamie's Kitchen Australia* – was involved in choosing a site for the new restaurants and overseeing renovations. In both shows building and renovation timelines were seldom met, associated costs always seemed to be escalating, and we were encouraged to think that the restaurants were in danger of not opening on time, or opening with styling and decoration incomplete. This was a dramatic thread that ran through many of the episodes.

---

[Episode Three opens with camera on Jamie and his accountant Mike Prost at either end of a couch discussing the financial situation of the Fifteen venture.]

*Jamie Oliver:* On paper I'm doing a very stupid thing, I know my old man hasn't said it, but I know he thinks the same as what I do, he thinks I'm crazy.

*Mike Prost:* We went to the Development Agency, we said to them this couldn't cost 450 thousand and they said fine, we'll contribute and then they actually did an about turn and it's 1.3 million.

*Jamie Oliver:* This has sort of turned into a bit of an animal really, hasn't it?

*Mike Prost:* Are you going to change your mind? You're going to change your mind I can see.

*Jamie Oliver:* Yeah, but I had some geyser come around to the office the other day with a notebook and pen. I said, 'Who are you'? 'I'm from the Bank', 'What are you doing'? 'I'm getting a quote for the office.' 'Why?' 'Because you're borrowing money. And if it all goes tits up we're having your offices.'

[Laughter]

*Jamie Oliver:* Oh God. Oh God.

*Voice Over (footage of construction activity at site of restaurant):* Jamie Oliver's money is on the line. So is his reputation. He's up to his neck in a risky new venture, a non-profit making restaurant and the costs are rocketing.

[Footage of Jamie holding new baby, arm around his wife, Jools, posing for throng of photographers outside hospital.]

Jamie's also taken on the job of a lifetime. He's become a dad. To top all that he's signed up to another big time commitment. He's chosen 15 unemployed young people to cook for his new restaurant.

[Footage of trainees at stoves performing various tasks.]

The trouble is they can't cook. They'll train with Jamie once they've mastered the basics. For that he's put them on a crash course at chef's school. They'll have to cram a year's normal training into just four months.

> (*Jamie's Kitchen*, Episode Three, Broadcast in
> Australia on Channel 10, 5 August 2003)

Once the final 15 had been selected, the following episodes saw the initial excitement exhibited by the new recruits wane as the enormity of the task dawned on them. Like all apprentices they had to learn the basics, and the glamour of working in *Jamie's Kitchen* wore off in the face of the tedious repetition of hours spent chopping and dicing and being continually told to do it again until you get it right.

*Voice Over [footage of a particularly fraught vegetable chopping exercise under the tutelage of the austere trainer Herr Bosey]:* Top, the immaculate slices of Kerryann Dunlop. Rock-bottom the chunky lumps of Dwayne Montford.

> (*Jamie's Kitchen*, Episode Two, Broadcast in
> Australia on Channel 10, 29 July 2003)

*Jamie:* It's not all what they see of me, you know, TV chefs and book tours, that's rubbish. It never happens. It's going to be hard work. Scrubbing out fridges. It is about getting on your knees and scrubbing rubbish out of the floor

> (*Jamie's Kitchen*, Episode One, Broadcast in
> Australia on Channel 10, 21 July 2003)

The drama in the shows also derives from the sometimes volatile interactions between the trainees and Oliver and the other trainers. In the first series the London trainers included a number of Jamie's friends and mentors. Food writers, restaurateurs, and hoteliers Zoe Collins and Ruth Watson, and Jamie's mentor Gennaro Contaldo helped Jamie with the judging when the final 30 were required to prepare a salmon dish in the kitchen at WKC. This task was the final test to determine who the final 15 trainees would be. In the training kitchen we were introduced to a range of characters/figures including Herr Bosey, an imposing German chef; Peter Richards, Jamie's old college tutor described as being from the *old school*; and Mark Gautier, a lecturer at Hammersmith College. Oliver's use of friends and mentors was not only a sign of respect for those who trained him and assisted him to success but also an important plot device because it established Jamie's credentials as one who knows, as someone who is respected in the industry, as someone, who having done *his* apprenticeship, can be the *Master* to his own *apprentices*.

Oliver is of course integral to the drama of the first series. In this series we saw his judgement questioned; seemingly impossible deadlines looming and passing; the increasing friction in his relationship with his pregnant wife Juliette (Jools); his enthusiasm and energy wax and wane, and his concern increase as he saw his money disappearing before his eyes while building deadlines came and went. In *Jamie's Kitchen Australia* Jamie had a lesser role to play – he made only occasional appearances in the flesh, by phone or online to check on progress and offer advice and sometimes criticism. His place was taken by Australian chef/pal Toby Puttock who assumed the primary management/organizational role with the help of an enlarged support team put together and managed under the auspices of the Fifteen Foundation.

The Fifteen Foundation was established after the first series of *Jamie's Kitchen* in the UK. The Foundation is responsible for funding, managing and developing the training programme and ensuring that best use is made of their assets and resources. The Foundation's website states its purpose is 'to make Fifteen a global social enterprise brand providing fantastic opportunities for young people' (Fifteen Foundation, 2007). At the time of writing the Foundation has opened franchises in London, Cornwall, Amsterdam and Australia; has plans for a US version; runs a catering service; and provides continuing assistance to former trainees to open their own restaurants, or secure positions in restaurants around the globe.

So what is *real* about this sort of reality TV? What is real about this drama that is staged and framed and edited in ways that promise to produce dramatic entertainment that will, in turn, produce advertising revenue and be successful in the terms of commercial TV? Australian Cultural Studies academic and commentator Catharine Lumby (2003, p. 13) outlines, in broad terms, the characteristics of the reality TV genre. These include: 'the use of ordinary people as opposed to trained actors; editing which emphasises character and narrative; a multi-stranded narrative (normally characteristic of soap opera and drama) ... contrived locations; pieces-to-camera delivered by contestants; dramatic tension (the audience sometimes knows things the contestants don't) ... documentary style voiceovers'. Lumby also argues that reality television borrows from an assortment of different genres; the use of raw footage and voiceovers are aligned with news and current affairs; and the analysis of human nature (which some commentators have dubbed 'Lab Rat TV') is a feature common to documentaries. As well, the use of repetition – 'at the beginning of each nightly episode there are synopses, and at the end, tomorrow's episode is previewed' (Roscoe, 2001, p. 481) – is a common feature of soap opera. We can see in this characterization the themes, threads and narrative structure we were witness to in the *Jamie's Kitchen* series.

As with all representations we know – at one level – that we are watching a carefully edited and contrived version of *reality* in this reality TV series. For example, those trainees who were the least controversial and problematic got very little airtime. Indeed, some trainees whose faces were unfamiliar appeared at the end of both series. These young people apparently had less *drama* in meeting the demands of the training, and of the processes of self transformation that characterize the training processes in both series. This is perhaps not surprising given that the reality television format, in a similar fashion to that of soap opera, relies on 'conventional development of identification with particular contestants and narrative outcomes' (Turner, 2005, p. 419). That is, as the audience for these shows we are presented with a limited set of characters, and characterizations, that we can form some sort of attachment to. An attachment that can be sustained over the duration of the series and which will keep us viewing as advertisers try to sell us *stuff/things*.

There is continued debate in the media, in academic circles, in staffrooms and around the dinner table (and more recently in houses of parliament both here in Australia and in the UK) about the pros and cons of the cultural phenomenon known as *reality* TV. Discussions abound about whether or not it is real, hyperreal, fiction; whether it simply mirrors or makes *reality* in terms of, for example, promoting racism, sexism and promiscuity (mainly debated in relation to various permutations of the *Big Brother* series). In a recent review of *Jamie's Kitchen Australia* journalist Melinda Houston (2006, p. 58) described the series as 'a perfect microcosm of the nation'. She argued that the series has provided a 'stunning insight into Australian society' portraying 'drug addiction, abuse and homelessness' and making 'middle-class' Australia sit up and take notice, when they normally would turn off, through 'attaching Jamie Oliver's marquee name to proceedings and ensuring – through clever editing and a robust sense of humour – that it was never anything but entertaining'. The interest that these programmes generate among *real* people whom we know certainly suggests that they produce *real* effects. In this sense Arjun Appadurai's (1996) concept of *mediascapes* is useful in identifying and analysing the realities that provoke, and are provoked by, the genre. These mediascapes – newspapers, magazines, TV shows, films, the WWW – enable us to justify focusing on the figures of Jamie Oliver and his trainees, and the drama of *Jamie's Kitchen*, as legitimate objects of our academic work. For Appadurai (1996):

> Mediascapes, whether produced by private or state interests, tend to be image-centered, narrative-based accounts of strips of reality and what they offer to those who experience and transform them is a series of elements (such as characters, plots, and textual forms) out of which scripts can be formed of *imagined* lives, their own as well as those of others living in other places. *These scripts can and do get disaggregated into complex sets of metaphors by which people live as they help to constitute narratives of the Other.*
>
> (1996, pp. 35–6, emphasis added)

Series such as *Jamie's Kitchen* are successful, then, because we, as members of the globalized audience for these and similar shows, are able to form scripts of *imagined* lives from the devices, techniques and narratives that shape the genre. We recognize plots, characters, dispositions and emotions generated in and through these mediascapes. We are able to imagine ourselves and our lives in relation to these mediascapes, or to empathize with those individuals, groups, relationships that are represented there. In short, many aspects of these narratives *ring true*. The more such narratives ring true the more successful they are.

For Paul Willis (2000, p. 117) this *ringing true* can be thought of as the *Ah-ha effect*. In ethnographic research and representations this effect provokes moments of recognition or creative imagining, in what Willis describes as 'evocative' representation. For us the depictions of the young trainees in *Jamie's Kitchen* produced just such an effect. The sketches we provide of selected trainees later in this chapter – drawn in part from their lives on screen along with other media representations – are evocative of the many young people we as educators and researchers see both in and out of education and training settings. For some commentators our experiences, of ourselves and of others, are understood and made sense of by reference to our previous experiences. We can understand these processes in terms of their *intertextuality*: a term that signals the ways in which events, practices, contexts are understood as more or less familiar in relation to previous experience (see, for example, Johnstone, 2002). We would suggest that the power of reality TV such as *Jamie's Kitchen* exists, in part, as a consequence of its intertextuality.

Reality TV can also be understood as one example of what Kenway and colleagues (2006, p. 25) term the global/local nexus. *Jamie's Kitchen* and *Jamie's Kitchen Australia*, as elements of the Jamie Oliver franchise, have what might be termed *global* formats: characteristics, settings and narrative structure that are easily recognized regardless of the country of manufacture. However, these series also have *local* inflections such as geographical locations, language, accents and sometimes different, although importantly still recognizable, cultural interpretations and meanings. Appadurai (2000, p. 100) has argued that global cultural processes are 'products of the infinitely varied mutual contest of sameness and difference on a stage characterised by radical disjunctures between different sorts of global flows and the uncertain landscapes created in and through these disjunctures'. In this sense we can argue that identity in a globalized context has global, national, regional and local components as well as particularities of gender, race, class and sexuality. Moreover, 'the dialectics of the global and the local' produce 'hybrid identities' and, at the same time, reassert 'traditional modes of identity' (Kenway *et al.*, 2006, p. 26).

It is within this type of conceptual framework that we can situate the two series of *Jamie's Kitchen* as studies of the new world of work; Jamie Oliver (and his work with the Fifteen Foundation) as the *figure* or exemplar of the entrepreneurial self; and the trainees as *figures* or exemplars of youth at risk of not developing the entrepreneurial forms of selfhood that the twenty-first-century worlds of work demand. It is to a sketch of a number of trainees that we now turn. *Who are the Master's Apprentices and what are they really like?*

## Section Two

### The master's apprentices

> When house-mates leave the house they are often asked to reflect on the experience of being part of a TV show, and to reveal the perceived gap between their 'real' selves and their representations
> (J. Roscoe, 2001, 'Big Brother Australia: Performing the "Real" Twenty-Four-Seven', p. 485)

Of the original Fifteen trainees, five went on to secure cooking careers. Elisa Roche (the only girl to graduate), Ralph Johnson, Tim Siadatan, Ben Arthur and Warren Fleet all ended up working in some of London's best restaurants. Given the marginalized, personal, work and educational backgrounds of many of the trainees, these successes are substantial. Not only did the trainees start off at-risk of leading wasted lives, they were also expected to do in one short year what other trainee chefs are expected to do over three or four years. And all while under intense media scrutiny, and with producers, directors and editors in control of the ways in which they would be represented, in the ways in which we get to see and imagine them. Some of the trainees obviously handled this much better than others. As a result of the media interest generated by the two television series, trainees have been asked to endlessly reflect on their experiences before, during, and after their selection, training and appearances on our screens. These representations and the forms of reflexivity they require and generate say something about the influence of media on modern forms of identity construction in which the ability to be a reflexive subject is, more often than not, taken for granted (Giddens, 1991). We would argue that this taken-for-granted-ness masks the uneven development and exercise of such dispositions. The gendered and classed dimensions of the modern reflexive subject are played out in various ways in *Jamie's Kitchen* and we explore the nature of twenty-first-century reflexivity in later chapters.

In the remainder of this chapter we will sketch details of aspects of the lives of a number of these trainees. These details are drawn largely from transcripts of the TV shows and provide a sense of the lives the young people have led up to the time of their recruitment. We also detail their experiences of work and training. Some of the Master's Apprentices we introduce here were largely unsuccessful in their attempts to transform themselves. Others were more successful – even inspirational – in their capacities to develop and transform their lives. The mix is not accidental, but it is also not representative of the cohorts. We intend these descriptions to be illustrative of some of the experiences, some of the histories/biographies, some of the problems, issues, tensions and dramas that were brought to, and emerge from, *Jamie's Kitchen*.

## Jamie's Kitchen: the 1st series

### *Kerryann Dunlop*

Kerryann was one of the trainees in the first intake of *Jamie's Kitchen* and featured heavily in this first series. At the time the series was broadcast she was 19 years old and came from Hackney in East London. A dedicated Arsenal fan she was often quoted as saying, 'cooking is the only thing I am good at'. In a web interview Kerryann stated that 'eating and cooking are my passion. As a kid I used to watch my mum and my nan in the kitchen – they are both great cooks – and I would be saying: "Can I do that? Can I taste this?"' (Fifteen Foundation, 2007). When Kerryann was selected she had already done a year's training at Butler's Wharf Chef School but this organization had closed down. During this time she had completed National Vocational Qualification (NVQ) 2 for front of house and kitchen so was not a complete novice when she entered *Jamie's Kitchen*.

In a profile that appears on the Fifteen Foundation website Kerryann describes herself as hard-working, boisterous and happy, although later in the article she contradicts this by professing she loves tasting new things but hates 'hard work' (Fifteen Foundation, 2007). Kerryann missed a lot of classes in the first series; finding it hard to make her money stretch to meet all of her needs. She was choosing to spend it on 'magazines and stupid things' rather than leave enough for transport. She finally thought 'I could get silly things for the rest of my life or get a life'. In this interview she cites being part of a team, communication and interpersonal skills as the most important things she has learned in the course. She also said that she 'has learned to taste things in a way I never could before: to recognise and identify individual flavours in a dish, instead of just liking it, or not liking it'. She thinks she has become more instinctive in her cooking and her growing confidence has meant that she can 'feel [her] way and judge quantities, without weighing ingredients'. At the time of this interview Kerryann was working as an assistant pastry chef at Baker & Spice in Chelsea.

In an article that appeared in *The Observer* (UK) on 12 October 2003 she is described as the real star of the show and being famous for 'skiving and moaning' (Kelly, 2003). In an article in Melbourne's *The Age* in December 2003, a spokesperson for the Fifteen Foundation admitted that she had been suspended, although the website profile indicated she had an enforced absence due to illness (Connolly, 2003). The spokesperson for *Jamie's Kitchen* went on to say: 'While the show was on the air in the UK, people were wandering into the restaurant saying, 'Where's that Kerryann girl? I want to sort her out for not turning up'. Kerryann's dramatic, starring role in the series exemplified many of the issues that trainees brought to the table when they enrolled in the training programme. Why did many of the trainees appear to be *looking a gift horse in the mouth*? What were they thinking in not turning up to work-placement, or not attacking the opportunities and challenges with passion? What sort of *slackers* were some these young people? All good TV, and manufactured to attract and provoke responses in viewers. However, there are more serious questions here about what an employer, a training organization, a social enterprise can or should know about the individual who they employ, train or work with. These questions exercised the minds of Jamie and his colleagues on many occasions in the first series as they struggled to understand the likes of Kerryann and how she appeared to be behaving. Early in the original series the drama was being shaped by these concerns as Oliver and Peter Richards (chef/trainer) were confronted with the need to understand and explain what influences might be shaping trainee attendance and engagement in the context of continuing absenteeism by Kerryann and others.

Voice Over: *After turning down thousands of other eager applicants Jamie can't turn a blind eye to the three kitchen truants – whatever they're going through.*

Jamie: *There's stuff going on that I don't know about and I can't relate to because I've never been through some of the things they go through. You know problems with family and stuff. So I think I have to consider situations ...*

Peter Richards: *I look at it from the point of view, you know, you're going to employ these people and how comfortable would you feel as an employer?*

Jamie: *Hmmm.*

(*Jamie's Kitchen*, Episode Two, Broadcast in Australia on Channel 10, 29 July 2003)

Kerryann was a particular concern in terms of no-shows throughout different elements of the training programme. Her behaviours and dispositions certainly tested the limits of the patience of people like Oliver, but also the processes and systems that Cheeky Chops had put in place at this time – systems and processes that would be subsequently criticized because they did not sufficiently account for the circumstances many of the trainees found themselves in.

---

*Jamie:* I don't know what to say to you darling because it's not the money.

*Kerryann:* This week there was a delay in Hackney with the line and ...

*Jamie:* Don't cry sweetheart. I'm not bollocking you I'm giving you a last chance.

*Kerryann:* I know I'm wasting it. I want this more than anything in the world.

*Jamie:* Let's cut the shit right. One more day not turning up is really not good enough. I have to see you really meaning this because, you know what, I'm putting myself out for you guys. I really am. Not just for you guys but on the whole bloody project.

*Kerryann:* I feel so shit at the moment.

*Jamie:* Why do you feel shit?

*Kerryann:* Because I feel like I'm relying on everybody else and I shouldn't be.

*Jamie:* Relying on everybody else?

*Kerryann:* Yeah, they're always giving me cigarettes and stuff because I've never got any money because I've got a debt to pay.

*Jamie:* What are you going to do? Where are you going to go after if you don't do this?

*Kerryann:* Nothing. It will break me if I don't do this anymore.

*Jamie:* Do you think you can do it? Should I give you another chance?

*Kerryann:* Please.

(*Jamie's Kitchen*, Episode Two, Broadcast in
Australia on Channel 10, 29 July 2003)

Regardless of her 'star' status, and perhaps because of the 'skiving and moaning' Kerryann did not graduate with the others in this cohort, but did get a chance to go back and complete her training later. Jamie Oliver explained some of the problems with the trainees this way:

> The problem with some of the trainees was that they were starstruck. Their celebrity status took over from their cooking. With the latest round of intakes he has told the cameras to keep out. 'It actually impacts on their learning. They start to think they are celebrities without being chefs first', he says. 'For some, it just wasn't for them. Some couldn't hack it. Some just disappeared ... because they couldn't be bothered to turn up.'
>
> (Connolly, 2003)

A later interview on the Tesco website sees Kerryann running the pastry section in the Fifteen restaurant and declaring: 'I'm going to be a chef' and despite some well-documented 'run ins' with Oliver asserting: 'Aww, he's great. He's like a big brother or best friend to me now.' She is 'too scared to' swear at Jamie now because 'the newspapers might say I'm getting sacked again!'

### Michael Pizzey

Michael Pizzey was 17 when he was selected into the first intake of trainees for *Jamie's Kitchen*. He was dyslexic and had been diagnosed with ADHD and, perhaps typically and unfortunately, had a poor school record and was an early school-leaver. The similarities between Michael's troubled academic history and Jamie Oliver's are evident. In the interview which appears on the Channel 4 website Michael declared: 'I've always loved cooking and wanted to be a chef since I was five but, because of my problems, I didn't think I would be able to do it.' Michael had poor concentration and as he said himself had 'a short temper'. He was prescribed Ritalin, which helped him concentrate and kept him relatively calm. Michael described himself as 'loud, sociable, caring' (Channel 4, 2007).

In Episode One he started off badly by refusing to eat an oyster and gagging on his ravioli in the initial taste test. Subsequently he became the object of much discussion in selection meetings between the trainers and Jamie Oliver. He was championed by Zoe Collins who stated: 'He's obsessed with food. I spent 20 minutes on the phone with him talking about the perfect pizza crust so I really think we should put him through.' In the end he was selected into the final 30 despite failing his taste test.

The final 30 were required to prepare and cook a salmon and vegetable dish so that Jamie and his team could select the final 15. The trainees were asked to comment on their experiences.

> Michael Pizzey: I love every second of it. The way you have to make everything perfect and on time. It is undescribable how I feel. I am so chuffed with myself.
> 
> (*Jamie's Kitchen*, Episode One, Broadcast in Australia on Channel 10, 21 July 2003)

His commitment and enthusiasm, at least at the beginning, were unmistakable. However, when the final 15 commenced training Michael was soon in trouble. He was unable to keep up with the pace, often made mistakes, became anxious and was prone to lose his temper.

> *Voice Over:* Michael Pizzey is finding it hardest of all. Dyslexic – he's also got an attention deficit disorder. He should be on medication to help him concentrate but he's not taking it.
> 
> *Peter Richards (Chef/Trainer also has concerns):* I don't know whether Michael is going to cope in a commercial situation.
> 
> (*Jamie's Kitchen*, Episode Two, Broadcast in Australia on Channel 10, 28 July 2003)

To make things worse, soon after Michael set a tea towel on fire.

> *Mark Gautier (Lecturer at Hammersmith College, comments):* It's double jeopardy, a lighted tea towel and a pot of boiling water. All he'd need was a pair of roller skates and we would have lost him completely.
> 
> (*Jamie's Kitchen*, Episode Two, Broadcast in Australia on Channel 10, 28 July 2003)

Despite all of this Michael's attendance record was the best of all of the trainees – but this was largely as a result of Jamie Oliver intervening and trying to find out why Michael had, at one point, failed to attend classes over a significant period.

*Voice Over:* This isn't Michael's first run-in with his teachers, in a fit of peek he stomps out threatening to jack in the whole course. To keep him on board, Jamie makes a twenty mile round trip to see him at home.

[Footage of Jamie in car on motorway, then walking up path to front door, knocking – hears dogs inside.]

*Jamie:* I can't stand dogs, I don't like dogs.

[Inside house – following scene is an exchange between Michael Pizzey and Jamie Oliver in living room of Michael Pizzey's house.]

*Jamie*: So what's going on then?

*Michael Pizzey:* I'm just totally … I'm just bored at the moment.

*Jamie:* Bored?

*Michael Pizzey:* Yeah, because nothing really exciting is happening.

*Jamie:* Right, what do you mean by that?

*Michael Pizzey:* Well, my colleagues were cooking and enjoying it, and some of the staff [inaudible] doing it all over again, but when it comes to Mondays and all we do is parcel these boxes upstairs … It's just not really exciting me much.

*Jamie:* Unfortunately, the start is always the most boring. We're only two months away from opening the restaurant. Our restaurant. You know what I mean, I just think it's a real, I mean, at the end of the day I'd be really disappointed in myself if we lost you at this point, because we haven't started cooking yet. You know sometimes things in life are a bit boring …

*Michael Pizzey:* I know that, if I do basically quit, I've just wasted three months … And I'm going to disappoint a lot of people.

*Jamie (in car, to camera):* I don't know what to say really, I'm quite shocked, I thought he was going to give me a whole load of reasons why he didn't want to do the course. But I was bombarded with the one thing, which is, 'I was bored.' I like the boy, I want him to do well, that's why I came all the way out here to sort him out. He's being a fucking baby.

(*Jamie's Kitchen*, Episode Three, Broadcast in Australia on Channel 10, 5 August 2003)

Michael's relationship with the trainers, particularly Peter Richards, became progressively more volatile, especially after he broke his arm playing basketball with the other trainees outside the college.

---

*Voice Over:* Michael Pizzey has a good attendance record but a bad attitude. Playing on his broken arm, he hopes to duck out of the cookery lesson, but his teacher Chef Peter Richards has other ideas.

*Peter Richards (Westminster College, standing over Michael):* Well, that's it, now see when I spoke to you yesterday I said you would come in today and you would help me with the stores.

*Michael Pizzey:* Well I'm up and down stairs and everything and carrying … .

*Peter Richards:* It's only your hand that's hurting, it's not your legs.

*Michael Pizzey:* Yeah, but I can't carry things, that's the thing.

*Peter Richards:* If you can't come in and do the work that everybody else is doing, then I will find you something to do.

*Michael Pizzey:* I've had a lot going on this week which really just done me properly in, just properly just done me in, physically and mentally.

*Peter Richards:* We'll draw a line under it, but next week you're either here to work in the kitchen and if you're not here to work, then I will find you something to do.

*Michael Pizzey:* I can't see any point in being here when I'm in this state, but as he says, 'Chef knows best' [heavy sarcasm as Peter Richards walks away]. Tosser!

(Jamie's Kitchen, Episode Three, Broadcast in<br>Australia on Channel 10, 5 August 2003)

---

Because of his learning difficulties Michael also found it difficult to pass the theoretical components of the course (NVQ Level 1). His struggle with this side of the programme in particular made Michael anxious and when he was confronted by the Head of School, Sheila Fraser, for not handing work in on time he became aggressive and yelled at her – he was ultimately suspended from the programme for what follows.

*Voice Over:* Two weeks on the students who failed the NVQ are back to try again, but there's been a bust up. Michael Pizzey has turned up without his written work and had a row with the head of school. Student counsellor Tony Elgin has got to calm Michael down, but first he's got to find him.

*Tony Elgin (to Mark Gautier):* Mark. What's happened?

*Mark Gautier:* Basically, Michael Pizzey has had a confrontation with the head of school. He's verbally abused her and he's been instantly suspended because of that ... Obviously you just fucking can't do that. You do not threaten or abuse your head of school, it's just not done.

*Sheila Fraser (to Tony Elgin):* I spoke to Michael and I said, I said you just can't hand in things whenever you feel like it, it would be nice if you came to me ... I said don't shout at me, and he just kept shouting and then I said [inaudible] You're withdrawn and then that's when it erupted.

*Tony Elgin:* Well he's thrown his books down and he's gone, so I'll call him.

[Scene of angry confrontation with Michael – inaudible conversation – Michael Pizzey punches a locker in the locker room of the college.]

*Tony Elgin:* Calm down mate ... I can get you back in here.

*Michael Pizzey:* Why should I when I've [inaudible] things to work and she just keeps knocking.

*Tony Elgin:* It's not just today is it, it's an ongoing thing with lots of different people. You know what I mean, OK? OK? OK? Well that's because of the way you spoke to her.

*Michael Pizzey:* I don't like being spoken to like a little prick.

*Tony Elgin:* OK, but you've got to calm down, you've got to see what the situation is, then you've got the choice of whether you want to kind of continue.

*Michael Pizzey:* I've only got two days left.

*Tony Elgin:* Exactly, exactly.

*Michael Pizzey:* She had a go at me and I had a go back, why should I take that?

*Tony Elgin:* You can't speak to people like that. Because for example you're in the kitchen, you're a bit busy, you're a bit stressed, you can't go around speaking to people like that. So you've made a mistake. You appreciate that because you can't speak to people like that. You know that. So you're going to have to kind of undo that. It's a hiccup, it's not the end. So you've got to keep calm and do the right thing. Yeah? Yeah? Yeah?

*Michael Pizzey:* Right.

*Tony Elgin:* Cool.

(*Jamie's Kitchen*, Episode Three, Broadcast in Australia on Channel 10, 5 August 2003)

Michael organized his own work experience while suspended and was accepted back at the college after a disciplinary hearing in which he agreed 'not to fly off the handle and do my work on time and pass my NVQ1'. Once he met these conditions he would be allowed to join the rest of the trainees. He found it difficult not being part of the main group, stating, 'I feel quite left out.'

Michael learnt to be reflexive about his shortcomings and health issues through his interactions with counsellors, psychologists and other experts before, during and after *Jamie's Kitchen*. Understanding himself in these terms, learning to govern himself (sometimes more successfully than at other times) through these understandings is central to his reflexivity (Giddens, 1991; Foucault, 1991).

*Q:* **What is the most important thing you have learned on this course?**

I've learned a lot. I've done an anger management course to learn how to control my temper. I've learnt not to bottle things up but to tell people how I am feeling and not leave it until I fly off the handle. I've also learnt that my way of always saying what I think might not be the best way. I stop and think more now.

(Channel 4 (2007) *Return to Jamie's Kitchen: Meet the Trainees*)

Michael joined the following year's trainees on an induction weekend in Wales but despite time away and various interventions designed to keep him on track things didn't work out and Michael did not rejoin the other trainees after this weekend.

> He has returned to college to study catering: 'I've wanted to be a chef since I was five but, because of my problems I didn't think I'd be able to do it. I'm glad that Jamie took me on. I'm sorry I could not do it for him'.
>
> (John Aldridge, 2004, 'Q. What do a chef and a pizza boy have in common?', *The Observer*, Sunday 16 May 2004)

### Dwayne Montford

Dwayne Montford, who was 18 years old at the time of the first series, had a school history that saw him suspended from his school 126 times. Like Michael Pizzey, Dwayne was an early school-leaver, his student career punctuated by numerous suspensions and time spent at a behaviour correction school. By his own admission Dwayne found it hard 'to toe the line'. He was eventually suspended from the training programme for 'repeatedly failing to turn up for work placements' (McNeil, 2002). This admission mirrors the adversarial relationship that Dwayne had with teachers and school authorities, developing a learner identity as unsuccessful and as a troublemaker. This learner identity did not set him up well for his time as a trainee in *Jamie's Kitchen* and it was not long before Dwayne found himself in trouble in this environment.

Dwayne had trouble taking direction and liked doing things his own way:

> *Voice Over:* Dwayne's his own man. He's just been told how to peel and segment grapefruit but he decides he knows best – [He gets taken to task for doing it wrong]. The fruit salad shows that some of them still haven't mastered the art of cutting. Dwayne's cut himself, as well as the fruit. It's too late to undo the damage but Dwayne has come up with a novel way to improve his marks. With the teacher's back turned, Dwayne pulls a fast one and swaps his plate with Peter's.
>
> (*Jamie's Kitchen*, Episode Two, Broadcast in Australia on Channel 10, 28 July 2003)

In this incident Peter Richards (Chef/Trainer) did not take kindly to Dwayne's prank, stating: 'I know my work because I know it is good. You know your work because at the moment it's crap.' This set in train a relationship between trainers and trainee marked by suspicion and criticism that went from bad to worse.

> *Peter Richards:* I have doubts about Dwayne. I was bloody angry because he was taking the piss out of me. Now he doesn't need to do that [Dwayne pokes his hand into the chef's hat when he is judging his food]. Now he doesn't need to do that. I give him far more than he gives me. All I expect him to give me is commitment and I've told him this.
>
> *Voice Over:* Dwayne has written BLACK BOY next to his name on the roll.
>
> *Peter Richards:* Did he do that? Hell.
>
> *Herr Bosey* (another trainer) *to Dwayne:* One time explaining, two times explaining acceptable, three times explaining then we have a serious problem.
>
> (*Jamie's Kitchen*, Episode Two, Broadcast in Australia on Channel 10, 28 July 2003)

Dwayne demonstrated an ability to be reflexive about his behaviour, stating in a voice-to-camera sequence in Episode Two:

> *Dwayne:* When I started, I started off crap cos I was messing about, mucking around. Doing things I shouldn't be doing and then I had this big talk with chef and he told me I had to pick up or I'm coming off the course. Sometimes I go too far on the funny side. First I started off in a really good school called Woolidge polytechnic. I used to be really naughty, badly behaved. Didn't do my work. Throwing chairs everything. Got excluded. I made a record in that school for getting excluded the most which was 126 times – well I've never been expelled. If I got kicked off the course I would never be able to live with myself.
>
> *Voice Over:* What would you end up doing?

> *Dwayne:* I don't know. It would make me think that I am shit so I would end up doing something shit like working in a crappy restaurant. It would bring me down basically.
>
> (*Jamie's Kitchen*, Episode Two, Broadcast in
> Australia on Channel 10, 28 July 2003)

Of course, brief moments of insight do not mean that learned behaviours are easily overcome. In Episode Three we saw Dwayne up to his old tricks when he added a range of strange (and somewhat random) ingredients to his *designer* sausages.

> *Pete Gott (owner of the organic piggery in Cumbria which the trainees and Jamie Oliver visited to understand food production):* And you as upcoming chefs, it's your job not just to cook it right, but you've got to make sure that they know they've got the right meat.
>
> *Voice Over:* Next they have to design their own sausage with whatever ingredients they want, as always Dwayne goes for broke.
>
> *Jamie:* Tell me what's gone in there?
>
> *Dwayne:* Everything, ketchup ... that, that, that ... [pointing to tubs of condiments, flavourings, etc.]
>
> *Jamie:* And what about *confusion of flavours.*
>
> *Dwayne: Confusion of flavours?*
>
> *Jamie:* What does this say about you?
>
> *Dwayne:* That I'll try anything.
>
> [Jamie laughs.]
>
> (*Jamie's Kitchen*, Episode Three, Broadcast in
> Australia on Channel 10, 5 August 2003)

Relationships between Jamie and Dwayne deteriorated when Dwayne did not show up for work experience. Jamie was visibly upset at this behaviour. Jamie subsequently phoned Dwayne to try and find out why he did not show up.

> *Jamie (making a phone call to Dwayne):* Dwayne, it's Jamie, can I just tell you that your head chef thinks I'm a complete tosser. He thinks I'm a tosser because every time you don't turn up I stick up for you right and then he's laughing at me. He's going: 'He ain't going to turn up, he ain't going to turn up'. And then what happens the next day? You don't turn up. Seriously Dwayne we need to have a chat tomorrow. I'm not going to have a go at you. I just need to talk to you man to man – and you are a man now, you're not a fucking kid alright. And let's get it sorted out. See you mate, you take care. Fucking hell.
>
> *(Jamie's Kitchen,* Episode Four, Broadcast in Australia on Channel 10, 12 August 2003)

The next day Jamie had a 'chat' with Dwayne:

> *Jamie:* You're a funny guy, you love to tell gags, but do you know what you're out of school now. I can't believe, can't believe you've gone on work experience and not turned up. And not only have you not told anyone in this building, you haven't even told your own head chef. It's really bad, really bad, cringe-able. If you understood the business a bit more, you'd understand how cringing it is. I go to bed at night cringing.
>
> *(Jamie's Kitchen,* Episode Four, Broadcast in Australia on Channel 10, 12 August 2003)

In spite of repeated warnings and chances Dwayne did not turn up for work. An article in *The Observer* on 16 May 2004 gave readers an update on the fate of the original trainees. At that time Dwayne was cooking pizzas in a Pizza Hut in south London, studying for an NVQ in catering at a local college and thinking about what might have been.

> I regret dropping out. I feel like I let everyone down, Jamie, me, the others on the course. I wish I could rewind and start again. I'm vexed. I could have been one of the top kids there ... I'd like to be working in a Michelin-starred restaurant but I'm squeezing cheese onto pizza base ... I know Fifteen was about giving people like me who were expelled from school a second chance but I want another chance. I wasn't ready for it. I didn't see what a great opportunity

I was being given. I always played the idiot at school and that was what I did at Fifteen. I thought I was being funny swapping plates around when I didn't get something right but I was really being an idiot. I don't blame Jamie. I blame myself. I wish someone had told me to knuckle down sooner. But no one said anything. And by the time they did, it was too late.

(John Aldridge, 2004, 'Q. What do a chef and a pizza boy have in common?', *The Observer*, , Sunday 16 May 2004)

## Jamie's Kitchen Australia

*Dovid*

Dovid was a homeless 20-year-old when he applied to be a Fifteen trainee and during the series lived in a Melbourne refuge. He had not had parental support since he was 11. He didn't know his father and was unsure why he left the family home and his mother is deceased.

*Dovid:* My dad left when I was younger and stuff. Don't know what happened there you know. Like before mum passed away I spent a little bit of time with her and stuff like that and knowing her really well, but as you get older you realise how you haven't got a mum, haven't got a dad. What's going on? On days I cry and stuff you know because I miss her.

(*Jamie's Kitchen Australia*, Episode Seven, Broadcast in Australia on Channel 10, 26 October 2006)

At his initial interview Dovid stated that he 'didn't really pass school'. He confessed to having a nervous disposition and stated that he does not follow through with things, preferring to take the easy way out. In Episode Four, when many of the trainees were starting to hit their straps, Toby Puttock had this to say about Dovid.

*Toby:* Dovid is incredibly quiet and I don't know where his self-confidence is at. Like he always hesitates about doing things. He's really smart so I am sure if he just jumped in he'd nail it and it would be fine but he thinks 'What if I'm doing it wrong?' and he's kind of looking around at what everyone else is doing and I think he just needs to trust himself and just go with it and I've said that to him.

(*Jamie's Kitchen Australia*, Episode Four, Broadcast in Australia on Channel 10, 5 October 2006)

Dovid found the going difficult for most of this series but others believed in him when he didn't. Another trainee Erin, a young mother on methadone treatment for a drug addiction, tried to help him out by swapping her successful rice dish for one that he had made a mess of.

> *Erin:* Take it up [to chefs for inspection]. Don't be scared. They're not going to know. They're going to think you did it. It's a cracker. And they're going to go 'Oh that's a pass'. Don't worry so much. Don't be so picky and hard on yourself. You're too hard on yourself. By next week you'll probably do it better than anyone. Go Dov. I believe in you.
>
> *Erin (to camera):* It's not my place to be helping Dov. But just like I think the damage it can do to somebody when they're not getting helped, and I think this is just such a good opportunity. For them to fall through the cracks and for no-one to even notice that it's happening. Maybe I'm not helping him, but in the other sense, I can't not. I don't know.
>
> (*Jamie's Kitchen Australia,* Episode Four, Broadcast in Australia on Channel 10, 5 October 2006)

Dovid did the swap but confessed to Toby that he 'had help' when Toby asked him: 'Where did you pull this one from?' Toby took a measured approach to the situation and was supportive and encouraging. Despite Erin's concerns that no one was noticing, it is obvious that they were.

> *Toby:* Take a deep breath. Don't worry about it too much. Let's have a look anyway [tastes the meat Dovid has prepared]. You've done a wonderful job of the meat man so you can do it. You've just got to relax a bit and go for it.
>
> (*Jamie's Kitchen Australia,* Episode Four, Broadcast in Australia on Channel 10, 5 October 2006)

This concern, however, did not stop Andrew Sankey from Box Hill TAFE putting Dovid on notice. Despite the willingness of chefs and trainers to support them, the trainees still had to pass the theory and training hurdles put in front of them – and in a short period of time. Episode Five saw Dovid in further difficulty when he studied recipes for the wrong day and quickly became overwhelmed.

*Andrew Sankey:* He can't organise himself. He did work for the wrong day. He had it all wrong.

*Voice Over:* After a slow start it's an apprehensive Dovid serving up his first dish. The clock's ticking. Despite having three dishes still to cook Dovid's been sprung by Glenn taking a break.

*Dovid:* I don't want to say I don't want to do it and stuff but it's confusing.

*Glenn:* Look you're going okay. You're giving it something but you are not giving it enough. Do you think you've got what it takes to make it in the kitchen?

*Dovid:* No.

*Glenn:* See you've already quit before you've even started. If you think like that you'll never get anywhere.

*Dovid:* Yeah.

*Glenn:* You're like 45 minutes before your exams due and you've got something boiling there on the stove and you're not even a quarter of the way into what you need to be done. You're down here having a cigarette. To me that's not commitment. That's running away. That's not stepping up to the plate and getting back in the kitchen and putting it out.

*Dovid:* It's not running away … It's saying … I'm sorry that you see it that way and stuff.

*Glenn:* I'm just saying it the way I see it. I've got all you guys. I'm here to help. Don't get me wrong mate, I'm on your side 100% but if you don't pass this TAFE … If Andrew doesn't give you a pass through you're not going to make it into the restaurant and we want all you guys to go through cos that's why you're here. Okay so you need to really put your head down. Alright? And get into it. Keep focussed and make it happen.

*Dovid to camera:* It just seems that they can see more in me than I can actually see in myself. You know they can see that I can do this but really … you know what I mean? Like put yourself in my shoes. I don't think I'm doing a real perfect job.

> (*Jamie's Kitchen Australia,* Episode Five, Broadcast in
> Australia on Channel 10, 12 October 2006)

Dovid, here, displays a particularly limited sense of self, of the possibilities and choices that he imagines are open to him, of the skills and capacities that he thinks he brings to the training and work environment of Fifteen. Throughout the series we develop a sense of a lifecourse characterized by loneliness and ongoing failure, marginalization and exclusion from mainstream institutions and relationships. On the evidence of this drama Dovid exemplifies the potential for material and social oblivion that Bauman and Beck identify.

> *Andrew Sankey:* Dovid must be used to failing everything and then everything is such a strain for him he started to have a little meltdown because he thought he was going to fail ... I can honestly say there's been good progress in the last week. Only last Tuesday I told him that based on what I had seen in the previous six weeks and his test results he probably wouldn't pass and probably wouldn't go through and unbeknownst to me he'd been sleeping rough. He'd been homeless for a week or so and I was telling him his uniform's all wrinkled, he's not clean and he's a mess and he was tired and dishevelled. Of course if you're sleeping in a park in the middle of a Melbourne winter ...
>
> (*Jamie's Kitchen Australia,* Episode Six, Broadcast in Australia on Channel 10, 19 October 2006)

Dovid observed that 'If I didn't pass it then I guess there's no more chances from this point on' and with this realization he put in the extra effort. Despite Andrew Sankey's predictions, Dovid managed to pass his theory and practical tests. His success seemed to mark a turning point in his progress.

> *Dovid:* That just shows I am learning a lot of things out of this. I was impressed with myself but at the same time I was like confident about what I had done as well. I didn't want to get the perfect score I just wanted to get a little bit of good feedback you know, on what I'd actually done.
>
> (*Jamie's Kitchen Australia,* Episode Six: Broadcast in Australia on Channel 10, 19 October 2006)

Even though Dovid appeared more confident in the training environment where he was well supported, this confidence was very fragile and work experience at La Luna in Melbourne saw him struggling again.

> *Dovid (speaking to camera):* I'm trying my best but something keeps holding me back. You know what I mean? You can just tell. People get frustrated you know. They show you something that's so easy you know. Something a five year old can do this guy here can't even do something a five year old can do. So fuck ...
>
> *Head Chef Adrian Richardson (to camera):* It seems like he's kicking himself. He doesn't want to fail. He's scared that people might think he's an idiot.
>
> (*Jamie's Kitchen Australia*, Episode Seven, Broadcast in Australia on Channel 10, 26 October 2006)

Adrian Richardson decided to work with Dovid one to one and slowly his confidence in the kitchen grew.

> *Dovid:* I've been given a shot to try some things that I want to do. I think I need more practice and stuff. There's still a lot to learn. The more days I actually spend here I tend to feel more comfortable with the guys I'm working with so then you know, so that keeps your confidence up so then you should have no problems doing a task.
>
> (*Jamie's Kitchen Australia*, Episode Seven, Broadcast in Australia on Channel 10, 19 October 2006)

Despite some further setbacks, Dovid seemed to find his feet amid the heat and noise of the kitchen when they were preparing food for a group of possible corporate sponsors. Later at the media launch he reflected on his journey.

> *Dovid:* I guess I've started to come out of my shell a bit and started to socialise with people. Try to do my best with things. Thought I couldn't do it and had doubts. I passed my training and stuff really doing all this. And I just think if I stop doubting myself there's no reason why I can't do it.
>
> (*Jamie's Kitchen Australia*, Episode Nine, Broadcast in Australia on Channel 10, 9 November 2006)

In the final episode the trainees cooked and played host to the chefs that welcomed them into their restaurant kitchens for their work experience. Dovid was selected to stand up in front of everyone and thank the chefs on behalf of the rest of the trainees. In many respects the processes of self-transformation that we witness with Dovid exemplify the sorts of outcomes Fifteen aims for. Processes, systems, support structures and rationalities come together to facilitate Dovid in developing new forms of self-understanding that promise, at the very least, to create new options and choices, new fields of possibilities in which Dovid might imagine and fashion a future; a future where there are still no certainties or guarantees.

*Kat*

We were introduced to Katherine Wilson – aged 23 – in the first episode of *Jamie's Kitchen Australia* when she attended the initial selection interview. Kat, as we came to know her, was slightly built, dark-haired, and pale. When we first saw her she was having an awful lot of trouble speaking. It is not just that she was nervous, as so many of the would-be trainees were. Her speech was slurred and her eyes glassy. In the words of one Melbourne reporter: 'Kat turned up to her interview looking very much like she was stoned off her tree' (Houston, 2006, p. 58).

> *Kat:* I'm getting over drug addiction and I'm ... but um ... I've got a lot of support from family ... [long pause during which Kat is trying to control her emotions]. Just a very touchy subject at the moment.
>
> *Interviewer:* Would you like the cameras to go away for the moment?
>
> *Kat:* Yeah.
>
> *Voice Over:* Katherine's now desperate to escape the clutches of heroin. For the last three months she's been on a methadone program trying to kick her habit. Katherine sees Fifteen as an opportunity to straighten herself out.
>
> *Interviewer:* I mean who am I to judge her but I would say she's looking for a respite in the kitchen – she wants to hide.
>
> *(Jamie's Kitchen Australia,* Episode One, Broadcast in Australia on Channel 10, 14 September 2006)

In a later episode Jamie asked Kat 'Where did it all go wrong?' after she indicated that she came from a good supportive family and that she had wanted to be a footballer from the age of 8 – an ambition she said her family encouraged her in.

> I used to like happy hard-core music and I started going to raves and that's where I got into ecstasy and speed and that was by about the age of 13.
>
> (*Jamie's Kitchen Australia*, Episode Nine, Broadcast in Australia on Channel 10, 9 November 2006)

On the first day at Box Hill TAFE several students were missing and Kat was one of them. She finally arrived an hour and a half late. An electrical failure at home caused her to sleep in and, on top of this, her partner had lost his keys and wallet. Cancelling his credit cards for him on the way in delayed her further. On arrival she declared: 'I'm here and that's cool enough for me.' Later that day there was a video link-up with Jamie so that he could meet and greet the new recruits. When it was her turn, Kat surprised everyone by speaking forcefully and articulately to Jamie.

> *Kat:* What got to me was the fact that Melbourne couldn't even admit to the problem and yet you're willing to come here and help us when our country can't even admit to the problem in the first place. And that is something that is inspirational and has motivated me. And I love the fact that you have the belief in all of us I guess to give us that opportunity. So thank you very much.
>
> (*Jamie's Kitchen Australia*, Episode Three, Broadcast in Australia on Channel 10, 28 September 2006)

After Kat spoke to journalists at the media launch televised in Episode Nine, Jamie likened her to a poet.

> *Kat:* I've changed my life for it and I've given it everything I can give. It's gonna give me a career so … I'm going to be here. I'm going to do everything I need to do and give the guys everything that I can.
>
> (*Jamie's Kitchen Australia*, Episode Nine, Broadcast in Australia on Channel 10, 9 November 2006)

Kat's willingness to speak positively about her Fifteen experiences makes her a good spokesperson for the Foundation and she is often featured praising the work they do. In Episode Eight she spoke to a group of would-be sponsors from the Australian business community about the opportunities provided to them:

> *Kat:* Being around people with the same focus to change their lives and get on the right track and having a great support base behind us and people that want something better for us and realise that we are young adults with talents and with dreams just like everyone else but ... and they want to give us a go.
>
> (*Jamie's Kitchen Australia*, Episode Eight, Broadcast in Australia on Channel 10, 2 November 2006)

Kat's journey of self-transformation was one of the most inspirational of all of the trainees. Her struggles were written on her face. She was open about how hard it had been for her, and also how determined she was to grab this opportunity to transform her life. Kat was particularly forthcoming in a group meeting where trainees were encouraged to comment on their experiences so far.

> *Kat:* I've managed somehow to change so much and I didn't even see it happen. I definitely found so much motivation and drive and being pulled through by the great group of people I'm surrounded by. It's helped so much for me [getting emotional] to reach the personal expectations I set and I want to reach higher levels and higher qualities but I have to relax and breathe ... and give it time and work hard and it will come.
>
> When I was using drugs every hit to me was kind of meaning ... or hoping that I overdosed without even knowing. It was just good gear or a dirty needle or ... who knows. Just something to take me over the edge. It's only just changed and that would have to be the biggest thing that I've got out of this and everyone has been a big part of that so it's awesome for me.
>
> (*Jamie's Kitchen Australia*, Episode Six, Broadcast in Australia on Channel 10, 19 October 2006)

It was clear that Kat's journey had inspired everyone, including the other trainees. Lauren Oliver told Kat that she had been considered for work experience with Jamie in the UK (Chase and Vanessa were chosen for this) but her health problems prevented them from selecting her. Rodney, another trainee who was ultimately a drop-out from the programme, had this to say about Kat's influence on him.

> *Rodney:* You know I remember you saying at the start you didn't really have much to get out of bed for and go outside and do things for and now every time I see you you've got so much to … and it's such a big thing to see and if that's all I've gotten from this then that's worth it for me. Is your happiness and your joy for life again. I think it's so fucking beautiful.
>
> (*Jamie's Kitchen Australia*, Episode Six, Broadcast in Australia on Channel 10, 19 October 2006)

*Alan, also known as Amos, also known as AJ*

In his initial interview 16-year-old AJ stated: 'I was always a really A grade student all my life and then my parents sort of split up and everything went downhill.' This family breakdown resulted in him leaving school early. Throughout the series AJ was in and out of the family home and we can only guess at the level of conflict he lived with outside the controlled environment in Jamie's kitchen.

> *AJ:* I came to have a problem with authority. I didn't really listen to many people.
>
> (*Jamie's Kitchen Australia*, Episode Four, Broadcast in Australia on Channel 10, 5 October 2006)

This confession proved to be rather prescient as AJ struggled with his relationships with authority figures in the series, particularly with TAFE teacher Andrew Sankey. Many of the episodes involved these two in a tussle for the high ground. As the Voice Over in Episode Four informed us: '16 year-old AJ doesn't like being told he is wrong.' Their first big conflict occurred when AJ overcooked his spaghetti.

> *Voice Over:* Andrew thinks AJ can do better so now he has to start all over again.
>
> *AJ to camera:* I reckon it's great. I can't tell if it's overcooked or not. I'd eat that every night of the week.

[Andrew Sankey has told him the next version is ok but AJ fiddles with it and then leaves it on the stove top to do something else.]

*Andrew Sankey:* I said let's go. That means pick it up. It's gone all oily again. You've cooked the water out of it.

[AJ looks very angry.]

*Andrew Sankey:* that's worse than before. Why didn't you put it on the plate when I said?

*AJ:* You never said put it on a plate you said let's go.

*Andrew Sankey:* What does 'Let's go' mean?

*AJ:* Hurry up or something.

*Andrew Sankey:* Hurry up for what? What's left to do? Are you going to cook it until it's black top and bottom? I've cooked better than that in the toilet. It's just gross. I don't know. You've mucked about with it for twenty minutes. It's a five-minute dish. Get yourself cleaned up.

[AJ walks out and Andrew follows him.]

*Andrew Sankey:* You don't think you can have a hard time and just walk out do you?

[AJ vents his anger with Douglas Patterson [Box Hill TAFE Course Director] out in the corridor.]

*AJ:* He goes 'Let's go' and I thought he meant hurry up. Instead 'Let's go' means chuck it on a plate ... He's pushing his luck. Swear to God.

*AJ to camera:* I was ready to hit him ... or stab him or hit him with something.

(Jamie's Kitchen Australia, Episode Four, Broadcast in<br>Australia on Channel 10, 5 October 2006)

This event took up a lot of airtime as the two of them traded threats back and forth. AJ was honest in his responses: 'The only reason I walked out to be honest with you ... another thirty seconds you would have felt something hit you.' But this only made Andrew Sankey more aggressive. As a result it became a bit of a boys *pissing contest* with Andrew asserting that: 'That's never going to happen under any circumstances.' Finally, Andrew tried to diffuse the situation by taking a more measured approach and bringing AJ's outburst back to a lesson about what not to do in the kitchen.

> *Andrew Sankey:* Now you were cross with me because I got you to do it again. So whilst you're in anger you're not thinking properly so you have to change something in yourself to cope with situations like that because they're going to happen every day in the kitchen. There's noise, there's people telling you what's what, there's customers sending meals back, there's a chef riding on your back. All sorts of things going to happen under pressure. If you're not ready for it or if you're just going to down tools and walk out or even hit somebody ... You won't last ten seconds. It's not going to happen. So you have to change ... not anybody else.
>
> ... You have to change so that it doesn't happen again because I was you ... I was that ... I know what it's like.
>
> (*Jamie's Kitchen Australia*, Episode Four, Broadcast in Australia on Channel 10, 5 October 2006)

Andrew's final response here is telling and perhaps the reason why he came down so hard on AJ. The problem of course is that his self-confessed trouble with authority left AJ with few alternatives – back down and lose face or revert to the behaviours that he has used in the past and challenge those trying to bend him to their will.

> *AJ:* So I have to change to suit your needs?
>
> *Andrew Sankey:* No. You have to change to fit into everybody else's needs. Otherwise all of your life you're going to be an aggressive little punk in a society that doesn't want you there like that. It doesn't work that way in a kitchen. There's no room for behaviour where you think fuck you all, I'm out of here.
>
> *AJ:* You can't change five or six years of my life in what ... two weeks.
>
> *Andrew Sankey:* I'm not asking you to change now in the next five seconds. I'm asking you to take this on board and over the next six weeks you do have to change otherwise I won't pass you.
>
> *AJ:* That's your choice.
>
> *Andrew Sankey:* No it's your choice. I'm asking you to develop as a person. As a human.

> *AJ:* I'm telling you right now I am not going to change just for something like that so then it's your choice whether you pass me or not.
>
> *Andrew Sankey:* What are you going to do with your life every time the pressure comes on? Run away? That's not productive. What are you going to gain out of it? What are you going to gain from running away?
>
> *AJ:* Well that's still to come isn't it?
>
> *Andrew Sankey:* I don't want to hold you up too long.
>
> *AJ:* Goodbye.
>
> *Andrew Sankey to camera:* What an interesting lad. I think he's going to go away and think about it and I'm going to be positive and I think he's going to change over six weeks.
>
> *(Jamie's Kitchen Australia*, Episode Four, Broadcast in
> Australia on Channel 10, 5 October 2006)

After this *chat* AJ arrived late to an important practical exam and was totally unprepared. Andrew told him to sit the test another day. AJ had been fighting with his family all weekend. He was kicked out of home the week before – which would have coincided with the altercation with Andrew Sankey – and was now looking for another place to live. After sexually harassing Lauren Tyler, one of the female trainees (we discuss this incident in detail in Chapter 5), AJ was suspended for five days. When he came back, the time he had lost made it very difficult for him to catch up as he was already behind.

> *AJ to camera:* It hasn't hit me yet but it will and I'll be pretty cut about it but I brought it upon myself I guess. I really have to figure out what I'm doing instead of sitting around and fucking hoping for the best. I might as well make it the best I can … I'm putting everything I can into this. It's anything and anyone that can help me is sort of helping me and I'm taking help from anyone about anything.
>
> *Interviewer:* Do you think you can do it?
>
> *AJ:* I sure bloody hope so and I reckon I can make it just as long as I put me head down and get all this stuff done.
>
> *(Jamie's Kitchen Australia*, Episode Six, Broadcast in
> Australia on Channel 10, 19 October 2006)

AJ arrived late for his final chance to pass the practical exam. He didn't think he had passed the theory exam as he 'had a shitload of guesses'. During his preparation he dropped a tomato on the floor, which rattled him, but after some time-out to compose himself he finished his dishes with three minutes to spare. Somehow he managed to pass his practical exam and Andrew praised his efforts. It was, however, very difficult for AJ to accept his praise after their various heated clashes.

> *AJ to camera:* Can't even describe the pressure. It's like nothing I've ever felt before. Really hard to come back and get into it all – and the main pressure is just doubting yourself all week you know ... made me feel sort ... shit.
>
> Yesterday I did four theories and practical and went into two of the theories not even knowing what the subject was.
>
> *(Jamie's Kitchen Australia,* Episode Seven, Broadcast in Australia on Channel 10, 26 October 2006)

Unfortunately for AJ his results were not good enough to get him through. There were other issues as well that had more to do with his age and immaturity which made the team reluctant to pass him through to the next stage.

> *Toby:* My feeling is that I think that you would benefit personally from not being in the Fifteen kitchen and from working in another kitchen and my reasons for that are I think you would benefit from being around older guys in the kitchen. I think if you're in the Fifteen kitchen with all of these guys you may be led astray again.
>
> *Andrew Sankey:* Given the effort you put in yesterday ... huge effort and it was such a good thing to see. If I was an employer and I saw that I would be thinking wow this kid has the ability to change and produce work like that! So that's a huge plus for you and now you can go off and do whatever you want with that.
>
> *(Jamie's Kitchen Australia,* Episode Seven, Broadcast in Australia on Channel 10, 26 October 2006)

The bottom line, however, despite the praise, is that AJ would not be continuing his Fifteen journey with the rest of the trainees. We end this chapter with his final voice to camera.

*AJ:* Fifteen's my family. That's it. Everyone's always there for me. Everyone went through the same thing. Had the same problem. You could talk to anyone about anything. It's not going to come back at you. For the next week or so it's just going to feel pretty bad but ... I don't know.

Other than that you get over everything I guess.

(*Jamie's Kitchen Australia*, Episode Seven, Broadcast in Australia on Channel 10, 26 October 2006)

# 2
# Jamie's Kitchen and the problem of young workers

## Introduction

In this chapter we will introduce detail about the Fifteen Foundation's training programme – the development of which is reflective of some of the drama we witness in the original *Jamie's Kitchen* TV series. This discussion will centre on the ways in which the Foundation identifies, understands and represents the individuals that it sees as the target population in its programme. The Foundation targets its training, education, work-placement and employment programmes to a particular population: a population that can be characterized as marginalized, unemployed (even unemployable) young people, aged 16 to 24 who have little or no employment history, or marketable employment (life) skills and capacities. Often, these labour market-related deficits are further complicated by drug- and alcohol-use issues, criminal activity, homelessness, and histories of abuse and violence.

These, for want of a better term, are the factual descriptors of the population that the Foundation targets – we can readily see which young people are of interest to the Foundation. However, at the level of representation, and of meaning, these signifiers open up for discussion and analysis ways of understanding a population that over the past 30 or 40 years has provoked community concerns about its transition into the adult world of work, autonomy and relationships. Indeed, what this focus on Fifteen's representation of its trainees does is provide a basis for a wider discussion of young people, youth labour markets, and the contemporary fetishization of 16–24-year-olds as *Generation Y*. This wider discussion, which draws on various constructions/representations of young people from fields such as youth studies, education, cultural studies and sociologies of work, can contribute to more critical understandings of young workers and generations in fields such as management, organization and labour studies.

## Fifteen and (the) problem (of) youth

> *Voice Over:* After turning down thousands of other eager applicants Jamie can't turn a blind eye to the three kitchen truants – whatever they're going through.
>
> *Jamie:* There's stuff going on that I don't know about and I can't relate to because I've never been through some of the things they go through. You know problems with family and stuff. So I think I have to consider situations …
>
> *Peter Richards:* I look at it from the point of view, you know, you're going to employ these people and how comfortable would you feel as an employer?
>
> *Jamie:* Hmmm.
>
> (Jamie Oliver and Peter Richards, chef/trainer, considering what influences might be shaping trainee attendance and engagement in the context of continuing absenteeism by some trainees)
>
> (*Jamie's Kitchen*, Episode Two, Broadcast in Australia on Channel 10, 29 July 2003)

As we discussed in the previous chapter, the entertainment value of the drama of both the *Jamie's Kitchen* series works at a number of levels. If this book was primarily about *Jamie's Kitchen* as a reality TV text we might focus our discussion on the techniques of staging, filming, framing, and editing that work to manufacture the drama that makes large numbers of viewers watch these and similar shows. We might also focus on the dialogue; or the use of Jamie Oliver, the celebrity brand, in various ways to structure and narrate the action to produce the drama; or the ways in which certain of the trainees figure more prominently in the drama than others. Indeed, this last technique is significant in creating a sense that the *type* of young person that the Fifteen Foundation targets to work in *Jamie's Kitchen* has a range of issues in their life (historically and in the present) that make them a *problem*; a problem that is often difficult to manage and regulate. And which continually places their position in the programme in jeopardy.

*Will they stay or will they go? Why are they looking this gift horse in the mouth? Don't they know that Jamie – who could be doing lots of things as a celebrity chef – is putting himself out for them? Sacrificing his time. Risking his money. Stuffing up his marriage. Why would anyone – any boss, employer, manager – bother with these kids? They're slack. They don't show up where and when they should. They can't follow simple directions. You have to watch their every move, and mood. Because they often show up angry, annoyed, tired, pissed off. And they're not backward in letting any and everyone know this.*

All of which makes for good drama and spectacularly successful TV. And as reality TV it is manufactured so that it will be dramatic and successful. Another significant reason for, and dimension of, the success of these series is that this drama, this focus on the problems and issues that might lead to failure, also produces a range of emotional responses in the audience – to the trainees, to those that train and manage them, and to Jamie Oliver. Again, these responses are varied – but they are not our main interest. What is of relevance though is that many of the marginalized, unemployed 16–24-year-olds who participate in the TV shows, and the ongoing training programmes, are successful in developing new skills, abilities, behaviours and dispositions that offer them the possibility of finding ongoing employment in the hospitality industry. And they do so despite circumstances, histories and contemporary relationships that would result in most of us missing work or appointments, losing motivation, or resisting management and regulation. Indeed, we too might appear as problematic or risky propositions in the world of work under these circumstances.

We will return to certain elements of this drama at various stages of the narrative that follows. For now we want to focus on a more systematic discussion and analysis of the Fifteen Foundation training programme and the young people it targets. The Foundation has produced a document entitled *What's Right with these Young People* that outlines the Foundation's training programme. Its target audience is prospective Fifteen franchisees, and its aim is to inform potential franchisees (and others interested in the training programme) 'about what goes on with our young people during their time with us' (Fifteen Foundation, 2005, p. 2). As such it provides a useful introduction to the purposes and processes associated with the training programmes Fifteen conducts on an annual basis with marginalized young people.

Fifteen exists to reach out to young people who are disregarded in society – the focus all too often is on what's wrong with them. Fifteen focuses on what's *right* with them, providing opportunities and

> support through which they can find and develop the best in themselves.
>
> (Fifteen Foundation, 2005, *What's Right with these*
> *Young People*, p. 3)

Embedded in this discourse are references to social understandings of the *type* of young person that Fifteen targets – understandings that are often negative and which attach themselves to a variety of problem behaviours, attitudes, histories, contexts and relationships. The nature of these problems is made explicit in the following manner.

> We work with young people who often come from troubled families, who have 'failed' at school and who have experienced homeless-ness, drug and drink problems, have been ensnared in the criminal justice system, and consequently have low self esteem, self defeating patterns of behaviour, and social networks that serve to keep them locked in to poverty and underachievement.
>
> (Fifteen Foundation, 2005, *What's Right with these Young*
> *People*, p. 3)

The narrative here indicates that the often negative understandings associated with these behaviours, contexts and relationships are influ-ential in perpetuating the circumstances that these young people find themselves in. The widespread focus on what is *wrong* with young people in these circumstances – by schools, businesses and managers, state and non-government authorities and agencies – is something we will return to shortly. At this stage though it is worth highlighting that the Founda-tion is keen to be seen as *realistic* about its potential for *fixing* the young people they target.

> We are under no illusions that we can 'fix' them. We cannot sort out family problems, undo a criminal record or compel them to give up smoking weed. What we can do is provide them with more choices, open doors to new networks and opportunities and invite them to step through, helping them develop new skills to deal with their old problems.
>
> (Fifteen Foundation, 2005, *What's Right with these*
> *Young People*, p. 3)

At this point the Foundation's story about what they set out to achieve is more about changing the settings and circumstances in which young people live their lives – often in ways that further marginalize them from work, education and training or productive engagements with various businesses, authorities and agencies – rather than with *fixing* individual lives. The logic suggests that new opportunities, new responsibilities, new settings and activities, new relationships will provide the possibility for young people to transform themselves. Again, the Foundation is explicit in communicating this logic and how they envisage this transformation occurring.

> This involves a unique encounter with food and Jamie's inspiring approach to cooking and service. But Fifteen is so much more than a chef training project. Food and cooking are the means to the end. The purpose is personal transformation for each young person.
>
> (Fifteen Foundation, 2005, *What's Right with these Young People*, p. 3)

In this sense – as we suggested in the introductory chapter, and which we will further explore in the following chapter – the Foundation positions certain understandings of food, of its production, preparation, presentation and consumption, as a technology of self-transformation. The purpose is not so much to train chefs, but to utilize food, cooking and the work environment of a commercial kitchen that thinks about, prepares and presents food in particular ways, as a means to transform the opportunities, choices and self-understandings of young people previously at risk of living and leading *wasted lives*.

As the Foundation indicates, with the *type* of young person that Fifteen deals with this is not necessarily an easy task. Indeed, processes that seek to enable these young people to transform themselves into passionate, creative, entrepreneurial workers in a commercial kitchen can be demanding on the young people involved, and on those that manage and train them, and attempt to support and facilitate these processes of self-transformation.

> Having to leave your past behind is a difficult task and not all the trainees make it. At least one in four of the London recruits do not get to graduation.
>
> (Fifteen Foundation, 2005, *What's Right with these Young People*, p. 3)

This significant attrition rate is explained by the Foundation in the following manner.

> Working long hours, early and late shifts, sometimes weekends, while your mates are out partying or worse, and turning up for college when you really don't want to be there, is bloody hard to do.

> They might drop out because they commit another offence and go back to jail. They might discover they don't like the hard work involved. They might turn out to have mental health issues which we simply cannot deal with. There are many reasons why.
> (Fifteen Foundation, 2005, *What's Right with these Young People*, p. 4)

The demands on the young people for this sort of commitment should not be underestimated. Indeed, in one episode of *Jamie's Kitchen Australia* one trainee's attitude, presentation and attendance was causing some concern to College trainers and Foundation staff. Yet, as the episode's narrative revealed, this trainee (Dovid) was *sleeping rough* in a park because he had no permanent housing. Of course the question arises as to what responsibilities employers, trainers, managers have to know about these types of issues in a trainee's/employee's life: and, once knowing about these issues, what obligations exist in organizations and work-places to manage them. In the social enterprise context of Fifteen such issues are not peripheral – they are fundamental to the mission of the Foundation and the work it undertakes. However, the point we want to return to at this stage is that the nature of this work with marginalized young people also creates demands on those who work with them.

As we have already suggested, managing a for-profit social enterprise presents a range of different issues and challenges to other forms of organization. Managing trainees – as individuals, teams, or groups – in a social enterprise context is different to managing and training and inducting individuals/teams in a work organization where employees who don't or won't or can't display preferred behaviours and dispositions can be (often are) sacked. In a social enterprise such as the one that the Fifteen Foundation operates, the core business of the franchise is to train, work with, support and encourage those young people that other orga-nizations wouldn't employ – for any number of reasons. Yet, we would argue, in this social enterprise context a whole range of issues that exist in organizations take on a starker, more explicit, *more in-your-face* character. Here we are thinking of issues associated with gender relations in organizations; differences in thinking, understanding and values based in social class, ethnic background, sexuality; differing models, modes and means of teaching, training and learning where the development and exercise of certain skills, behaviours and dispositions are the desired outcomes. The list could go on.

> It's exhausting and frustrating work: tracking down missing trainees, dealing with housing issues, money management, relationships and alcohol and drug abuse. Balancing the demands of a high profile professional restaurant business with the personal and social needs of young people in transition is a constant challenge for trainers, chefs and front of house staff.
>
> (Fifteen Foundation, 2005, *What's Right with these Young People*, p. 4)

In the glare of successful reality TV programming these difficulties produce good drama. However, in the ongoing work that the Foundation undertakes away from this glare, practices and processes are developed and deployed to enable the Foundation, and the restaurant, to deal with these issues in ways that can enable the business to operate successfully, and the training programme to run productively. Included in these processes are programmes such as the Buddy System outlined below.

> We introduce the Buddy System, linking each trainee up with a member of the Fifteen front of house team. This serves two purposes. It gives the trainee a 'special friend' outside of the kitchen who can help ease them into the hurly burly of restaurant life and help sort small niggly problems as they arise. Bigger issues are referred on to the Foundation team to sort. Secondly, by volunteering to be a buddy, the Fifteen staffer is given a clear role to play in the project and this involves restaurant staff in the core purpose of Fifteen.
>
> (Fifteen Foundation, 2005, *What's Right with these Young People*, p. 13)

In a later chapter we will return to discussing additional aspects of the Foundation's programme: a discussion that will look at the detail of the programme in terms of the variety of rationalities and technologies deployed in processes that seek to produce passionate, entrepreneurial trainees. The final point to make here though is that the programme also involves a number of 'collaborators' in providing a variety of training-related experiences. These collaborators are, *ideally*, individuals and organizations that 'understand and buy into the core mission of Fifteen and are able to offer the students the support they need' (Fifteen Foundation, 2005, p. 4). These collaborators include other restaurants that host trainees on work experience; primary producers that the Fifteen restaurants use to source ingredients and produce (meat, vegetables, olive oils, etc.); agencies with expertise in youth housing, health and support services. As the Foundation indicates, significant issues confront the programme in terms of the understandings and perceptions that collaborators and restaurant staff bring to their engagement with what Fifteen calls 'our challenging group of students' (Fifteen Foundation, 2005, p. 4). The Foundation recognizes a need to work with collaborators and its professional staff to develop different understandings of the trainees.

---

It is easy for professional chefs to jump to judgment on young people from very different backgrounds to themselves who respond in very different ways to pressure and hard work. When the heat is on, it is easy for a chef to get very angry with a trainee who is late and to make all sorts of assumptions about his or her perceived laziness, lax attitude and ingratitude for the chance they have been given. Working with the chefs and other staff to help them understand what the young people are going through is vital to a successful project and a harmonious and productive kitchen.

Greg Marchand, Head Chef in London, says this: *'They (the trainees) are receptive for the first four weeks, then they try to push just how far or how much they can get away with: time keeping, standing around, shouting, phoning in sick. I think they were a bit scared of their new environment, which would explain why they were quiet at first, but as soon as they sussed the place out, they were trying to act like they were tough cookies. A very important time for the chef is when you have to show them the line not to cross.'*

(Fifteen Foundation, 2005, *What's Right with these Young People*, p. 13; italics in original)

---

The main purpose of this discussion has been to identify that *Jamie's Kitchen* and the Foundation not only work with marginalized, unemployed young people. They also work with, and often against, a variety of perceptions and understandings that have attached themselves to these types of young people. These *ways of knowing* have consequences – intended or otherwise – for the ways in which the Foundation works with young trainees, professional staff, and collaborators, and with the work it does to establish and grow its social enterprise brand. In the following section we will extend this discussion of the ways in which young people are made known in *Jamie's Kitchen* to develop a conceptual framework for understanding the problem of Youth in a more general sense. This discussion plays a pivotal role in situating the Fifteen Foundation in time/space/place – in particular histories, issues and problematizations related to contemporary populations of young people. As such, the discussion is vital for understanding the ways in which this social enterprise – and the processes, practices, rationalities that shape its management of marginalized young people – emerges as a particular solution to the problem of young people.

## The problem of youth

> ... when I talk about power relations and games of truth, I am absolutely not saying that games of truth are just concealed power relations – that would be a horrible exaggeration. My problem, as I have already said, is in understanding how truth games are set up and how they are connected with power relations. One can show, for example, that the medicalization of madness, the organization of medical knowledge [*savoir*] around individuals designated as mad, was connected with a whole series of social and economic processes at a given time, but also with institutions and practices of power. This fact in no way impugns the scientific validity or the therapeutic effectiveness of psychiatry: it does not endorse psychiatry, but neither does it invalidate it.
> (Michel Foucault, 2000a, 'The Ethics of the Concern for Self as a Practice of Freedom', p. 296)

> You see, what I want to do is not the history of solutions ... I would like to do the genealogy of problems, of *problematiques*.
> (Michel Foucault, 2000b, 'On the Genealogy of Ethics', in Rainbow (ed.), p. 256)

For the past 30 years or so the Anglo-European Liberal democracies have experienced, and been reshaped by, profound social, economic, cultural and political change. Processes of globalization; transformations in labour markets, education and training systems and pathways; gender, ethnic and sexual identity politics and social movements have, in a very broad sense, reshaped the social, economic and political landscape in which individual and collective biographies and lives unfold, are fashioned, and are governed. One consequence of the institutionalized and individual anxieties and uncertainties that have accompanied, indeed contributed to, these transformations is that community, policy and academic discourses are marked by widespread adult anxieties about contemporary populations of young people. Important here are concerns related to the ways in which young people should be schooled, policed, housed, employed, or prevented from becoming involved in any number of risky (sexual, eating, drug-abusing or peer-cultural) practices.

In these settings, adult anxieties about the public and private behaviours and dispositions of young people means that Youth looms large, and often threateningly, in community perceptions and in policy areas and academic disciplines such as juvenile justice, youth work, education, health promotion, adolescent mental health, family and social work. The training and commercial practices and processes of the Fifteen Foundation make sense, are relevant, in the context of these widespread concerns.

An examination of the many ways in which Youth is represented is an exercise that focuses on a series of problematizations. That is, how do various experts (psychologists, sociologists, management consultants, etc.), policy advisers and politicians, community agencies and the media represent young people, and under what circumstances? What 'Youth' issues or problems are the objects of this attention? Which populations of young people are the targets of these problematizations? What purposes are served by these forms of representation?

A sense of what we are discussing here, and why it is relevant to the work of this book, can be illustrated by a number of examples. Richard Eckersley's *Casualties of Change* (1988), *Youth and the Challenge to Change* (1992), and 'Values and Visions' (1995) represent a consistent, prolonged attempt by one commentator to construct a view of Youth in 'crisis' in the Anglo-European democracies. This sense of crisis has echoes in any number of discourses that render youth knowable in terms of the 'risks' associated with life in the Liberal democracies at the turn of a new millennium. Indeed, the pages of any number of Youth, Psychological, Public Health, Education, Labour Studies, Gender Studies Journals are testament to the ways in which a globalized knowledge economy has an insatiable demand for the truths that make youthful behaviours and dispositions knowable, calculable, governable and manageable.

In Eckersley's (1992, pp. 3–7) framing of the impact of profound social, economic and political change on today's young people we encounter a narrative that suggests that society 'has become increasingly hostile to our well being'. In this context we are able to see 'the worsening plight of young people, expressed in rising suicide rates, drug abuse and crime, and also more widely in their social conservatism, political apathy and materialism'. Moreover, in the 'cultural and social turmoil' that characterizes 'Western civilisation' during the last 30 years or so, 'the young suffer most' as they 'face the difficult metamorphosis from child into adult, deciding who they are and what they believe, and accepting responsibility for their own lives. It is a transition best made in an environment that offers stability, security and some measure of certainty.' Eckersley argues that 'the problems of youth suicide, alcohol and drug abuse and delinquency' are indicators of a 'constellation of psychological traits: alienation, anomie, frustration, confusion, hopelessness, impotence, loneliness. At the end of it all is a crippling lack of self esteem.'

Eckersley's representation of a crisis of Youth is indicative of the ways in which profound social, economic and cultural transformations frame various community, policy and academic discourses which give expression to adult anxieties about today's young people. In these contexts powerful narratives of risk, fear and uncertainty structure a variety of emergent processes and practices aimed at regulating the actions and thoughts of young people. These practices include:

- An increasingly widespread use of electronic surveillance technologies (video, audio) in spaces such as shopping malls, streets and schools;
- The proposed and actual introduction of state and local government laws and by-laws allowing night curfews, zero-tolerance policing and electronic tagging of young offenders;
- By-laws which set limits on the number of young people who may gather in certain public spaces, and which allow police (public and private) to move young people on if they cause others anxiety;
- Anti-Social Behaviour Orders (ASBOs) in the UK that criminalize nuisance behaviours.

In association with these more direct policing practices, increased levels of anxiety and uncertainty provoke new forms of adult interventions into young people's lives on the basis of professional concerns about young people's welfare. These practices include:

- The involvement of youth, community and health workers in street work with young people on projects which attempt to regulate *anti-social* practices;

- Various education programmes that target the risky sexual, eating and drug practices of young people, or the nature of their transitions to adulthood;
- A general concern for any youth activity that gives the appearance of being beyond the management or surveillance capacities of various agencies. These concerns are evidenced in the countless research projects which seek to better understand all aspects of Youth in a manner which promises to develop more 'sophisticated' ways of identifying, differentiating and naming populations of young people with regard to diverse professional and lay concerns (Kelly, 2000a, 2000b, 2000c; McLeod and Malone, 2000; White, 1993).

---

**The vexed question of today's youth**

Beneath two portraits of a girl and boy in their early teens a full-page newspaper advertisement announces that from 'today' over 150 corporations, government departments and research centres, will 'understand our generation a whole lot better'. The advertisement, which lists the names of these organisations, heralds the merger of two Australian market research companies, ACNielsen-McNair and Reark Research. The merger, it is claimed:

*'will offer the most comprehensive range of services in retail and media measurement and customised research. And, most importantly, we'll now have the added ability to integrate all this vital marketing information. Meaning a more complete picture of today's consumers for our clients. Which in turn, gives our clients an even greater edge in the global marketplace. **We might even find the answer to the vexed question of today's youth**'.*

(*The Age*, advertisement, 9 December 1997, p. A13)

---

Our interests in this discussion are not so much with young people – in the *unruly*, embodied, flesh and blood sense – but, rather, with the ways in which *unruly* young minds and bodies provoke concerns in the community, business, policy and academic spaces of adults. At the outset, though, it should be recognized that adult anxieties about young people are not new phenomena. Youth has historically occupied the 'wild zones' in modernity's imagination. Indeed, the concept of Youth, with its roots in the study of adolescent *storm and stress*, youthful *identity crises*, *delinquency* and *resistance*, has emerged from, and been shaped by, ideas of ungovernability, and by particular ideas about how social class, gender and race are influential in shaping this ungovernability (Bessant and Watts, 1998; Kelly, 1999, 2000a, 2000b, 2000c; Tait, 1995). Young people are *young*, at a quite fundamental level, because they are not *adult*. Adulthood, with its associated ideas about autonomy, responsibility, self-regulation has stood, historically, as the point of arrival in many of the problematizations of Youth. However, many of the labour market, relationship and identity transformations of the past four decades have unsettled the view of adulthood as a relatively stable space of arrival.

This manner of discussing the meaning of Youth is indebted to Michel Foucault's problematizations of the Subject and Power within Liberal practices of government. In the following chapter we will return to a discussion of Foucault's later work on the care of the self to identify and examine the processes in *Jamie's Kitchen* that seek to develop a passionate, entrepreneurial form of selfhood in the young people recruited by the Fifteen Foundation. At this point Foucault's governmentality framework, and the extensive literature that is indebted to Foucault's later work, will be used to situate this discussion of the problem of youth and young workers. A principal concern in Foucault's (1991) investigations of the forms and effects of modern 'governmentality' was to foreground the emergence of the idea of *population*. Foucault's investigations were grounded in the proposition that, from the sixteenth century through to the early nineteenth century, there was a transformation in the ways in which European government was imagined. This transformation involved a movement from a concern with the nature of the relation between the Prince and his subjects (an issue of sovereignty), to a concern with the nature of the relations between the State and the management of its populations (a concern with the art of government). In thinking of government in this manner, Foucault imagined government as the 'conduct of conduct'. Government, in this sense, 'is a form of activity aiming to shape, guide or affect the conduct of some person or persons' (Gordon, 1991, p. 2). As Rose and Miller (1992, p. 174) have pointed out, Liberal government is practised 'through a profusion of shifting alliances between diverse authorities' in a variety of projects which seek to govern various 'facets of economic activity, social life and individual conduct'.

Foucault's work highlights the ways in which power relations have, in the space of the modern Liberal democratic nation state, become 'governmentalized'. Foucault (1983, p. 224) argued that the forms of the 'government of men by one another in any society are multiple'. These power relations, these actions upon actions, can be 'superimposed, they cross, impose their own limits, sometimes cancel one another out, sometimes reinforce one another'. However, what is of concern with regard to the particular forms of power in contemporary Liberal Democracies is that 'the state is not simply one of the forms or specific situations of the exercise of power – even if it is the most important – but that in a certain way all other forms of power relation must refer to it'. Here, Foucault's argument rests not on the notion that these other specific relations of power are derived from the State. Instead there is a sense in which other forms of power relations – in schools, in the justice system, in families, in workplaces and organizations – become 'governmentalized, that is to say, elaborated, rationalized and centralized in the form of, under the auspices of, state institutions'.

The point here is that the Fifteen Foundation takes on the task of salvation, of transforming (in a variety of ways) the circumstances in which certain young people live and lead their lives – lives that are understood largely as problematic in terms of their education and training, employment, criminal and drug-use histories. The Foundation undertakes this task in a training framework built and regulated by particular state agencies; in labour markets that are regulated in a variety of ways, including at the level of forms of appropriate behaviours and dispositions; and with young people who have a history of being seen as problems within, and by state-regulated education, training, work, criminal justice and public health systems. Foucault's framework provides a way of understanding the ongoing management and regulation of the behaviours and dispositions of young people across diverse domains, at various levels of practice, and from a variety of intellectual and political positions. Drawing on Foucault's legacy, Nikolas Rose's (1990, p. ix) concern with examining the 'powers that have come to bear upon the subjective existence of people and their relations one with another' provides a useful way to link the problematization of Youth to the ongoing management and regulation of the young trainees – at Fifteen, in schools and colleges, in other settings such as commercial kitchens and work experience sites. Central to Rose's project is an examination of the ways in which the government of human subjects 'has become bound up with innovations and developments in a number of scientific discourses that have rendered knowable the normal and pathological functioning of humans'. The *Psy* sciences, criminology, sociology, feminism, management and organization studies – all are implicated in processes that have 'taken up and transformed problems offered by political, economic, and moral strategies and concerns, and ... have made these problems thinkable in new ways and governable with new techniques'.

Thinking about Youth as a distinct, largely institutionalized population enables us to engage with long-run historical processes of expert knowledge production about the truths of Youth; an engagement which suggests that Youth can be understood as an *artefact* of diverse forms of expertise; and of attempts by these expert systems to regulate the behaviours and dispositions of populations of Youth by producing and telling the truths of Youth.

As an artefact of expertise Youth can be understood as consisting of a constellation of signifiers that enable us to *know* who or what it is we are talking about when we talk about, for example, marginalized, unemployed 16–24-year-olds. As a construction, an abstraction, Youth emerges from and shapes our understanding of flesh and blood young people. Indeed, the Fifteen Foundation identifies in its document *What's Right with these Young People* that it has to struggle with the ways in which its trainees, the *type* of young people it works with, are *known*. Instead of thinking about, and looking at what is *wrong* with these young people (an easy enough task) it attempts to see what is *right* with them. The point to stress here is that this is not a process that can be dismissed as an organization ignoring the *reality* of these young people (their histories/records/problems) and indulging in *touchy-feely*, politically correct revisionism (rewriting the history and reality of the lives of these young people). Rather, from the perspective we are developing here, the Fifteen Foundation is involved in re-problematizing Youth: re-conceptualizing understandings of *problem* young people in ways that focus on providing different opportunities, on developing processes, activities, forms of management, regulation and training that enable trainees to transform themselves. This is not a representation, problematization, regulation-free zone – there is no such thing. Instead it is a space in which different representations, problematizations and regulations aim to produce different outcomes for groups of marginalized, unemployed young people. And, as a for-profit social enterprise the Foundation is largely successful in meeting the objectives that are core to its business.

Foucauldian genealogies of Liberal government point to the processes of individualization and normalization at work in the practices of modern Liberal government. Increasingly, these practices take as their objects the *unconscious*, the *soul*, *desire*, *aesthetics*, the *body* as well as the rational, cognitive *mind* of the individuals and the populations they attempt to govern. In this sense the *why* aspects of young people's behaviours and dispositions emerge as the objects of expertise impelled by concerns for certainty and mastery and order. Here the soul, desire and the unconscious become *governmentalized*: they become *elaborated* and *rationalized* by processes, in institutions, by experts, who manufacture and/or meet the demands of schools, colleges, business, and governments to *know* young people in better, more sophisticated ways.

A further example illustrates this claim. Contemporary understandings of young people and young workers are principally structured by a narrative which suggests that it is *only* by productively engaging in an extended period of compulsory and post-compulsory schooling, that young people will 'adequately develop into the kinds of adults who can function effectively in the complex and demanding world of modern society' (Faye, 1991, p. 66). Elizabeth Faye (1991) argues that this discourse of Youth as students emerged as a 'compelling truth' in the context of post–Second World War reconstruction throughout the Anglo and European economies. This *truth*, argues Faye, should be analysed in such a way as to examine the rationalities and techniques mobilized in the diverse programmes which took as their object this particular view of young people as students. Faye's analysis foregrounds the representation (*fantasy*) of the adolescent – in various efforts to make schooling *work* – as a 'desiring', 'motivated' subject who wanted to learn:

> who wanted to belong, who willed his/her own membership of the democratic community, willed in fact his/her own *subjection* as a democratic citizen. This subject would not need persisting and external forms of coercive discipline, because s/he has successfully internalised the normative social rules and was self disciplined, had in fact chosen 'the right path, not merely by making it impossible ... to do otherwise, or through fear of punishment, but from a *desire* to do the right thing!'
>
> (Faye, 1991, p. 68, citing Ramsay, 1949, original emphasis)

This construction of the adolescent as the 'self guiding/self governing subject', is principally shaped within psychological discourses. These discourses were largely successful in translating this psychologically based truth of human motivations, behaviours and dispositions to concerns about how to *make up* (Rose and Miller, 1992) active citizens within the institutional spaces of schooling. Faye's (1991, pp. 67–70) analysis highlights certain processes which enabled this representation of adolescents as 'repositories of hope and objects of desire' to take hold. In the first instance, Faye discusses the concern within the domain of Educational Psychology to construct a narrative of *progressive* education in which schools could be conceived as: 'happy, democratic communities, full of interest and reality and activity, where the educational programme is fit-ted to the pupil and not the pupil to the programme'. Faye's analysis of the emergence of these discourses in the context of Australia's postwar efforts at reconstruction also foregrounds the processes which resulted in the establishment, within the Victorian Education Department, of the Psychology Branch (in 1947). This particular centre of expertise emerged, partly, as a consequence of various submissions from the Department's first official psychologist, who argued that an extension of psychological services to all schools would meet a concern to understand 'all aspects of the cognitive and the *normal* emotional life of the child'. This problem space was to constitute the domain of:

> the psychologist, the medical officer, the psychiatrist, the research worker ... if instruction and development of well integrated personal-ities are to proceed on the sound bases of a full understanding of each child, his [*sic*] native endowments, restrictions placed upon him and his future needs, and a good adjustment of the educational process to the individual as he progresses through our schools.
>
> (Jorgensen, 1945, cited in Faye, 1991, p. 70)

Of interest here is Faye's (1991) proposition that it matters little when, how and why schools would inevitably *fail* in their attempts to produce this ideal adolescent subject of Educational Psychology. What matters here is that such *failures* provoked renewed discussion, argumentation, critique and propositions with regard to these *failures*: debate which con-tinues to emerge from within diverse ways of conceiving the problem (Liberal, Critical, Conservative, Radical, Feminist), and the measures appropriate to attempts to alleviate the problem. Indeed, as Faye (1991) argues:

> the more that attention was drawn to the reasons why schools did not or could not achieve this objective – whether it was because of inadequate and inappropriate accommodation, inadequate numbers of teachers, or inappropriate curriculum and teaching methods – the more the truth which linked the adolescent to the school in this particular way was consolidated.
>
> (1991, p. 68)

Thus, at the start of the twenty-first century it is *natural* to imagine young people as students. Indeed it is almost an absurdity to think otherwise. A history of 150 years of mass compulsory schooling, including 50 years of mass compulsory secondary schooling, weighs heavily on attempts to problematize this truth. Moreover, the historical *truths* of Youth as *delinquent, deviant, maladjusted, disadvantaged, marginalized* and *at-risk* have been constructed in relation to this truth of *normal* Youth as a self-governing student. These historical problematizations of *not normal* Youth have assisted in consolidating this truth of normal Youth. It is primarily through attempts to school these Youth that delinquency, deviancy, maladjustment, disadvantage, and risk will be regulated (treated).

This particular truth – and the processes that work to construct it, circulate it, and enable it to function as a truth – has strong echoes in the ways in which human resources discourses, and the forms of management and regulation that are shaped by these discourses, construct the truth of the self-actualizing and self-governing worker whose interests in work, performance and productivity can match the organization's demands for performance and productivity from employees who require minimal supervision (Rose, 1990; Miller and Rose, 1990, 1995; Townley, 2000). Peter Miller and Nicholas Rose (1995, pp. 435–6), for example, examine the continuing influence of Elton Mayo's Hawthorne studies on the meanings and purposes of work in worker's lives, and how it should be managed with these interests in mind. As they argue, the moral dimensions of work to be found in human relations discourses continue to be influential in shaping the truths of employment and unemployment in the industrialized democracies.

Again, the often cited failure of the figure of the self-governing employee to *appear* in organizations, and/or the failure of training, management and culture-change programmes to *produce* this ideal worker is not the issue. The issue is more that the *will to knowledge* (Foucault, 2000c) which drives these processes, produces ways of knowing – young people, team members, crew, talent – that are reflexive and institutionalized, and circulate in ways that produce hybridized representations of individuals, groups and populations (Kelly, 2003). The contemporary fetishization, in various management and marketing circles, of *Generations X* and *Y* is an example of these processes that we will discuss in the final chapter of this book. At this point we turn to a more detailed account of the problem of youth labour markets in the developed economies in order to understand why a social enterprise such as the Fifteen Foundation needs to frame the sorts of interventions it has developed to train unemployed 16–24-year-olds.

## The problem of the youth labour market

> The world is facing a growing youth employment crisis. Both developing and developed economies are faced with the challenge of creating decent and sustainable jobs for the large cohort of young women and men entering the labour market every year. The issue features prominently on the international development agenda. Youth employment is a major focus of the Millennium Development Goals (MDGs) and was reaffirmed by the Ministers and Heads of Delegations participating in the High-Level Segment of the Substantive 2006 Session of the Economic and Social Council (ECOSOC) who committed themselves to 'develop[ing] and implement[ing] strategies that give youth everywhere a real and equal opportunity to find full and productive employment and decent work'.
>
> (Foreword, International Labour Office (ILO), 2006,
> *Global Employment Trends for Youth*)

It should be established by this point that the Fifteen Foundation targets a particular population for its training programmes in the hospitality industry: marginalized, unemployed 16–24-year-old young men and women at the start of a working life. At the time of writing these training programmes operate in three countries: the UK (London and Watergate Bay, Cornwall), Holland (Amsterdam), and Australia (Melbourne). Moreover, the Foundation has ambitions to turn itself into a global social enterprise brand that trains, inspires and provides opportunities for young people around the globe. In stating this goal it appears to suggest that there is a demand for the sorts of intervention, support and training that it offers. And at an empirical level it could draw on any number of regional, national, or international agencies and authorities (for example, UNESCO, ILO, OECD) – and the masses of data they produce, analyse and interpret – to support a claim that significant numbers of young people experience the labour markets of a more globalized, flexible, 24/7 capitalism in ways that highlight the precarious, casualized, uncertain nature of these labour markets (Sennett, 1998, 2006; Beck,

2000; Bauman, 2005). Indeed, a recent OECD Working Paper (Quintini and Martin, 2006) suggests that:

> high youth unemployment remains a serious problem in many OECD countries. This reflects a variety of factors, including the relatively high proportion of young people leaving school without a basic educational qualification, the fact that skills acquired in initial education are not always well adapted to labour market requirements, as well as general labour market conditions and problems in the functioning of labour markets.
>
> (2006, p. 3)

In this section we will identify and discuss a number of the key characteristics of youth labour markets. We will situate this discussion in recent commentaries by influential sociologists of work in order to problematize a key element of much business, policy and community debate about the problem of youth labour markets – namely, that young people experience problems in transitioning into labour markets because they lack the characteristics of the self (a work ethic) that labour markets demand. Those young people who are successful in these labour markets are so because their behaviours and dispositions, their self-understandings and presentation of self make them employable. Young people who are unsuccessful – so the story goes – are so because there is something wrong with them. We want to suggest that one thing that *Jamie's Kitchen* and the ongoing work of the Fifteen Foundation clearly illustrates is that this work self, this ethical orientation to work is important, but that it is not fixed, or innate, and can, indeed, be cultivated if opportunities, support structures, and meaningful work can be brought together to alter the circumstances in which young people live and lead their lives.

> Perhaps the most poignant aspect of the school to work transition is the deflation of dreams that occurs for so many
> (Borman and Reisman, 1986, *Becoming a Worker*, p. 25)

The *reality* of contemporary labour markets has come to be dominated by stories of globalization, increased competition, high technology and uncertainty as these impact on labour markets in ways that result in, or demand, *flexibility, casualization, core* and *peripheral* workforces, *upskilling, multi-skilling* and *life-long learning* for employees. There are also powerful and widespread arguments that the risks associated with these emergent *realities* can no longer be wholly managed by collective forms of insurance, as enacted, for example, through the collective bargaining processes which dominated the Australian Industrial Relations landscape from the early 1900s up until the 1990s. Rather, these risks are *best* or most efficiently managed through processes that require individual workers/employees to assume new forms of responsibility to identify and manage the risks that they face in contemporary labour markets:

> The Workplace Relations Act offers a new approach to industrial relations in Australia. The legislation moves away from a collective, centralised system of wage fixing and bargaining to a system of industrial relations where the focus is on the individual and employer and employee negotiations at the workplace.
>
> (Australian Workplace Relations Act, 1996, p. iii)

As a consequence of these changes in the nature and understanding of the labour/employment relation in the developed economies a number of prominent sociologists have highlighted the emergence of widespread anxieties and uncertainties in globalizing contexts, and the processes of individualization which accompany, and indeed structure, these feelings as individuals work away at their increasingly Do-It-Yourself (DIY) biographical projects (Beck, 2000; Beck *et al.*, 1994; Giddens, 1991). This DIY Self will be discussed in more detail in the following chapter.

Ulrich Beck's (2000) *The Brave New World of Work* provides a useful means to develop a discussion of a number of issues that emerge from these claims, and the ways that these issues impact directly on how we can understand the problem of youth labour markets. A central theme of Beck's book is that contemporary labour markets in the more developed 'first world' are changing in ways that see them taking on some of the central characteristics of labour markets in the less developed 'third world' – what Beck refers to as the Brazilianization of labour markets in the developed world. Beck argues that an important feature of these transformations is the 'spread of temporary and insecure employment, discontinuity and loose informality' into 'first world' labour markets, labour markets that through processes of postwar reconstruction, and the so-called long boom of the 1950s, 1960s and first years of the 1970s, had not only enjoyed full employment, but had indeed pursued full employment through various forms of social policy and labour market regulation. Of course full employment was understood differently in different national contexts, and differing policies and regulations were developed to pursue this social and economic goal. In addition, full employment was largely framed by understandings of the employee as a full-time male breadwinner who needed employment security and social policies to support a dependent spouse and family (Fraser and Gordon, 1994). In the 1950s, in Australia and the UK for example, the majority of young males entered the labour market at the end of the period of compulsory schooling. They would hope/plan to remain in the labour market until retirement at age 65 or later. At this time rates of labour market participation among males were almost universal in both the UK and Australia. However, in both countries, females exhibited different patterns of economic activity. They too would tend to leave school at age 15 and enter the labour market although even among 15–19-year-olds rates of participation were lower than for males. In the 1950s there was a tendency for young women to withdraw from the labour market once they married or had children. As a consequence labour market activity was relatively low among young adult females. However, since the 1950s rates of labour market participation by young males and females have steadily declined to be replaced by longer periods of educational participation, including lengthy periods of post-compulsory education and training. It is predicted, on these trends, that by 2010 labour market participation rates for 15–19–year-old men and women in the UK and Australia will be in the range of 40 per cent to 45 per cent (Furlong and Kelly, 2005).

In effect, full-time employment opportunities for young people aged 15–19 have virtually disappeared, to be replaced by prolonged periods of schooling, and part-time and/or casual work concentrated in a relatively few industrial and occupational areas. In Australia the Australian Bureau of Statistics (ABS, 1998a, 1998b, 2004) argues that the youth labour market is characterized by 'higher levels of job mobility, lower average incomes and a different occupational profile to the rest of the working population' (1998a, p. 1). Casual and part-time work, periodic unemployment, complex education and employment pathways, and a concentration of young workers in the retail and food service industries are other key characteristics of the youth labour market (Lewis and McLean, 1999). The Australian supermarket and retail chain Woolworths (2002), for example, claims to be the biggest employer of apprentices in Australia. It employs more than 45,000 young people, one third of whom are under 20: '*We take very seriously our responsibilities to give their working lives a great start'*. At a more general level, in the OECD economies the two industries that employ the largest numbers of young people (as a proportion of total number of workers in these industries) are the *wholesale and retail trade*, and *hotels and restaurants*. As the OECD indicates, these two industries tend to pay below-average wages and are often characterized by temporary, part-time and casualized forms of employment. At the same time young people across the OECD tend to be under-represented as workers in high-wage, expanding sectors of the economy such as *financial intermediation*, and *real estate and business activities* (Quintini and Martin, 2006).

---

**Some global trends in Youth Labour markets (15–25-year-olds)**

The share of the youth labour force in the youth population (the youth **labour force participation rate**) decreased globally from 58.9 to 54.7 per cent between 1995 and 2005, which means that in 2005 only every second young person was actively participating in labour markets around the world.

In 2005, the number of **employed** young people was 548 million, an increase of 20.1 million from ten years before. However, because the youth population grew at a quicker pace than youth employment, the share of youth who are employed in the youth population (the youth **employment-to-population-ratio**) saw a decrease from 51.6 to 47.3 per cent between 1995 and 2005.

Compared to adults, the youth of today are still more than three times as likely to be unemployed; the **ratio of the youth-to-adult unemployment rate** was 3.0 in 2005, up from 2.8 in 1995.

The youth unemployed make up almost half (43.7 per cent) of the world's total unemployed despite the fact that, in comparison, the youth share of the total working-age population (ages 15 and over) was only 25.0 per cent.

(International Labour Office (ILO), 2006, *Global Employment Trends for Youth*, pp. 2–4)

---

Beck's (2000, pp. 1–3) Brazilianization argument suggests that in a 'semi-industrialized' economy such as Brazil, full-time paid employment is a secure form of existence for 'only a minority of the economically active population; the majority earn their living in more precarious conditions'. For Beck a life-world characterized by 'nomadic "multi-activity"' is not a 'pre modern relic', nor is it any longer *just* a feature of the female labour market. Rather, these labour market insecurities emerge in the more developed world as a fundamental characteristic of the movement from a *work society* to a *risk society*. Beck's (2000) thesis echoes concerns that are also covered in a number of other texts including Richard Sennett's *The Corrosion of Character* (1998) and *The Culture of the New Capitalism* (2006); Zygmunt Bauman's *The Individualized Society* (2001), *Wasted Lives* (2004), and *Work, Consumerism and the New Poor* (2005); and Jeremy Rifkin's *The End of Work* (1995). All these texts share a series of key themes including claims that processes of globalization, facilitated by electronically enabled, micro-processor-based technologies, have transformed the physical reality of paid work in many of the industrialized nations. In addition, these processes have transformed the spaces in which work is imagined, so that new narratives of work, of its value, of those who participate in it, and the way this participation is structured have emerged and been articulated by employers, unions and governments.

Beck (2000) illustrates his argument by quoting labour market figures for Germany which indicate a rise in the number of employees in the *precarious group* from 10 per cent in the 1960s, to 25 per cent in the 1970s, to nearly 33 per cent in the late 1990s. Definitions of what is meant by precarious employment across different national contexts, and comparisons across these settings, are fraught with difficulties. The exact nature and calculations of precarious forms of employment and comparisons between different settings is not our chief interest here (see Campbell, 2004 for a useful discussion of these matters). Rather, our interest is in the ways in which casualized and part-time employment has grown in many developed labour markets at the expense of full-time and/or more secure forms of employment; a change often accompanied by calls for forms of labour market regulation that introduce or encourage flexibility, enterprise and individual responsibilities and rights – at the same time as they remove or combat labour market *rigidities* (collective bargaining, minimum conditions) that supposedly stifle enterprise and participation.

---

**Misconceptions concerning youth and youth labour markets**

*Misconception 3: Young people like to 'shop around' to find the best job. Therefore, they will choose to take up numerous short-term, temporary posts in order to gain experience and find the 'best fit'.*

A young person can 'shop around' for the best job only in an economy with robust economic growth that results in strong demand by employers for her/his particular skills. A good example would be the strong demand for computer programmers in the United States in the 1990s that resulted in a situation in which the prospective computer programmer could 'bargain' for the best employment contract terms and could choose to change jobs even numerous times in one year. The system of moving in and out of temporary employment and only eventually (if ever) into permanent employment, worked for some young people in a boom economy like that of the United States in the 1990s, but the situation there was clearly unique.

Even in developed economies, however, the desire of young people for job security remains a primary concern. France is a case in point. In February 2006 the Government of France introduced the 'first employment contract' (Contrat Première Embauche, CPE) with the aim of encouraging companies to hire young people by introducing a flexible system allowing them to hire those under the age of 26 for a period of two years during which the employee could be dismissed at any time and for any reason. Widespread popular opposition to the reduction in job security for young people that the introduction of the CPE was perceived to create led to its early withdrawal.

(International Labour Office (ILO), 2006, *Global Employment Trends for Youth*, p. 7)

In this context Beck (2000, pp. 2–3) makes the argument that the developed economies are/will be confronted with challenges to debate the emerging characteristics of a 'political economy of insecurity'. The parameters of this debate are important for our discussion of the problem of youth labour markets. In the first instance he argues that there is a need to examine the rules and consequences of a new power game played between 'territorially fixed' participants, such as governments, trade unions, and the majority of workers, and 'non-territorially fixed' participants, such as capital, commerce and finance. Many labour markets are geographically bounded, as well as being marked by opportunities/lack of opportunities as a consequence of different forms of economic activity and histories of economic activity. *Industrial economy coal towns often struggle to remake themselves as chic tourist destinations in a postmodern, global, leisure economy.* This location in time, space and place is particularly important for young people who are dependent on family and/or access to public and private transport. Mobility and movement within and between different labour markets is, for many young people, a matter of constrained choice. The Fifteen Foundation acknowledges the difficulties that mobility and movement can pose for the population it targets, and is explicit in its recruitment processes that applicants must live in close proximity to the restaurants.

What this means is that the idea of a singular youth labour market should be qualified by an acknowledgement that gender, ethnicity, geography, and family employment and education histories and opportunities impact on the labour market experiences of different young people. (Kenway and Kelly, 2000; Kelly and Kenway, 2001; Lewis and McLean, 1999). In effect there are a variety of labour market characteristics that structure early employment opportunities for different populations of young people (Kelly and Lewis, 2000). Yet what often emerges in many discussions of young workers is that they are 'vocationally immature', inadequately prepared for the workforce and display poor attitudes towards work (Borman and Reisman, 1986). Over 20 years ago Borman and Reisman (1986, p. 3) argued that there was a need to move beyond this sort of 'fault finding' to look at the relationship between young people's 'values', 'personality' and work experiences and the 'constraints and opportunities of labour market structures' and 'labour market opportunities'. Here Borman and Reisman (1986) identified the 'opportunity structure' of youth labour markets – an opportunity structure that is increasingly shaped by the contingencies and uncertainties of a globalized risk society, and an opportunity structure that also sees young people preferred as employees in certain labour markets and not others. Choice, initiative and enterprise take on different meanings if these structural elements are taken seriously in any discussion of contemporary youth labour markets.

> **Misconceptions concerning youth and youth labour markets**
> *Misconception 4: Unemployment is the key labour market challenge for youth.*

> Youth unemployment is only the tip of the iceberg. Although more difficult to quantify, there are two other groups that together outnumber the unemployed youth but suffer from the same frustrations as the unemployed: the discouraged youth and the working poor.

In countries without effective unemployment support mechanisms, concentrating on unemployment also runs the risk of excluding from the analysis the less privileged population who simply cannot afford to be unemployed. In several developing countries, young people of higher socio-economic backgrounds are over-represented in the unemployment numbers because it is only they who can afford to spend time looking for work, without incoming wages. The problem is not so much unemployment, therefore, in developing countries but rather the conditions of work of those who are employed.

> (International Labour Office (ILO), 2006, *Global Employment Trends for Youth*, pp. 7–8)

**Misconceptions concerning youth and youth labour markets**

*Misconception 5: Youth unemployment rates give an accurate picture of youth labour market challenges.*

This misconception is closely related to the previous one. If we accept that some young people who are working (the working poor, young workers without a contract, young people in hazardous work, as examples) and some young people who are inactive (the discouraged workers) are also in situations that place them far from the goal of achieving full and productive employment, then looking at youth unemployment rates to the exclusion of other indicators would mean ignoring a large portion of the youth population that requires equal attention by policy-makers aiming to improve the productive potential of youth populations.

> (International Labour Office (ILO), 2006, *Global Employment Trends for Youth*, pp. 7–8)

A related concern, in terms of debates about what a political economy of insecurity means for young workers, is the apparent need by the territorially fixed players to choose between higher unemployment accompanied by relatively low levels of poverty; or lower levels of unemployment existing alongside what Beck (2000, pp. 2–3) calls 'spectacular poverty'. This focus on unemployment levels, on economic activity made calculable through *headline numbers*, is often a positive for governments – especially if these numbers are declining. Yet, as the ILO indicates, this focus can mask other characteristics of youth labour markets that can be as important for understanding young people's activity and orientations to activity in various labour markets. In many respects unemployment rates are a poor reflection of the opportunities available to young people. Young people may prolong their education in the knowledge that few opportunities exist in the labour markets that they are most able/likely to access. Moreover, governments are able to manage unemployment figures within politically acceptable limits via policies that facilitate various forms of non-participation by young workers. It can be argued, for example, that the expansion of higher education is an effective strategy for reducing the number of economically active young people. In both Australia and the UK, levels of unemployment for young people and adults are currently lower than they have been for several decades. To repeat the point: official and popular focus on these types of headline numbers can deflect analysis/discussion from the labour market experiences and outcomes of particular populations such as young people – whose transition into labour at the start of a working life can present a variety of challenges.

Further concerns for Beck in terms of thinking about the emerging nature and consequences of a political economy of insecurity, include the ways in which 'technologically advanced capitalism', and its displacement of labour, mean that 'all paid work is subject to the threat of displacement' – a situation which Giddens (1990, 1991) and others have addressed through discussions about the anxieties and uncertainties that are said to characterize the start of the twenty-first century. In addition, Beck argues that there is a need to explore the ways in which the emergence of large measures of precarious employment spill, domino-like, into other aspects of the institutional fabric of the work society: 'the foundations of the social-welfare state are collapsing; normal life stories are breaking up into fragments; old age poverty is programmed in advance' (2000, p. 3). Finally, Beck suggests that there is a need to investigate and analyse the ways in which the economic and political gospel of 'labour market flexibility' in First World economies results in a redistribution of risk away from the social insurance technologies of the welfare state, to the capacities, behaviours, dispositions and choices of individuals – a so-called *individualization of risk management* (Kelly, 2001a, 2001b).

In a discussion of labour markets and the relationships between global/local processes in shaping the experience of labour market participation Bauman (2001, p. 24) argues that working lives have become 'saturated with uncertainty'. Bauman acknowledges that there is little that is 'particularly new' about this situation – 'working life has been full of uncertainty since time immemorial'. What Bauman suggests though is that contemporary workplace uncertainties are of a 'strikingly novel kind' – these uncertainties are a 'powerful *individualizing* force'. For Bauman, contemporary uncertainty 'divides instead of uniting, and since there is no telling who might wake up in what division, the idea of "common interests" grows ever more nebulous and in the end becomes incomprehensible. Fears, anxieties and grievances are made in such a way as to be suffered alone.' For Bauman the uncertainty and risks character-istic of 'flexible capitalism' (Sennett, 1998) also have a structural element to them. That is, flexibility looks different, feels different, and has differ-ent consequences depending on the element of choice that shapes this flexibility. Little choice in the matter – because of circumstances that are influenced by age, social class, gender, ethnicity and geography – is different to a wealth of choice and opportunity that is delivered by comparative social, economic and cultural advantage.

The debates about the nature of contemporary youth labour markets, of ideas and practices of flexibility, of enterprise, of choice and of under-standings of dependency, autonomy and responsibility have provoked debate about how youth transitions should be characterized (Wyn and White, 1997; Sweet, 1995; Bessant and Cook, 1998; Furlong *et al.*, 2003). These debates are not merely rhetorical. In Australia, for example, they have framed, for a number of years since the mid 1990s, policies such as the Common Youth Allowance which takes as a key point of reference levels of parental/guardian income up until the young person is aged 24 – assuming a relationship of dependence until this age. Much of this debate is framed by spatial metaphors. It is suggested, for example, that transi-tions are linear or non-linear, are more fragmented (Furlong *et al.*, 2003). Historical time enters these discussions when present-day transitions are positioned as being less linear, more fragmented, and longer than for previous generations of young people. As Wyn (2004, p. 17) suggests terms such as 'post-adolescence', 'over-aged young adults', 'generation on hold', 'extended transitions' and even 'parasitic youth' (Takahashi and Voss, 2000) have entered debates about the nature of the transitions for post-1970s generations.

In much of this discussion there is a tendency to individualize both the risks associated with these transitions, and the management of these risks. Current community, commercial, policy and academic discussions are strongly flavoured by a voluntarist logic – *life is largely the sum of the choices we make, and risk management is a matter of individuals making better choices.* For instance, Wyn (2004, p. 17) argues that young people 'are now navigators of their own biographies and careers', even if they are sailing in uncertain and risky waters, and they have different levels of support, capacity and skill to navigate with. The risk here is that we can discount the ways in which age, social class, gender, ethnicity and geography continue to structure life courses, chances and choices – particularly for young people whose life world is determined by relationships of dependence. In terms of Beck's Brazilianization thesis, the risks and uncertainty that accompany casualization in contemporary youth labour markets impacts on different labour market sectors, and on different groups of young people in a variety of ways. For these groups, choices in relation to participation and activity in these labour markets are not solely a consequence of individual capacities, skills and dispositions.

## Conclusion

> *Man makes his own history, but he does not make it out of the whole cloth;*
> *he does not make it out of conditions chosen by himself, but out of such*
> *as he finds close at hand.*
> (Karl Marx, 1852, The Eighteenth Brumaire of Louis Bonaparte)

To paraphrase Marx: we make our own choices in many areas of life, but not always under the circumstances of our own choosing. Individualization, as a concept of significant importance in contemporary social theory, is a powerful tool in trying to understand the ways contemporary settings increasingly open up more and more aspects of a person's life to the idea, and to the very practice of choice. Individualization, the compulsion to be free and to make choices as individuals, is accompanied by what Foucault (1983) calls 'normalisation', and what Beck (1992) calls 'standardization'. These processes, which we discuss in more detail in the following chapter, have profound consequences for the development of a sense of self, and for the forms and types of relationships that this self can be involved in, even *must* be involved in.

Individualization suggests that many aspects of life were often a matter of fate, or of duty, or were predetermined by an accident of birth. Many still are. But increasingly, for more and more people, life has become – as Giddens (1991) would say – a reflexive project that is both a life of choice and, as a consequence of this, a life of uncertainty, risk and ongoing anxiety about the choices to be made and the consequences that flow from making these choices.

As we will argue in the following chapter, the ways in which we know, understand and imagine young people – as individuals or members of a team or group that need to be trained, developed, managed, regulated – are largely made known within a calculus that suggests that the individual is a person who is free to choose is, indeed, both capable of choosing and compelled to choose. What the drama of *Jamie's Kitchen* illustrates – often explicitly and with much passion – are the tensions, even paradoxes in relation to a life of choices, a life given meaning or value through the choices that we are able to make. These include:

- Choices are great – until you have to make one;
- Not everyone has the same choices;
- The consequences of different choices must be carried by the individuals who make the choices;
- These consequences are not the same for everyone;
- We are compelled to choose, but we must practise these choices within a limited range of what might be regarded as appropriate or normal – if not we risk punishment, prosecution, medicalization, imprisonment, marginalization (what Foucault calls processes of normalization).

# 3
# Becoming the Passionate, Entrepreneurial Self

## Introduction

Food – its meanings, its production, its preparation, its transformation, its presentation and, finally, its consumption – is central to the stories, the drama and the appeal of *Jamie's Kitchen*. Food, understood in the way it is in *Jamie's Kitchen*, promises to provide the means to provoke passion in the young people targeted by the Fifteen Foundation. This passion, its relationship to food, and its location in a workplace such as *Jamie's Kitchen*, promises to transform these young people into the entrepreneurial workers so valued by twenty-first-century capitalism. These ideas are made explicit in a discussion with Jamie Oliver on CBS's (2006) *60 Minutes*. Every year Fifteen trainees in the UK are taken on a tour of Tuscany to develop understandings of the origins of quality produce and the sorts of passions this produce might provoke. For Oliver this trip offers the following to his trainees:

> They get a purpose of what it's all about, you know, they get a romance ... I think with Giovanni and this particular vineyard it's kind of, they meet him, they get to know his personality and generosity and they see how he makes his wine and then they drink his wine and they finally realize that every damn thing in his life is consistent. And, actually, if you start acting consistent in a good way from today, it's only a matter of time before you, too, can be an expert and a master.
>
> (CBS, 2006)

Our argument that certain understandings of food can provoke and give focus to a passion that is not readily apparent as these young people enter the application processes established by the Fifteen Foundation; and that this passion, once provoked and disciplined, can actually transform the self, emerges from particular understandings of the self. Across the social sciences over the last 20 or 30 years two influential stories of the self have made significant contributions to the ways in which we can think about identity, subjectivity, the self. These stories have made uneven, sometimes unclear, contributions to the critical study of management, of work, of youth, of identity. However, these stories will make a significant contribution to the tales we tell about *Jamie's Kitchen* and young workers.

The first of these stories is sociological in the sense that it seeks to understand the self and its transformations in terms of large-scale sociological narratives of the globalized, post industrial, postmodern, late twentieth-, early twenty-first-century world. This story sees the self as reflexive: as a largely rational, cognitively competent agent capable of, indeed compelled to, continually remake itself in light of the ongoing, reflexive monitoring of myriad settings and understandings of human action and interaction. This reflexive, Do-It-Yourself (DIY), individualized self is the central character in the reflexive modernization literatures shaped primarily by the work of Ulrich Beck and Anthony Giddens.

The second of these stories, and the one that we will give most attention to, is a genealogical orientation to the self. This orientation owes much to the later focus by Michel Foucault on *the care of the self*, and to the governmentality literature that has emerged under the influence of Foucault's legacy. In this story the self is the product, always in process, of diverse undertakings/projects that seek to guide, direct, encourage, compel the self to know itself in certain ways, to act in certain ways, to govern and regulate itself in certain ways. In this story there is a focus on the techniques/technologies and rationalities that promise to produce certain forms of selfhood. These technologies of the self are contextual, shaped and put in play via the practice and relationships of different forms of power, and, as we will argue, involve individuals in the ongoing practice of freedom. It is this story of the self as an ongoing, regulated, ethical achievement that we see as most powerful in understanding the ways in which the Fifteen Foundation seeks to provoke in young people a passion that is focused on particular understandings of food: a passion that holds out the promise that an entrepreneurial self can emerge from the training facilitated by the Fifteen Foundation. In this sense, passion is technical, a technique of self-transformation and salvation.

## Fifteen and the passionate self

*Voice Over:* To sort the wheat from the chaff Jamie's devised a taste test. The wannabes will sample dishes that most of them have never eaten before let alone cooked.

[Jamie is seen walking around the test kitchen talking to his staff.]

*Voice Over:* Without being told what they are eating candidates will be marked out of 10 on their opinion of the master chef's butternut squash ravioli and deep fried tempura oyster.

[The hopefuls are talking to the camera telling the audience what they don't like – things like squid, mussels.]

*Jamie:* None are formally trained as far as we know. They are all unemployed and not in education. So all we can look for really is a bit of passion with food.

[The trainees file in one at a time for the taste test.]

*Jamie:* What are you tasting? What do you like about it? What does it make you feel?

[They have trouble expressing themselves.]

*Jamie:* Would you say you are not good at expressing yourself? [Pause] … with regard to flavours? [Young man agrees] If you want to be a chef it comes from the palate really, and from the heart. I think you've got it from the heart and don't mind a bit of hard work but you haven't got a clue what any of these tastes are. You can't even say sweet or sour or hot or spicy or soft and crunchy. You've got to think about that seriously because you've obviously been putting stuff in your mouth without tasting it.

[Michael Pizzey comes in. He can't eat oysters and he puts the ravioli in his mouth and gags – has to spit it out.]

*Voice Over:* Jamie soon sees that his biggest problem is not eliminating the 30 guys he doesn't want but finding those he does want.

*Jamie:* No disrespect but if I ask you to taste something. We've got to serve customers and if you can't taste something you can't season it and, like, the customer's going to get a bland bit of old food.

[One young woman tastes the oyster and pronounces it bland. The kitchen staff, including Jamie, are seen rolling about laughing and mimicking her.]

*Jamie:* I thought the people coming here were supposed to love food. They're just going through the motions. I am not even sure why they've come. I'm offering to do them a favour. You know what I mean.

*Voice Over:* In the end Jamie grants a reprieve to some of the low-scoring rejects.

*Zoe Collins (talking about Michael Pizzey):* He's obsessed with food. I spent 20 minutes on the phone with him talking about the perfect pizza crust so I really think we should put him through.

[Jamie is back in the big room with all the candidates. He is greeted by shouts and applause.]

*Jamie:* I don't really like this kind of pop star getting rid of people thing. It's quite tough and there are two more rounds. Remember you guys are down from a thousand. You're from all over London and from different walks of life. I think that's the beauty of it ... We're down to 30. From 30 we go to 15. Then we start. So from now start thinking food. Live it, breathe it, read it and in a year's time you could have something to really shout about, you little buggers. Nice one (applause and shouting).

*Jamie (as Voice Over. Footage of young hopefuls leaving, laughing, playing to camera):* It now feels like the ball's in motion. It now feels like this is real. But also, even though I wasn't expecting loads, only inspiration, the guys were completely cold to cooking. These guys are probably less than your average TV foody. They're wannabes. We're really talking about basic knowledge. That kind of scares me a bit. But it's self inflicted so it's my problem really.

(*Jamie's Kitchen*, Episode One, Broadcast in Australia on Channel 10, 21 July 2003)

This extract from *Jamie's Kitchen* is illustrative of a number of issues that are particularly relevant to the story we want to tell in this chapter. At this point in the drama of the first episode of *Jamie's Kitchen* we see and hear about an apparent lack of passion, of energy, of excitement, of entrepreneurial flair in the young people making the first steps in trying to become employed.

*An alternative reading might suggest that given the starting points of many of these young people these first steps are pretty substantial and indeed provide evidence of the existence of traits they supposedly lack. Particularly in the context of having their failings and relative lack of sophistication subjected to the glare of reality TV under the gaze of a global celebrity brand such as Jamie Oliver – who for all his laddishness inhabits a different world/planet to these young people.*

Second, the possibility of self-transformation, of being somebody different, of doing something different within the space of a year is held out to these young people. And this possibility is something that can be realized if they embrace food in the ways that Jamie envisages it – if they *live* it, *breathe* it, *read* it. Third, we see the emphasis on the individual as the figure who must recognize his or her deficits and lacks, who must develop, know, and understand him- or herself as being an agent who can transform his or her own life and circumstances through their own efforts. These issues, as we see them, emerge from the conceptual frameworks that we will discuss and elaborate in the sections that follow.

## The DIY self: risk, reflexivity and individualization

> Nor only that pedagogy and medicine, social law and traffic planning presume active 'thinking individuals', as they put it so nicely, who are supposed to find their way in this jungle of transitory finalities with the help of their own clear vision. All these and all the other experts dump their contradictions and conflicts at the feet of the individual and leave him or her with the well intentioned invitation to judge all of this critically on the basis of his or her own notions.
>
> (Ulrich Beck, 1992, *The Risk Society*, p. 13)

The reflexive modernization narratives of Ulrich Beck and Anthony Giddens offer our discussion of the processes of self-transformation in *Jamie's Kitchen* a sociological framework that attempts to identify and analyse various relationships between social processes (at the local, national and global level), and forms of selfhood that emerge from, and indeed shape, these processes. These theories of the character and transformations of our times, and the DIY self that emerges in these settings, can be understood in terms of the following key ideas: the *Risk Society*, reflexivity, and processes of individualization. These concepts have had a degree of use in the literature on organization studies, but less so in the management or human resource literatures (Reimer, 1998; Alvesson and Deetz, 2000). Our suggestion is that these concepts provide a useful framework for thinking about the complexity and uncertainty of globalized relationships between individuals and the social processes and structures that shape contemporary life-worlds – particularly for young people at the start of a working life. There is a need, in this context, to develop an understanding of processes of individualization in an increasingly globalized world: processes that open us all to uncertainties, risks and opportunities, as we are forced to construct a life and sustain a more or less coherent narrative of this life. To do this we provide a sketch of these concepts in the following pages, and we will return to them at a number of points in the discussion throughout this book.

## The risk society

Beck's (1992) *The Risk Society* has been one of the most provocative and influential sociological texts of the last two decades. His arguments about risk and individualisztion have been developed in subsequent texts (1994a, 1994b, 2000; Beck and Beck-Gernsheim, 2002) – largely as a consequence of responding to critiques of his early work that have tended to take two forms. The first of these has emerged from governmentality theorists who draw on the work of Foucault to argue against the totalizing tendencies of the risk society/reflexive modernization thesis of a *radical break/rupture* between a simple and a more reflexive modernity. The argument here is that different and particular risk rationalities need to be situated in the contexts and relationships that give them certain forms and consequences (see, for example, Dean, 1999a; Rose, 1999a). The second avenue of critique has emerged from a perspective that tends to confuse an analysis of *institutionalized individualism* (Beck and Beck-Gernsheim, 2002) with an endorsement of individualism as *liberal ideology* – a position that questions the extent to which individualization processes do, indeed, dissolve class, ethnic, age or other structuring elements in the shaping of life histories and trajectories (see, for example, Mythen, 2005; Abbott and Kelly, 2005).

For Beck (1992, pp. 9–10) there is a sense that in the last half of the twentieth century, and at the start of the new millennium, we are 'eye witnesses' to a 'break within modernity, which is freeing itself from the contours of the classical industrial society and forging a new form' – the *risk society*. Beck argues that in much the same way as industrial modernity 'dissolved the structure of feudal society', so processes of reflexive modernization have '*consumed and lost its other*' (original emphasis), and now undermine 'its own premises as an industrial society along with its functional principles'. These processes signal a 'demystification' of the roles and functions of science and technology in industrial society. Similar processes of doubt and uncertainty are attaching to 'modes of existence in work, leisure, the family and sexuality'. Here Beck is commenting on profound social, cultural, economic and political transformations that have reshaped global, national and local contexts through the last decades of the twentieth century. In other contexts these transformations have been identified and analysed as signalling the emergence of post-industrial, postmodern, knowledge/information-based social, cultural, economic and political relations.

Importantly, in terms of Beck's (1994a) thesis on the 'reflexive' character of these processes, the transformations in these principles are occurring largely outside the political, planning, or regulatory ambit of Liberal democratic nation states and the 'democratic self understandings' of these societies. These processes are not the result of rational, cognitive contemplation about the direction (progress) of modernity. These processes occur, largely, 'unplanned in the wake of normal, autonomized modernization' (p. 3). Autonomous here refers to the manner in which these processes are generated within rationalities, and forms of regulation and management peculiar to particular settings, institutions, organizations, businesses, research centres and centres of expertise. These processes answer not to a single logic, or rationality or overriding national or community interest. The consequences of these processes are, then, uncertain, and the uncertainty of these processes can be on the scale of the global (the future state of the biosphere) or the personal (work, relationships, diet). For Beck (1994a) an inherent consequence of this autonomization is the 'emergence of a risk society' (p. 5).

Beck (1994a, pp. 5–6) constructs the emergence of the risk society as occurring in two phases. The first phase is a stage in which the characteristics of the risk society are produced via the systemic and institutionalized practices and processes of industrialized modernity – but these effects fail to figure in, or shape, community and political discourse and debates. At this point the *grand narratives* (Lyotard, 1984) of industrial society (Science, Progress, Democracy, Work, Education, Family) remain dominant. As a result a range of issues, problems, risks (environmental, industrial, personal) are legitimized as inconsequential and/or manageable. At this stage risks such as industrial pollution and industry closures and failures – with associated human costs – are conceived as tolerable side-effects. The second phase in the emergence of the risk society is a stage in which the dangers and risks of industrial society begin to dominate and frame public, political and commercial discussions and debates. In this phase the relatively autonomous, unforeseen, unplanned consequences of modernity become '*socially* and *politically* problematic'.

Under such conditions the 'certitudes of industrial society (the consensus for progress or the abstraction of ecological effects and hazards)' are rendered unstable. Yet these risks are not merely matters for/of reflection, as might be suggested by the notion of reflexivity. Indeed, Beck argues that the risk society is not something that has emerged as a consequence of rational, deliberate choices or decision-making processes. Rather, the risk society 'arises in the continuity of autonomized modernization processes which are blind and deaf to their own effects and threats. Cumulatively and latently, the latter produce threats which call into question and eventually destroy the foundations of industrial society'.

## Reflexivity

Reflexive modernization, then, 'means not less but more modernity, a modernity radicalized against the paths and categories of the classical industrial setting' (Beck, 1992, p. 14). The inherent dynamism of modernity, illustrated by Marx and Engel's aphorism *'All that is solid melts into air, all that is holy is profaned'* (cited in Beck 1992, p. 2, emphasis added), points to new processes of modernization, marked, not by the crisis of capitalism but by its successes. Here modernization processes undercut and dissolve the contours and principles of industrial society. Reflexive modernization ought to be understood as a process in which the 'self confrontation with the effects of risk society' cannot be accommodated within the 'institutionalized standards' of industrial society (Beck, 1994a, p. 6). This does not mean that at some stage these effects cannot, do not, become subjected to processes of reasoned public, political, scientific *reflection*. Rather Beck's (1994a, p. 6) argument suggests that this later reflection cannot 'obscure the unreflected, quasi-autonomous mechanism of the transition: it is precisely abstraction which produces and gives reality to risk society'.

In this sense Beck is gesturing towards a series of crises and/or transformations which bear directly on those metanarratives which have legitimated and been constitutive of processes of modernization. Indeed, these *stories* have been fundamental to the practices of government in the modern nation state. What these crises reveal are the institutional foundations and the effects of modernization processes. At the same time these crises indicate the limited capacity of these institutional practices to engage the consequences of modernity effectively. Beck (1994b, pp. 181–3) argues that reflexive modernization is marked both by the growth of 'obligations to justify things', and of uncertainty and insecurity; indeed, 'the latter conditions the former'. In the last half of the twentieth century 'uncertainty returns', as reflexive modernization provokes transformations which are structured 'not just by what is seen and intended but also by what is unseen and unintended'.

This way of understanding the processes which are at work in transforming the life-worlds and life chances of populations of young people, suggests that categories of risk are attempts 'to make the incalculable calculable' (Beck, 1994b, p. 181). For Beck (1994b, pp. 181–2), and others, the insurance principle (the dialectic of risk and insurance) emerges within the epistemological and philosophical frameworks of industrial society (see also, Castel 1991; Defert, 1991; Ewald, 1991). The spread of this 'calculus of risk and insurance' occurs within rationalities that are structured by 'two types of optimism: linear scientization and faith in the anticipatory controllability of side effects'. These forms of optimism represent ways of rendering reality thinkable which are embedded in the metanarratives of Science and Progress. In these *modern* stories more *intelligent* applications of newer, better forms of knowledge will render *problems* more amenable to human control (management and regulation). The irony, for Beck, is that as a consequence of processes of reflexive modernization, the insurance principle, and the 'technical and social institutions of the "precaution state"', are confronted by processes which 'nullify, devalue and undermine' the notion of calculability to its very core: the 'self-reflection of late industrial society remains and blinds us to the confrontation with incalculable threats, which are constantly euphemized and trivialized into calculable risks'.

British sociologist Anthony Giddens has explored similar territory over the past 20 years (1990, 1991, 1994a, 1994b, 1994c are most relevant to this discussion). His work on reflexivity, risk and globalization has been influential in shaping debate and commentary in the academy, but, also, like Beck, in wider contexts through his interventions in community and policy discussions. These two sociologists are very much public intellectuals. In addition, Giddens' writings on politics have been influential, and much challenged, in the development of Third Way discourses in Anglo-European contexts (see Rose, 1999a for a sustained and spirited critique). Of interest in this discussion is his understanding of the ways in which large-scale, globalized processes transform the arenas of self-production; and the manner in which we reflexively make and remake ourselves in these arenas.

In *Modernity and Self Identity* (1991, pp. 3–4) Giddens argues post-traditional modernity is a 'risk culture', a culture not necessarily more risky than prior orderings of the social, but rather a culture in which risk becomes fundamental to the ways in which experts and non-experts order social relations. Under the conditions of a more reflexive modernity the 'future is continually drawn into the present by means of the reflexive organization of knowledge environments'. Yet this colonization of the future, via the constant proposition of 'as-if' scenarios, is in effect an incomplete project. At one level these forms of future-oriented risk assessment suggest notions of certainty and calculability. At another level these probabilistic ways of reflexively organizing social relations and environments 'contain numerous imponderables': a situation which emerges as a consequence of the reflexive nature of modern institutions, and the 'mutability' of the knowledge claims of expertise and abstract systems.

For Giddens (1991) a distinguishing characteristic of modern institutions is 'not so much their size, or their bureaucratic character'; but rather 'the concentrated reflexive monitoring they both permit and entail' (p. 16). One consequence of this reflexive monitoring of various environments of human interaction is the prominence of institutionally structured risk environments. Risk is fundamentally concerned with constructing some sense of what the future might hold, and the ways in which these possible futures are related to what we do and think in the present. Risk, in this sense, is about the *'colonisation of the future'* (p. 111, original emphasis). Giddens (1991) argues that within this increasingly generalized phenomenon of institutionalized reflexivity, the future emerges as a 'new terrain – a territory of counterfactual possibility'. The unknowable (future) becomes a domain amenable to colonization by reason, measurement and calculation (the knowable) (p. 111).

The concern with risk, and with imagining possible futures, is not merely the domain of expertise. A preoccupation with risk is, for Giddens (1991), illustrative of the forms of reflexivity which structure identity in contemporary settings. Here Giddens is concerned with highlighting the manner in which reflexive monitoring of risk knowledge, and risk scenarios, informs the everyday understandings, behaviours and dispositions of lay populations who reflexively appropriate such knowledge. Diverse understandings of expertly generated knowledge about health risks (diet, sexuality, exercise, smoking); relationship risks (divorce rates, counselling and self-help therapies); education risks (league tables, catchment areas, university entrance scores, leaving school early); employment risks (redundancies, training, skills, opportunities); and financial risks (mortgages, retirement planning) inform and influence the behaviours and dispositions of us all. In turn, these dispositions (changed or otherwise) are reappropriated by forms of expertise to *better* understand our motivations and *choices* as we make decisions about the directions of our lives.

This reflexive monitoring of risk environments and practices, and the penetration of this expert knowledge about life-worlds into these life-worlds, generates and drives (relentlessly) the manufactured uncertainty which characterizes contemporary settings. Radical doubt in relation to the claims of expertise about diet, sexuality, relationships, employment, the economy and schooling, indicate that:

> we are all caught up in *everyday experiments* whose outcomes, in a generic sense, are as open as those affecting humanity as a whole. Everyday experiments reflect the changing role of tradition and, as is also true of the global level, should be seen in the context of the *displacement and reappropriation of expertise*, under the intrusiveness of abstract systems. Technology in the general meaning of 'technique', plays the leading role here, in the shape of both material technology and of specialized social expertise.
>
> (Giddens, 1994b, pp. 59–60, original emphasis)

## Processes of individualization

> When we take [a] larger view of what it means to be an entrepreneur, we realize that we are talking about skills, attitudes, and disciplines everybody needs nowadays – qualities it takes to succeed in every field of work ... We need to apply entrepreneurial, self-directive, self-promoting, me-incorporated thinking to every aspect of our lives – our participation in learning activities, the way we manage our careers, our finances and investments, how we market ourselves, our ability to treat our lives as business enterprises. An entrepreneurial perspective can help us become more adept at the business of life.
>
> (Your Business Network, 2000, *Are You a Career Entrepreneur?*)

Within processes of reflexive modernization this uncertain and apparently unconstrained openness *forces* individuals, groups and communities to be '*set free* from the certainties and modes of living of the industrial epoch' (Beck, 1992, p. 14, original emphasis). For Giddens (1994b, p. 75) these institutionally structured processes mean that 'we have no choice but to choose how to be and how to act'. Central to these processes are the diverse forms of expertise produced and mobilized within the discourses of the *human* and the *natural* sciences. These discourses are 'inherent elements of the institutional reflexivity of modernity'. The mass of intellectually grounded knowledge, and the plethora of 'guides to living' (in the form of self-help manuals, and the therapeutic industries), which take as their object the Self and its relations to itself and to others, are instances of the manner in which expertise energizes the 'reflexive project of the self' (Giddens, 1991, p. 2). The proliferation of self-help manuals, guides to living, on how-to-be a ... (success, winner, leader, manager, entrepreneur), and a flow of never-ending workshops, programmes, training sessions situate Giddens' arguments in the world of work, although they sit just as easily in relation to advice on diet, relationships, sexuality, and our bodies.

Under these conditions Giddens (1991, p. 14) argues that *self identity* becomes a work-in-progress; a biography which is reflexively lived and 'organised in terms of flows of social and psychological information about possible ways of life'. Modernity, in this sense, can be understood as a 'post traditional' social order in which questions about 'How shall I live?' assume both a novel significance, and indeed, become highly consequential to the outcomes of this reflexive project of the self. A post-traditional society, for Giddens (1994a, p. 5), is not one in which 'tradition disappears – far from it'. Rather, in a post-traditional order 'tradition changes its status'. Traditions, in this view, 'have to explain themselves, to become open to interrogation or discourse'. Forms of association, gender roles and expectations, generational relations, ways of working and managing, the forms of authority or knowledge which are referred (deferred) to: all aspects of the *social* and the *natural* are subjected to the manufactured uncertainty and the contingency which characterizes processes of reflexive modernization. Giddens (1994c, p. 189) takes as one example of these processes of de-traditionalization, the elements of choice and reflexive monitoring of expertise which increasingly attach to the question of human reproduction. This is a question which emerges as a question only as a consequence of processes of individualization: should I/we have a child? When? How many? What if we can't? It is also a consequence of the penetration (a never more appropriate masculinist signifier) of the *natural* by scientific knowledge (IVF, reproductive and contraceptive technologies, biogenetic engineering). Here 'many traits that used to be "naturally given" have become matters for human decision-making'.

It is at this level that confusion develops about the direction and nature of discussions about these individualization processes. For Beck (1992) processes of individualization are 'neither a phenomenon nor an invention of the second half of the twentieth century' (p. 127). However, as the discussion thus far indicates, processes of reflexive modernization foreshadow, for Beck, a 'new twilight of opportunities and hazards' within the 'contours of a risk society' (p. 15). These largely autonomous processes of reflexive modernization 'tend to dissolve' the 'traditional parameters of industrial society' in a 'surge of individualization'. While class, gender and ethnic inequalities continue to shape life chances and choices, individuals are increasingly released from prior groundings in a 'conscience collective' of class, gender, and family relations (p. 87). Under these conditions, where class, gender and family coordinates recede (but do not disappear), individuals themselves become *'the reproduction unit for the social in the life world'*. Here there is a sense in which individuals must assume the role of makers of their own 'livelihood mediated by the market as well as their biographical planning and organization'. These processes of individualization are carried by, and indeed, carry processes of *standardization*. The penetration of market relations, and of abstract systems into every aspect of the life-world, compel the individual to choose: at the same time these processes promote, paradoxically, forms of market and institutional dependency, forms of standardization (p. 130, original emphasis).

In the discussion which follows we want to suggest that Beck's framing of these processes of individualization and standardization in terms of their institutional characteristics, provides a powerful means for understanding the contradictory impulses which shape the ways that young people attempt to construct a life and secure a livelihood in contemporary settings. Beck (1992) argues that the reflexive shaping of biographies across 'institutional boundaries' emerges as a consequence of 'their institutional dependency'. Here 'liberated individuals' become dependent on labour markets. As a consequence, individuals become:

> dependent on education, consumption, welfare state regulations and support, traffic planning, consumer supplies, and on possibilities and fashions in medical, psychological and pedagogical counseling and care. This all points to the *institution – dependent control structure* of individual situations. Individualization becomes the *most advanced* form of societalization dependent on the market, law, education and so on.
>
> (1992, pp. 130–1, original emphasis)

These processes of individualization, carried increasingly by market relations, deliver individuals 'over to an *external order and standardization*' that was unknown in the enclaves of 'familial and feudal structures' (Beck, 1992, p. 132, original emphasis). This form of standardization is of a different order precisely because it occurs within processes which compel individuals to *choose*, which set them *free* from traditional coordinates, and which make them responsible for their own biographies. These '*inherent contradictions in the individualization process*', suggest that possibilities for individual choices actually diminish in the face of these processes (p. 131, original emphasis). Here Beck (1992, p. 131) suggests that forms of dependence on market relations, on mediated expert knowledge about how one ought to live, and on a myriad of institutionalized practices, mean that 'individualized private existence' becomes increasingly 'dependent on situations and conditions that completely escape its reach'. These largely autonomous institutionalized processes supersede or are superimposed on the class, gender and family coordinates of industrial society. Moreover, these processes enter into reflexive biographical projects in ways which are structured by, and indeed structure institutionalized conceptions of the life course: Childhood – Youth – Adulthood – Retirement.

These '*institutional biographical patterns*' are, suggests Beck (1992, pp. 131–3, original emphasis), 'determinations of and interventions in human biographies'. Institutionally patterned markers such as; school starting age, school leaving age, age at which income support is payable, the age of citizenship, retirement age, indicate that 'individualization thus means precisely *institutionalization*'. The ability to structure individual biographies institutionally is often not a consequence of coordinated, planned attempts to structure, reflexively (reflect on), the life course. Rather these outcomes have a tendency to be the side-effect or the unplanned consequence of diverse, largely autonomous, attempts by various experts in diverse centres of expertise to regulate assorted aspects of these institutionally structured biographies. In this framework the *private* – that space of the *freedom to choose*, that space of individual motivations, dispositions and behaviours – is, for Beck, 'not what it appears to be'. Indeed, the *private* ought to be conceived as the '*outside turned inside and made private of conditions and decisions* (original emphasis) made elsewhere, in the television networks, the education system, in firms, or the labor market, or in the transportation system, with general disregard of their private, biographical consequences'.

These twin processes of individualization and standardization generate contradictory impulses within and for certain generational clusters. Populations of young people, in this instance, are increasingly imagined, and imagine themselves, as being responsible for their own biographies. In this sense the future participation by young people in the *good life* is in their own hands. Individualization processes result, argues Beck (1992, pp. 133–5), in individual biographies becoming 'self reflexive' and 'self produced'. The self in this sense becomes a Do-It-Yourself (DIY) project. Individuals are compelled to choose; we must choose and decide about 'education, profession, job, place of residence, spouse, number of children'. The domains of existence, the aspects of the life-world 'which are fundamentally closed to decision-making' are diminishing, while those aspects of individual biographies which are 'open and must be constructed personally' are increasing . These processes force young people to 'learn on pain of permanent disadvantage' to imagine themselves, 'as the center of action'. Yet, as Beck argues, these individualization processes, which are institutionally structured, are also increasingly, institutionally dependent, and thus increasingly 'susceptible to crises', to institutionally generated risks. In the case of young people this susceptibility is shaped by a number of processes: processes which impinge in diverse ways on the DIY project of the self.

Livelihood, suggests Beck (1992), is secured, tenuously, in the labour market. Increasingly, suitability for the labour market is dependent, for young people, on participation in schooling. Individuals and groups who are 'denied access to either' are confronted with the very real possibility of 'social and material oblivion' (p. 13), particularly in the context of labour markets which demand *flexibility*, *generic skills*, *transportability* of credentials, *passion* and *entrepreneurial* dispositions. Here, argues Beck (1992, pp. 133–6, original emphasis), an absence of the 'proper training' is 'every bit as devastating as is training but without jobs'. The risks for the DIY Self under conditions of reflexive modernization are, thus, increasingly individualized: the 'floodgates are opened wide for the subjectivization and individualization of risks and contradictions produced by institutions and society'. These institutionally generated risk environments, and the consequences they have for individual biographies emerge as 'no longer just events and conditions' which are visited upon individuals. Rather these risks are the *consequences of the decisions they themselves have made*'. Here the problems and the issues associated with transformed labour markets, globalizing economies, and the types of education and training that might be appropriate for these changed circumstances, are concerns which affect large populations. Yet, as Beck points out, in the face of these largely autonomous processes of individualization, 'what does that mean for the forging of my own fate, which nobody else can do for me?'

The problem of youth labour markets, and of those populations of young people most at risk in those institutionalized risk environments are largely imagined in terms of the individual behaviours and dispositions that young people have developed over time, and which they bring to their engagements with state agencies, training providers and employers in these settings. Young people are meant to inform themselves, prepare themselves, position themselves so as to identify and manage the opportunities and risks that emerge from and shape these labour markets. The risk society and reflexive modernization narratives powerfully bring these processes to light. They do so with a sense that these individualization processes bring both new opportunities and risks. Yet, these narratives, while highlighting the institutionalized nature of these individualization processes, tend to gloss over the ways in which the self is capable of knowing itself, or developing the self in ways that these processes demand. For example, reflexivity, in the sense of a capacity to monitor, to reflect on, to be aware of a variety of opportunities, risks, demands and openings actually looks different in different contexts. It could be argued that many of the young trainees in *Jamie's Kitchen* have a well-developed form of reflexivity that we might know as *street smart*. This reflexivity – awareness, knowledge and skill sets – may have been developed over time and no doubt equips these young people to survive, in a manner, on the streets. But this is a different sort of reflexivity to the sort demanded by globalized, individualized labour markets, and various industries and occupations within these labour markets. So the DIY self is reflexive – needs to be, is compelled to be reflexive – but it is produced, more or less successfully, for now, not yet, in a variety of contexts and settings such as *Jamie's Kitchen*. At this level, these reflexive modernization stories are less useful in understanding how various techniques, rationalities, processes and practices attempt to produce a self that is capable of managing a DIY project of the self.

In Chapter 6 ('Don't be a smart arse') we return to these themes of reflexivity and individualization. At that point these themes provide powerful means to explain the processes of individualization that position workers in the twenty-first century as being responsible for conducting themselves as an enterprise. For now we turn to a more extensive and detailed examination of the work and legacy of Michel Foucault – particularly his later work on the care of the self and governmentality. Our purpose here is to situate the ways in which the training processes we see in *Jamie's Kitchen* set out to produce an orientation to, and an understanding of the self that is positioned as the norm in *Jamie's Kitchen* – and in the wider world of work. Here *normality* of the sort that marks a person as employable, passionate, entrepreneurial, is itself a product of processes of individualization – but these processes are examined at a more intimate, *micro*, level.

## The care of the self: power and the subject

### Governmentality

> I am saying that 'governmentality' implies the relationship of the self to itself, and I intend this concept of 'governmentality' to cover the whole range of practices that constitute, define, organize and instrumentalize the strategies that individuals in their freedom can use in dealing with each other. Those who try to control, determine, and limit the freedom of others are themselves free individuals who have at their disposal certain instruments they can use to govern others. Thus, the basis for all this is freedom, the relationship of the self to itself and the relationship to the other.
>
> (Michel Foucault, 2000a, 'The Ethics of the Concern for Self as a Practice of Freedom', p. 300)

At this stage we want to outline and discuss Foucault's concept of governmentality as providing a broad analytical frame in which to situate our concern with the sorts of injunctions, incitements, directions that both aim to govern our lives, and provide the frameworks and techniques by which we should know and govern ourselves as workers. Governmentality has been a generative and powerful analytic in the social sciences over the past two decades. As a concept it suggests that as subjects we practise our freedom in a more or less open field of possibilities. This field, though, is not completely open in any unconstrained way. The world of paid work, and the behaviours and dispositions seen as necessary for ongoing participation in this world, is a field of possibilities constructed, shaped and bounded by multiple, complementary, sometimes contradictory, suggestions, encouragements, incitements for the ways in which we should conduct our life.

Colin Gordon (1991) argues that governmentality signals Foucault's interest in 'government as an activity or practice, and in arts of government as ways of knowing what that activity consisted in, and how it might be carried on'. This focus on the *mentalities* of government directs attention to the systems of 'thinking about the nature of the practice of government (who can govern; what governing is; what or who is governed)'. These concerns were introduced in a series of lectures at the College de France in 1978 and 1979 which were entitled, respectively, 'Security, territory and population', and 'The birth of biopolitics'. Foucault's series of lectures developed this theme on the art of government in a number of historical domains: the classical Greek and early

Christian concern with government as a form of *pastoral power* (the 'shepherd-game'); the early modern European 'doctrines of government' which were 'associated with the idea of reason of state and the police State'; the emergence, from the mid 1700s, of Liberalism, conceived as an 'art of government'; and post-Second World War 'forms of neo-liberal thought in Germany, the USA and France, considered as ways of rethinking the rationality of government' (Gordon, 1991, p. 3).

Importantly, in terms of the ways in which Foucault's work is often used in management and organization studies (see, for example, McKinlay and Starkey, 2000b), these series of investigations need to be situated in relation to Foucault's earlier work, most particularly his investigation of the 'microphysics' of power in *Discipline and Punish*. Foucault's focus there was on the *disciplinary techniques of power* that emerged and gave shape to developing institutional spaces such as prisons, factories, schools, hospitals: techniques and relations of power that were mobilized to 'observe, monitor, shape and control the behaviour of individuals' in these settings (Gordon, 1991, pp. 3–4). In much of the use of Foucault in management and organization studies there is a tendency to *freeze* Foucault at *Discipline and Punish*. However, Gordon (1991) suggests that Foucault's lectures on governmentality were framed, in part, as a response to criticisms of this earlier work. Included here were suggestions that Foucault's focus on the microphysics of power neglected the broader context of relations between the State and civil society – it was suggested that there was no *theory of the State* in these formulations. At the same time this emphasis produced perceptions that Foucault's *disciplined* society appeared to rule out the possibility, indeed the idea, that individuals could experience or exercise freedom – there appeared to be no spaces or relations *outside* of these disciplinary regimes. Foucault's concerns with the arts of government can, then, be seen as an attempt to respond, both rhetorically and through various modes of analysis, to a number of these criticisms, and to continue his investigations of the ways in which, in modern liberal democracies 'human beings are made subjects' (Foucault, 1983, p. 208).

As we initially discussed in the previous chapter, a principal concern in Foucault's (1991) investigations of the forms and effects of *modern* governmentality was to foreground the emergence of the idea of *population*. Foucault's investigations are grounded in the proposition that, from the sixteenth century through to the early nineteenth century, there was a transformation in the ways in which European government was conceived. This transformation involved a movement from a concern with the nature of the relation between the Prince and his subjects (an issue of sovereignty), to a concern with the nature of the relations between the State and the government of its populations (a concern with the art of government). Foucault's (1991, p. 89) tactic for examining this transformation rests on positioning the literature on the problematics of government of this period in relation to Machiavelli's *The Prince*. *The Prince* was most often read as being concerned with securing the Prince's, always tenuous, sovereignty over his territory and subjects. Foucault, however, argued that this literature was not solely positioned in relation to *The Prince*. This literature also needs to be read in the context of that thing 'which it was trying to define in its specificity, namely an art of government'.

The art of government, argued Foucault (1991, pp. 87–92), is 'not at all the same' as 'the prince's ability to keep his principality'. To speak of the art of governing is to refer to the practice of governing, among other things, 'a household, souls, children, a province, a convent, a religious order, a family'; while a governor, one who practises the art of government, can be a 'monarch, emperor, king, prince, lord, magistrate, prelate, judge and the like'. This concern with the practices of government is indicative of a number of early modern problematizations of government which take as their focus: 'How to govern oneself, how to be governed, by whom the people will accept being governed, how to become the best possible governor'. Foucault is concerned here with constructing government, as the *conduct of conduct*. Foucault argued that in this early modern literature on the arts of government, the practice of government was conceived with regard to 'three fundamental types of government, each of which relates to a particular science or discipline'. There is the 'art of self-government' which is concerned with 'morality'. The 'art of properly governing a family' is a concern of economy, where economy is, principally, about the practice of 'managing individuals, goods and wealth within the family'. The 'art of governing the state' is a question of politics, a 'question of defining the particular form of governing which can be applied to the state as a whole'.

### The conduct of conduct

Gordon (1991) argues that the interconnections between these arenas and modes of government are a crucial concern for Foucault. In some quite fundamental ways a concern with government, conceived as a practice directed towards the conduct of conduct, is a mode of analysis which serves to problematize a form of binary thinking about power: where power is conceived through the form of oppositions such as Structure/Agency, State/Civil Society, Oppression/Freedom. Within these oppositions power is conceived in terms of domination, or in terms of disciplinary practices, as being possessed by some and lacked by the others. Dean (1994, p. 179) argues that this emphasis on the practices of government signals an attempt by Foucault to 'cut the Gordian knot of the relation between micro- and macro-levels of power'. In this mode of analysis there is a shift from an earlier focus on 'disciplinary practices' to a 'more general concern for governmental practices seeking the direction of conduct'. An analysis of the practices of government, as the conduct of conduct, provides a way of understanding the ongoing management, regulation and incitement of actions, thoughts, behaviours and dispositions of subjects (populations) across diverse domains, at various levels of practice. It should be apparent, as many writers have suggested, that this framework is particularly relevant to understanding various aspects of the myriad relations, acts and processes of management and regulation, and types and levels of interaction that characterize contemporary organizations (see, for example, Alvesson and Deetz, 2000, and the collections edited by McKinlay and Starkey, 2000b and Grey and Willmott, 2005a).

Government can be conceived, then, as the 'way in which the conduct of individuals or of groups might be directed', and where, further, this government might include the conduct 'of children, of souls, of communities, of families, of the sick' (Foucault, 1983, p. 221). Central to this way of thinking government is Foucault's play on the ambiguous meanings of *conduct*. For Foucault (1983, pp. 220–1) the 'equivocal nature of the term *conduct* is one of the best aids for coming to terms with the specificity of power relations'. Conduct, in this ambiguous use, points both to the action of leading others, and to a 'way of behaving within a more or less open field of possibilities'. This field of possibilities is always constrained, and is shaped by time and space, and by the relationships between processes and relationships such as social class, gender, ethnicity and age. By imagining particular labour markets, particular organizations, and particular workplaces (such as *Jamie's Kitchen*) as constituting particular fields of possibilities, we can analyse these spaces in terms of the rationalities and techniques that give them shape and which seek to govern and regulate them. In addition, we can identify and analyse the ways in which young people, as trainees in *Jamie's Kitchen*, are required to understand, know and conduct themselves, and the ways in which they practise their freedom in this field of possibilities.

## Sovereignty, discipline and government

Governmentality, as a mode of analysis of the arts and practices of management, regulation and government, is underpinned by an emphasis on a quite specific form of power. Foucault (1991) preserves a distinction between three forms of power, the operation and effects of which mark each as distinct from the other, at the same time as they are intimately connected through their concern with populations. Here, Foucault (1991) argued that:

> we need to see things not in terms of the replacement of a society of sovereignty by a disciplinary society and the subsequent replacement of a disciplinary society by a society of government; in reality one has a triangle, sovereignty-discipline-government, which has as its primary target the population and as its essential mechanism the apparatuses of security.
>
> (1991, p. 102)

In his investigations of modern Liberal governmentalities Foucault (1991, pp. 101–2) stressed the importance of not seeing the emergence of these *mentalities*, and associated forms of pastoral power, as signalling the disappearance of other forms of power – namely discipline and sovereignty. Indeed a concern with arts of government makes the problems of sovereignty and discipline 'more acute than ever'. The issue of how to manage the conduct of conduct of diverse individuals and populations across a heterogenous field of problems and possibilities 'renders more acute the problem of the foundation of sovereignty ... and all the more acute equally the necessity for the development of discipline'. Kevin Stenson (1996, 1999) has argued that Foucault's formulation has introduced a certain ambiguity and confusion into governmentality studies. Indeed, this confusion, which Stenson identifies in the use of governmentality concepts in the social sciences generally, and in youth studies in particular, is also evident in the *use* of Foucault in management and organization studies. A number of contributions to the collection *Foucault, Management and Organization Theory* (McKinlay and Starkey, 2000a) illustrate these problems. In 'Modernism, Postmodernism and Organizational Analysis: The Contribution of Michel Foucault', Gibson Burrell (2000) summarizes his review of the contribution of Foucault's archaeological and genealogical work to organization studies by suggesting that:

> Foucault maintains that the despotic character of the disciplinary mode of domination is built into the heart, the essence of contemporary society and affects the body of the individual, of whatever class, at the minutest level ... According to Foucault, since all of us belong

> to organizations and all organizations are alike and take the prison as
> their model, we are all imprisoned within a field of bio-power, even
> as we sit alone.
>
> (2000, p. 21)

This understanding of power in effect freezes Foucault at *Discipline
and Punish* (1977), or possibly the first volume of *The History of Sexuality*
(1978). It should be acknowledged that the original text of Burrell's contribution to this collection (McKinlay and Starkey, 2000a) first appeared
in *Organization Studies* in 1988. In this context it is less appropriate to critique his claim that the 'full relevance' of Foucault's 'final shift – to the
ground of ethics – still remains an open issue' (2000, p. 21). However, in
the same collection Stewart Clegg (2000), in 'Foucault, Power and Organizations', presents an analysis of the contribution that Foucault's work
can make to organization and management studies. Clegg suggests that
Foucault sounds the death knell for work that focuses on sovereign forms
of power. Instead the focus should be on discipline and bio-power. Yet,
in Clegg's discussion there is no mention of governmentality, or what
this concept might mean for management and organization studies.
One final comment on this sort of confusion at this point: in their editors' introduction to the collection McKinlay and Starkey (2000a, 2000b,
p. 10) argue that: 'Contrary to Foucault, monarchic power was not totally
displaced during the Enlightenment. Monarchic and disciplinary power
continues to co-exist in an uneasy, shifting relationship in the late twentieth century.' Indeed. However, as our discussion to this point suggests,
this is not *contrary* to Foucault, but, rather, firmly located on the ground
that should be explored in analyses framed by Foucault's work.

So, at this stage we want to sketch the nature of sovereign and disciplinary forms of power to add to an understanding of government as the
conduct of conduct. This Foucauldian triangle plays a vital role in examining the ways in which processes of self-transformation are instigated,
managed and regulated in *Jamie's Kitchen* – by Jamie Oliver, by trainers,
by the young people themselves. In Foucault's framework, sovereignty
is a form of power seeking to establish and maintain relationships of
legitimate authority so that this authority itself is maintained. Stenson
(1996, p. 12) sets out to situate various youth work practices in a 'complex of inter-related strategies of government: sovereignty, discipline
and government'. In doing so he argues that 'the struggle to establish
and maintain a legitimated sovereignty is functionally central to Liberal
rule' (1999, p. 68). In Stenson's (1996, p. 5) discussion, this struggle is

a 'struggle to control geographical territory in the face of internal and external threats, through a monopolisation both of the threat and use of force and attempts to establish the legitimacy of that force'. Sovereignty is exercised by, and through, a range of institutions and strategies – including the armed forces, public and private police organizations, and a range of laws, regulations and by-laws. Sovereignty is, in this sense, both territorial and metaphorical. As Stenson (1996, p. 5) argues, a great deal of the historical and ongoing (actual and imagined) challenges to the legitimacy and exercise of sovereign power – 'from behaviour construed as "anti-social" to public order, disturbances or major demonstrations such as the anti-poll tax riots' – have emerged from, or been centred on, diverse populations of young people. At another level, in *Jamie's Kitchen* sovereignty is exercised – as in many organizations – by the Foundation managers and by Jamie Oliver, all of whom have the capacity to make and enforce regulations/laws/rules in order that the training programme and social enterprise can continue to function and prosper – in order that management and regulation (government) can take place.

For Foucault, disciplinary power attempts to produce relationships of regulation and forms of subjection that promise a certain docility in subjects and populations (Foucault, 1977, 1983, 1991). David Kirk and Barbara Spiller (1993, pp. 110–11) suggest, in their historical analysis of the disciplinary role of gymnastics in the primary school curriculum at the turn of the twentieth century, that Foucault's use of the concept of discipline provides a 'means of locating educational practices as one set of micro-technologies which, together with other sets of "little practices" within domains like the military, medicine and so on, make up the infrastructures of disciplinary society'. Moreover, the consequence of discipline is/was not 'mere subjection (as in slavery), but controlled production' of subjects and populations characterized by a 'docility-utility'. For Foucault (1977, p. 138), 'discipline produces subjected and practised bodies, docile bodies. Discipline increases the forces of the body (in economic terms of utility) and diminishes the same forces (in political terms of obedience)'. Historically, the promise of much Youth-focused regulation has been to produce, 'through surveillance and education' – as disciplinary practices – the 'productive skills and capacities' that will 'enable young people to adapt to a modern industrial society' (Stenson, 1996, pp. 5–6). In this respect much of the Youth Studies work that White (1993) refers to as emerging out of the 'changing economic, social and cultural circumstances of young people' in the last decades of the twentieth century is energized by concerns about how it is possible to produce, from the *raw material* of today's Youth, subjects who are capable of exercising a well-regulated autonomy. In *Jamie's Kitchen* and in the colleges and other restaurants where the training of the young people occurs, a myriad of *little practices* – cleaning floors and preparation surfaces; maintaining utensils, knives and tools; chopping and preparing ingredients in the correct way – aim to discipline the trainees to meet the demands of rationalized, time-determined, work in a commercial kitchen.

## The subject and pastoral power

Towards the end of his life Foucault (1983, pp. 212–15; 2000d) argued that his concern was with that form of power which 'applies itself to immediate everyday life', a form of power which 'categorizes the individual, marks him by his own individuality, attaches him to his own identity'; and which, further, 'imposes a law of truth on him which he must recognize and which others have to recognize in him'. This understanding of power is centrally concerned with identifying the form of power 'which makes individuals subjects': subject, in one sense, to 'someone else by control and dependence'; in another sense, subject to and tied to 'his own identity by a conscience or self-knowledge'. Within the modern governmental State, this form of power, which Foucault argued is grounded, in many important ways, in the Christian technique of 'pastoral power', can be characterized as consisting of a 'tricky combination in the same political structures of individualization techniques, and of totalization procedures'. The modern State, in this sense, can be conceived as a 'matrix of individualization', in which a form of pastoral power takes as its object the integration of individuals, whose individuality 'would be shaped in a new form, and submitted to a set of very specific patterns'. There are a number of characteristics of this form of power which bear directly on this discussion.

Foucault (1983, pp. 214–15) argued that in its ecclesiastical mode pastoral power takes as one object the eternal salvation of the individual: a salvation which is made possible through a 'knowledge of the conscience and an ability to direct it'. Within the development of the institutional structures of the governmental State 'salvation' takes on new meanings. Here a more secular form of pastoral power takes as its object, the 'health, well-being (that is, sufficient wealth, standard of living), security' of the population, and of individuals within the population.

For Machiavelli's Prince the 'ensemble of objects' of his power consists of two things: namely territory and the continued sovereignty over the inhabitants of this territory. There is a fundamental concern here with questions of territorial and juridical sovereignty, and the practices which might be mobilized in the maintenance of this sovereignty. However, within the domain marked out by a concern with the art of government, there is a shift to conceive of government as the 'right disposition of things, arranged so as to lead to a convenient end'. To speak of 'things', in this instance, is not to speak, primarily, of territory, or of juridical sovereignty. Rather, what is of concern in this definition of government is the relation between populations and 'those other things' such as 'wealth, resources, means of subsistence, the territory with its specific qualities, climate, irrigation, fertility'. Further, this emphasis on the disposition of things takes as its legitimate concerns those relations between populations (and individuals) and their 'customs, habits, ways of acting and thinking', and the relations between populations and 'accidents and misfortunes such as famine, epidemics, death' (Foucault, 1991, p. 93).

This emerging concern with the right disposition of things, so as to lead to some convenient end, implies, for Foucault (1991, p. 95), a 'plurality of specific aims', a 'whole series of specific finalities' as marking the ends of the practice of government. A key element in this framework is the notion of *disposition*. To *dispose* signals a further shift from the notion of a transcendental sovereignty which achieved its end, of obedience to the Sovereign (Law), through 'obedience to the laws'. Law and sovereignty here 'were absolutely inseparable'. In the concern to conceive of the arts of government there is an acknowledgement that government cannot solely be a question of 'imposing law on men'. Rather, in emphasizing the *disposition* of things, the art of government becomes more a question of 'emphasising tactics rather than laws, and even of using laws themselves as tactics – to arrange things in such a way that, through a certain number of means, such and such ends may be achieved'.

This is a quite specific characterization of power in its pastoral form; a characterization which marks pastoral power off from power as domination, or from a relationship of violence. For Foucault (1983, p. 220), this form of power relation is defined, not as a 'mode of action' which acts 'directly and immediately on others', as in a relationship of violence which 'forces', 'bends', 'destroys' and/or 'closes the door on all possibilities', but rather, a power relation, in this sense, is characterized by 'action upon action', on existing actions or on those which may arise in the present or future. In this view, a power relationship is further characterized through two elements. First, in a power relation, the Other, 'over whom power is exercised', must be 'recognized and maintained to the very end as a person who acts'. Second, within a relationship of power, a 'whole field of responses, reactions, results and possible inventions may open up'. Power here is a 'set of actions upon other actions'; it is a 'way of acting upon an acting subject or acting subjects by virtue of their acting or being capable of action'.

Government, then, can be imagined in terms of the structuring of the 'possible field of action of others', where that action might well be different to that envisaged, and which, in turn, might well open up the possibility of inciting a variety of measures or responses which seek to conduct future actions: 'Power is exercised only over free subjects, and only insofar as they are free.' Freedom, in this context, indicates that individuals and groups (populations), as the subjects of power, are situated in a 'field of possibilities in which several ways of behaving, several reactions and diverse comportments may be realised'. Conceiving power in this manner avoids some of the problems associated with seeing power and freedom as *oppositions*, as being 'mutually exclusive (freedom disappears everywhere power is exercised)'. Foucault (1983, p. 221) sees the interplay between power and freedom in the 'shepherd-game' as being far more complicated: 'In this game freedom may well appear as the condition for the exercise of power (at the same time its precondition, since freedom must exist for power to be exerted, and also its permanent support, since without the possibility of recalcitrance, power would be equivalent to a physical determination).'

This complex relationship between practices of government and subjects, who in all probability might choose to act other than as envisaged within certain fields of action, is further characterized by Foucault (1983, p. 222) as a 'relationship which is at the same time reciprocal incitation and struggle; less of a face-to-face confrontation which paralyzes both sides than a permanent provocation'. This mode of analysis of the practice of government suggests that power relations are, indeed, 'rooted deep in the social nexus'. Government, as the conduct of conduct, is not 'reconstituted "above" society as a supplementary structure whose radical effacement one could perhaps dream of'. Instead, argues Foucault , this focus on government emphasizes the view that, 'to live in a society is to live in such a way that action upon other actions is possible – and in fact ongoing'.

### If we are free to choose...

It is this understanding of government, conduct, power relations and freedom that leads to Foucault's later work on ethics and on the care of the self. These formulations suggest, for Foucault, forms of research, and an analytic, that are concerned with *practices of freedom*, *ethics* and the *care of the self*. The development of these concerns through the three volumes of *The History of Sexuality*, and in accompanying lectures and interviews during the last years of his life was variously attached to analyses of Victorian discourses of sexuality, and on the ways in which ancient Greek and Roman citizens (free men) problematized the ways in which they ought to conduct themselves and their relations with others – women, boys, slaves – in relation to domains such as marriage, food, and sexual practices and behaviours. This historical focus was not so much driven by a concern with defining/describing the history of the past (in order to return to it), but rather with producing histories of the present (genealogies), so that we might be able to recognize the contingencies, possibilities and limits of ourselves, and our present: with the purpose and possibility of imagining and acting otherwise (Foucault, 2000c).

Foucault (2000a, pp. 283–5) argued that freedom was 'the ontological condition of ethics' insofar as 'ethics is the considered form that freedom takes when it is informed by reflection'. Foucault's historical analyses (themselves the object of stinging critiques by various classicists and philosophers – see Timothy O'Leary's *Foucault and the Art of Ethics* (2002), and Alexander Nehamas' *The Art of Living* (2000) for overviews of the analyses and critiques) suggested that among the ancient Greeks and Romans 'concern with self and care of the self were required for right conduct and the proper practice of freedom, in order to know oneself ... as well as to form oneself, to surpass oneself, to master the appetites that threaten to overwhelm one'. In this sense, suggested Foucault: 'Taking care of oneself requires knowing ... oneself'. *Care of the self*, understood in these terms is not just *knowledge of the self*, but 'knowledge of a number of rules of acceptable conduct or of principles that are both truths and prescriptions. To take care of the self is to equip oneself with these truths: this is where ethics is linked to the game of truth.'

For Foucault ethics constitute the diverse, often complementary, sometimes contradictory, encouragements, incitements, directives that suggest that we should think and act in certain ways in relation to particular ends. Given these incitements and directives, how do we choose to conduct ourselves and our relations with others? With these concerns in mind Foucault (2000a) argued that his interest was with 'practices of freedom' rather than 'processes of liberation':

> This is precisely the problem I encountered with regard to sexuality: does it make any sense to say, 'Let's liberate our sexuality'? Isn't the problem rather that of defining the practices of freedom by which one could define what is sexual pleasure and erotic, amorous and passionate relationships with others? This ethical problem of the definition

> of practices of freedom ... is much more important than the rather
> repetitive affirmation that sexuality or desire must be liberated.
>
> (2000a, p. 283)

If we are free to choose, even compelled to choose, if the cultural, social, economic, and political spaces that shape the West at the start of the twenty-first century are largely structured by discourses of choice, and we are positioned as individuals who must make choices, if all of this has some truth or resonance, then ethics are a fundamental dilemma in all our lives. As Timothy O'Leary (2002, p. 170) argues in his examination of Foucault's philosophical and historical analyses, the aim of Foucault's ethics: 'can be characterized as an *art* of freedom: the task of giving form to one's liberty, of moulding and giving a style to one's life and one's relations with others is a task, like that of the artist, which knows no completion'.

This reading of Foucault's work on power/knowledge/subjects, on the care of the self, on governmentality suggests not a champion of liberal individualism, but a provocateur of the idea that as individuals who are free (in ways more or less circumscribed by relations of class, gender, ethnicity, and in different contexts of interaction) we are confronted with the challenges (never-ending) of how we will practise or exercise our freedom in more or less open fields of possibility. An example: once the would-be trainees make the choice to apply for the Fifteen Foundation programme (for whatever reasons, and from a variety of places of relative marginalization/disadvantage – as constraints on their capacities to imagine and exercise choices), and more or less willingly agree to submit themselves to the processes, practices, forms of regulation and management that structure programmes which have as their aim processes of self-transformation, how do they practise and exercise their freedom? In the chapters that follow we will explore a number of the dilemmas and demands of freedom that shaped the experiences of the trainees' induction into the rationalized, globalized labour markets of the twenty-first century. Ideas of passion, gender, conformity and generation will structure this analysis.

In this analytical frame there are many questions about what forms of freedom are possible in different lives – especially the lives of the trainees in *Jamie's Kitchen* – but also in the lives of those of us who have, more or less successfully, developed a self that is employable, entrepreneurial, passionate in the labour markets of the twenty-first century. What circumstances, relations, understandings and knowledges facilitate or limit the ways we might imagine the lives that we lead, or could lead, and the choices, opportunities, risks that shape and confront us in our daily lives? In addition, how do these imagined and material circumstances position us to understand others, the choices they make (or don't) and the possible relationships they could have to and with us, and we could have with them? Here, we can suggest that the various ways in which Jamie Oliver, his trainers, his mentors, his collaborators, the managers and staff of the Fifteen Foundation understand and know themselves, and the marginalized young people who are their trainees, are instrumental in giving shape to the selection and induction processes, the support structures and services, the work placements, the experiences that characterize the Fifteen programme.

One of the things we are thinking of here in terms of this framework is the sense of self that someone like Dovid (*Jamie's Kitchen Australia* trainee introduced in Chapter 1) brings to a training/employment relationship with others who are much more confident, skilled, experienced than he, and the training, disciplining, governing relationships and practices that seek to transform his sense of self, with the aim (*telos*) of developing a range of skills, competencies, confidences and self-understandings that would produce a different Dovid: a Dovid that didn't sleep rough; a Dovid that was employed at something that he wanted to do; something that he could be passionate about; something that gave him different possibilities for understanding himself and his life.

The analytical, even political, work that emerges from this framework – quite apart from the work that we have to continue to do to fashion a self that must choose, and must live with others whom we must recognize as being *free* and capable of choice – is to map, explore and analyse the different fields of possibilities in which we live our lives, and the possibilities, limits and consequences of the choices we make (and do not make) as we practise our freedom. Foucault offers a number of different tools for undertaking these explorations and analyses. These include his formulation of power/knowledge/subjects and his closely related fourfold analytic of ethics that structure the analyses in volumes 2 and 3 of *The History of Sexuality*. We will discuss these in subsequent chapters.

## Conclusion

The analytical and political usefulness and power of Foucault's formulations is that we cannot prejudge what the outcomes of the analyses might be. We cannot adopt a principled, say, Marxist or feminist position that argues, for example, that the trainees in *Jamie's Kitchen* are being *dragooned* into a life of wage slavery via their, apparently, willing partic-ipation in the training programmes provided by the Fifteen Foundation or that their marginalized, disadvantaged starting positions (which have their own histories of imagined and materially limited choice, opportu-nity and possibility) present them with few options or that the choices they make to participate are forced, or alternatively, naive or that they don't realize what they are letting themselves in for in submitting to the middle-class values, beliefs and ethics of a workspace that demands particular practices of the self, and of self-transformation. As one youth studies academic commented at a seminar in which we presented and dis-cussed some of the issues we are examining here: *'He's just trying to make them middle class'*, as if this outcome/consequence were an inherently bad, unforgivable thing: a fate worse than a life of continued marginal-ization or of possible material and social *oblivion*, on the *rubbish heaps* of globalized modernity or, even, that there is something inherently virtuous (*romantic*) about the working classes or those who live these marginalized lives or, indeed, that there are some essential, timeless and free-floating characteristics, behaviours and dispositions that we can identify as working-class or middle-class.

The task, instead, is to explore the processes, forces, tactics, knowl-edges, self-understandings, practices of self-transformation and choices that become evident within this framework, and to identify and analyse the consequences – intended or otherwise – of the play of these forces and processes and forms of freedom. In this sense such analyses are situated in what Nikolas Rose (1992, p. 3) has called *critical sociologies of freedom*; soci-ologies that understand freedom as a *formula* of regulation, government, management: 'freedom as it has been articulated into norms and princi-ples for organizing our experience of our world and ourselves; freedom as it is realised in certain ways of exercising power over others; freedom as it has been articulated into certain rationales for practising in relation to ourselves'.

Critical or genealogical analyses of freedom of the type envisaged by Rose – the *texture* of which derives from the later Foucault – would explore and analyse the myriad ways in which freedom has informed, and informs, the liberal and neo-liberal rationalities of government that have given shape to individual and collective lives in Western democra-cies since the eighteenth century. As Rose (1992, pp. 3–4) argues, these 'investigations would not be critical *of* freedom. They would not try to reveal freedom as a sham, or to decry the freedom we *think* we have in the name of a truer freedom to come.' Rather, drawing on the formula-tions of power, government, ethics and the self that Foucault developed,

# 4
# Passion: The Vital Ingredient in the Quest for Salvation?

## Introduction

> Cooking is the most massive rush. It's like having the most amazing hard on, with Viagra sprinkled on top of it, and it's still there twelve hours later.
>> (Gordon Ramsay, cited in Bill Buford, 2006, *Heat*, p. 79)

> I believe that you have to have a passion for what you do. Now I want to run my own restaurant. Fifteen has helped me believe that I could actually achieve this. I also want to learn by example and use my restaurant to help other young people and give them the opportunities I've been given.
>> (Georgina, Fifteen trainee, 2004, quoted in Fifteen Foundation, 2007)

Earlier in this book one of us admitted to a passion for food: for reading about, for watching TV shows on, and for working with, different ingredients and different ways of preparing and presenting food. Being passionate about food is something that we have no trouble understanding or identifying with. Both of us, in different contexts, would also admit to a number of other passions: particular practices, behaviours, people, and objects that provoke in us a range of emotions and feelings and rationalizations. Now is probably not the place to go into what some of those might be. However, being passionate about certain things is something that can make us feel alive, responsive, excited, energized.

141

Being passionate about something can get you out of bed in the morning and keep you going throughout the day – or night. Passion in this sense need not be a positive, *nice* thing. Passion can also be about anger, violence, aggression – passionate football supporters spring to mind here.

Most commonly passion is understood as an emotional state – even thought it may not be an emotion. However, passion is also something that is understood differently, in different contexts and with a variety of consequences. The *idea* of passion – sketched all too briefly to this point – also has something to contribute to an understanding of contemporary work-related identities and self-understandings. In organizational and work contexts at the start of the twenty-first century we can imagine, for example, being passionate about our work (*or not*). We can also imagine the consequences of being seen by others (managers, supervisors, trainers, team-mates) as *not* being passionate about our work/job. We might, at various times and with a range of consequences, wonder whether we can *become* passionate about the job or tasks that we need to do – especially when someone else has told us to do the particular task/job. In these organizational spaces it is widely believed that *being* passionate will make us more effective, more productive, more creative in our jobs: because passion is seen as of some importance in understanding work-related motivations, performance, and levels and forms of commitment to a team, or section, or organization.

We have already suggested that passion, understood in quite particular ways, plays a central, pivotal – but not unproblematic – role in the narrative and drama of *Jamie's Kitchen*, and in the lives of key players in that drama. Passion's *starring role* in the drama of *Jamie's Kitchen* can enable us to analyse some of the consequences of this contemporary *passion* for *passion* in trying to understand organizational and work lives.

Before we outline the direction that the discussion will take in this chapter we want to illustrate some of the tensions that emerge from this focus on work, passion and the self. We would both – albeit differently – own up to being passionate about aspects of the jobs that we do – teaching, research, writing (including this book), but probably not the *administrivia* that accompanies much academic work in contemporary universities. Is this a bad thing to say, that we are passionate about various aspects of our jobs? If we admit to being passionate about at least some of the things we are paid to do, does that mean we approve of all of the things that our jobs demand of us? Or that we approve of, or agree with, the managers who require us to do certain things, approach our tasks with energy, enthusiasm and passion – including, for example, discussing with students why they should get an extension for an assignment because their guinea pig died or why they should get a re-grade for an essay that takes 2000 words to say nothing and references no one? Does admitting being passionate about teaching, research or writing mean that we agree with government policies, that in our context, have significant, often detrimental, impacts on the quality of our working environment? The answer to all of these questions is: *not necessarily*. But all of these aspects of our jobs can impact on the energy, commitment, passion that we are able to exhibit for the things that we do to secure a livelihood (our salvation) in the individualized, globalized labour markets of the twenty-first century. Passion, in this context and in the sense we will use it here, should, therefore, be seen as problematic. So, in a reflexive engagement with the idea that passion and paid work can come together to provide even temporary salvation, we seek to make problematic the emphasis on passion in the processes of salvation that are made explicit in *Jamie's Kitchen*. This does not mean that passion, that being passionate, about food and work and training is a *bad* thing. Rather, this problematizing analysis – that draws on Foucault's understandings of power, the self and the practice of freedom – would seek to explore and analyse the productive and limiting consequences of understanding passion in particular ways, in particular fields of possibility.

To situate this discussion we will first sketch a review of the ways in which, for want of a better name, the popular management literature frames passion, and the ways in which in this literature passion is something that might be provoked, harnessed and managed for the purposes of enhancing individual and organizational performance. This sketch will serve to situate the significance of the concept of passion in the drama of both series of *Jamie's Kitchen*, and in the material that the Fifteen Foundation publishes in relation to its ongoing work training marginalized young people. As we have already indicated Jamie Oliver and his collaborators are dismayed by an apparent *lack of passion* among many of the initial applicants for training positions in Fifteen; a lack that is situated against the expectations of Oliver: *'I wasn't expecting loads, only inspiration'*. This initial lack, and the efforts to overcome it, drives the anxieties, uncertainties, confrontations and collaborations that manufacture the drama which unfolds around the training and processes of self-transformation that we witness in *Jamie's Kitchen*. Against this dramatic backdrop the idea that trainees need to develop passion – to *be* or *become* passionate – is made concrete in the following ways:

- Being passionate about food – understood in particular ways;
- Being passionate as you present, fashion and transform yourself;
- Being passionate about work and training, and the demands they place on the self.

From these preliminary sketches we will turn to a more detailed analysis of passion that is framed by Foucault's fourfold analytic of the ethics of the self. Developing concepts that we introduced in the previous chapter we will argue that this analytic enables us to understand passion, and its particular manifestations in *Jamie's Kitchen* and in the training of marginalized young people, as a powerful technology of self-transformation. As a technology of the self, passion is analysable along the following axes:

- It emerges from particular forms of knowledge and ways of knowing the self, vocational training, paid work, the restaurant industry, food;
- It is produced, regulated and managed within relations of power – sovereignty, discipline and government – that emerge from and give structure/shape to particular fields of possibilities;
- It seeks to provoke and produce certain practices of the self – understood in terms of the development and performance of an entrepreneurial, passionate self.

## Passion, work and management

> **It's just a job, isn't it?**
> If you feel that work is just a job, you are wasting 40 or more hours a week of your life. You are shortchanging your employer who gets less than your best effort. You are shortchanging yourself by wasting time on routine or even drudgery instead of spending that time doing what you enjoy. You could, and should, spend those 40 hours instead doing something that makes you feel good.
> (F. Jon Reh, 2007, *Passion Pays*)

One day in June 2007, when we were doing some research for this chapter, we typed *passion and work* as a search request into Google.

In 0.10 seconds our request returned 73,400,000 results. Interestingly, Google Scholar only returned approximately 115,000 results. The sheer size of the return might render a large percentage of these hits meaningless – we must admit to only clicking through the first five pages of them!

In these first five pages (50 results) we entered a virtual space in which motivational aphorisms, new age incantations, management buzzwords and self-help ephemera came together in ways that turned passion into a saleable commodity, an essential element in any successful, sustainable enterprise of the self. Many of these sites promised to reveal, for a price, the formula, the ingredients, the elements that will get you bouncing out of bed first thing in the morning, and make you reluctant to go back there until late at night in case you might miss an opportunity to display and use your passion in the globalized, 24/7 labour markets of the twenty-first century.

> **Thank God it's Monday**
>
> Do you look forward to Monday morning? Are you raring to go back to work? Or are you a TGIF (Thank God it's Friday) kind of person who can't wait to get away from the job for a couple of days? You spend at least 8 hours a day at the job. That is almost 25% of your week. If you are a TGIF person you are missing something really important in your work life – passion.

> Being passionate about your job is more than the old adage 'do what you love'. It's looking forward to going to work. It's time flying by when you're there. It's working past quitting time, not because you're swamped with work, but because you were so intent you didn't notice the time.

> When you are passionate about what you do for a living you enjoy it more. You also do it better.

> You are more committed to the success of the operation if you believe in it passionately.
>
> (F. Jon Reh, 2007, *Passion Pays*)

An illustrative, arguably representative, example of the sorts of ideas, suggestions, and theories of the self (as largely autonomous, choice-making, self-regulating, entrepreneurial, passionate) that circulate in these spaces, comes from a contribution to a www site called *EyesOn-Sales*. The site describes itself as a 'social/professional networking hub for Sales Professionals around the world'. The network claims tens of thousands of members who contribute to, and receive free access to, articles, blogs, podcasts and 'last, but not least, educational and inspirational video segments' (EyesOnSales, 2007). In the virtual spaces of the early twenty-first century this sort of networking hub is commonplace and widespread. We can safely assume that like many such hubs it makes a contribution to the discourses that shape conversations in a variety of settings about a variety of issues. Indeed, it is unremarkable insofar as it is illustrative and representative of the ways in which many individuals, groups and communities interact and communicate in the developed (and developing) economies.

If you enter passion as a search request on this site, Mark Sincevich's (2007) article *5 Ways to Keep Your Passion at Work* is returned as the number two result but was number one at the time of our research. In what follows we present an edited account of the five-step programme/recipe that Sincevich outlines. In the bio-notes that accompany the article, Sincevich is described (autobiographically) as the founder, and 'Chief Perspective Officer' (CPO) of Staash Press, a member of the National Speakers Association, and the executive director of the Digital Photography Institute. In these various incarnations he consults with, and coaches, individuals and organizations to 'increase their communication power ... gain a fresh perspective, generate new ideas, sharpen the focus and create more business'. He claims to accomplish this by 'bringing a unique photography angle to his creative keynotes, meeting facilitations, and powerful presentation skills programs'. Again, these claims about individual skills, capacities, dispositions, and ways of packaging, presenting and selling the self in the marketplace of a knowledge/information economy are unremarkable and, in many respects, *banal*. But this banality, we suggest, can highlight the ways in which certain ideas of passion; of the autonomous, choice-making and self-regulating self; of work and management come together to structure the fields of possibility in which we try to secure our salvation in globalized labour markets.

By its very title, *5 Ways to Keep Your Passion at Work* suggests a technical understanding of passion. It is something that is able to be produced, cultivated, enhanced. Passion, here, is technical, but it is not *mere* technique, largely because it is embedded in particular psychologized, individualized understandings of the self. The self is not just a surface effect. But it can be moulded, manipulated, worked on, energized, enhanced to create both favourable surface impressions, and a different, improved, sense of self, of self-worth, even self-esteem. Passion, in this and many similar formulations, can make you want to get out of bed, work harder, try new things ... The *trick* though, is to discover and practise the techniques that can enable this passion to emerge, to flourish, to be sustained. And it is a trick because, as is implied or made explicit in many of these recipes, there are situations, demands, organizational practices and processes, fellow workers, managers, that conspire against you being able to exhibit or exercise passion.

> **Keep a file of awesome people**
>
> One of the best ways to start learning about what you are passionate about is by keeping a file. When you read an article that is really inspiring, tear it out of the magazine and put it into a file. When you get an e-mail from a colleague that really inspires you, print it and put this into your file. I started doing this many years ago with a file called 'Awesome People.' It has now morphed into many sub-files, but the concept remains the same. If you want to have a rich life, start by studying the positive lessons of others.
> (Mark Sincevich, 2007, *5 Ways to Keep Your Passion at Work*)

The suggestion here is that generating and sustaining passion can require some quite menial record-keeping and filing. The information – articles, magazines, emails – may be inspirational but it needs to be collected and collated in quite mundane ways so that you can go back to it when your passion needs a boost.

> **Reasons why**
>
> Make a list of compelling reasons why you are doing your work in the first place and put it in a place where you can refer to it constantly. Concentrate on your top 5 reasons. If your list is less than positive, it will serve as motivation for you to keep looking for other motivating factors. Maybe you need to get more training or to work with a colleague in another department.
> (Mark Sincevich, 2007, *5 Ways to Keep Your Passion at Work*)

Again, *reasons why* need to be noted, recorded and stored in a way that makes them readily accessible, so that the reasons why you get out of bed, or stay late, or feel that you are doing something worthwhile can be readily retrieved and used to invigorate a lagging sense of passion. At this stage we also sense that not all people's Top 5 will be positive; but if they aren't, the self is conceived as an autonomous, choice-making agent who can readily, easily move to spaces where passion can be energized.

> **Just launch**
>
> Are you waiting for somebody to come along and give you more passion? It won't happen. It has to come from deep inside. Now that you have a file of people you admire and the reasons why you are engaged in the work that you do, you need to launch into some new ideas that will help inject additional passion into your work. Sometimes just getting out of the starting gate is all that you need ... William Shakespeare said, 'Our doubts are traitors that make us lose the good we might oft find by fearing to attempt.'
>
> (Mark Sincevich, 2007, *5 Ways to Keep Your Passion at Work*)

Here passion is understood as something that is inside the self, possibly dormant and waiting to be energized by the work of filing and list making. These techniques should then be utilized as you take yourself to market, as you enterprise yourself as a passionate self. The things that might hold you back include self-doubts, but these should be minimized as a consequence of the passion the self has generated and can now exercise.

> **Make a commitment**
>
> Make a 'working plan of action' going forward to give you stability and comfort. I worked with a former employer to transfer to a different division within the same company. I made a commitment of at least a year to help me increase my passion. This is especially important when trying to deal with managing your stress when the road before you is not clearly laid out. It might take even longer depending upon the type of work. This commitment for a longer length of time not only gives you credibility, but it also takes into account The Law of the Harvest. Farmer's know this very well. What you plant

> in the spring will grow into a beautiful plant by autumn. This process can't be forced or rushed. However, all plants need constant watering, nourishment and a positive environment. Don't forget this! How many plans fail due to inattention and lack of support? Take this into account going forward and be open to constructive criticism.
>
> (Mark Sincevich, 2007, *5 Ways to Keep Your Passion at Work*)

The passionate self here is understood as a project; a project that is ongoing; that needs a plan; that needs some sense of being on a journey; that also requires a commitment to see the project through even in the face of inevitable obstacles. Importantly, though, the ability to sustain the passionate self as an ongoing project is something that requires the constructive criticism, support and attention of others (and of the self as a reflexive agent).

> **Have faith in yourself**
>
> How can you accomplish this? A large part is attitude! Surround yourself with people who support you in your organization and when you are with friends and family. I asked a very successful neighbor who sold his first company for many millions how he was able to manage the stress of uncertainty as he followed his passions. He said, 'I don't ask myself if something is going to work; instead, I ask how it is going to work?' With comments like these and a supportive work environment, you will start to feel more in control of your life. Another way to have more faith in yourself is to go to bed every night and visualize how excited you are about the work that you do. Your subconscious mind will work 'behind the scenes' to help make your dreams come true. What is your dream for increasing your passion at work and how are you going to make it come true?
>
> (Mark Sincevich, 2007, *5 Ways to Keep Your Passion at Work*)

Again, the final step is largely dependent on a view that the self is autonomous, is self-actualizing, and can achieve things if only it is has the right attitude and can surround itself with the right people. These things, and the ability to visualize the excitement you take to and from your work, are the things that will enable the self to be in control of the planning, implementation and ongoing delivery of the project of the passionate self.

In summary then, what we see in this framing of passion (and in many similar formulations) are particular understandings of the techniques that can be mobilized – by those who are able to know themselves in these terms – to generate and sustain passion in relation to work. Work here is paid; it is the activity that can secure us salvation in the globalized labour markets of the twenty-first century. *So we may as well be passionate about it, or find something we can be passionate about.* But work is also something that we must do on ourselves; our own, passionate, self is an ongoing, reflexive enterprise/project.

Debra King (2005, 2006) has provided a different, but in some ways similar, account of the manner in which ideas about passion have found a central place in discourses and practices related to facilitating and enhancing motivation, performance and management in organizations. Her 2006 paper presents a sketch of a larger analysis of 30 books and 39 articles in business journals from what she identifies as *the popular management literature*. She argues that ideas about passion, spirituality and emotional intelligence figure prominently in this literature: they function as powerful truths in making the nature of work, management, performance, motivation and commitment knowable. She argues that in these discursive spaces passion is 'constructed as a moral imperative, something that should be sought and utilised' (p. 1). Her intent is to make problematic a particular framing of passion as an always-positive element in discourses about performance, motivation, commitment (*What happens if these truths position you as not being passionate enough in the particular context of your work?*).

King's analysis, which we will spend some time discussing, is framed by an attempt to define the characteristics of passion. These four characteristics, which enable passion to function as a 'superordinate concept' in her analysis, provide a framework that is useful to the discussion that follows.

1 *Emotionality*. Although not an emotion in itself, passion provides a context for the expression of particular emotions; the ways in which emotions are combined and prioritized, and for the intensity of their expression.
2 *Energy*. Passion is embodied through the way it generates, uses and shapes physical and mental energy. In the literature ... energy is often used interchangeably with passion in discussions of 'drive' and motivation.

3 *Object of meaning*. The object of meaning provides passion with its direction and focus. The object has to have a subjective meaning, although there is ambivalence about whether such an object has to be uncovered (from within the self) or discovered (from interaction with the world).

4 *Attachments*. In addition to being attached to a particular object of meaning, passion also leads to attachments to other people and social groups interested in this same object. These attachments help to generate a shared vision, a sense of belonging, and stronger commitment.

(Debra King, 2006, 'Conceptualising Passion: Problematising "Positive" Emotions', pp. 2–3)

In analysing the ways in which passion gives particular substance to discussions and debates about performance, motivation and commitment King (2006, p. 3) references a further two distinctions that emerge from her review: *Emotional labour* – a concept which she characterizes as the object of the rationalization, utilization and management (the co-optation) of passion to meet organizational ends such as efficiency, productivity and profit: *Work feelings* – an idea that is illustrative of an approach that positions emotional states, and the management of these, as 'central to individual well-being, motivation and job satisfaction'.

These distinctions, argues King (2006, pp. 3–4), appear in different forms in discourses of *emotional management*, in which a prime concern is with appropriate, limited, value-bound emotionality in organizational contexts; and in discourses of *emotional intelligence* where the main interest is in a capacity to recognize, develop and utilize feelings and emotions (our own, and those of others) in the conduct of relationships that bear on processes and practices which, in turn, impact on organizational performance. For King, this preliminary discussion and clarification serves to situate a *frame analysis* of the roles that ideas about passion, spirituality and emotion play in framing, diagnosing, and providing a prognosis for a range of organizational and management problems and issues. Her analysis suggests that passion is largely framed in two ways. First, passion is conceived as an *extrinsic state* that can be mobilized to meet organizational ends. Here passion is a vital ingredient in the 'construction of emotional attachments' within organizations. Understood in this way passion is something that managers should 'generate and advocate ... amongst their subordinates, although their own passion may be either simulated or sincere'. Second, passion is understood as an *intrinsic state* that is valued for itself. In this sense passion might be seen as an antidote to the 'perceived hollowness of hyper-materialism and the need for meaning in people's lives. The answer is to find and be driven by passion, so that work becomes more intrinsically fulfilling and meaningful.'

King uses these two frames as a means to suggest that passion should not be seen as an unproblematic good, a win-win for individuals and organizations in all contexts, all relations. Rather, the promise of passion – 'of working with dignity, of a way of "being" in an organisation that is more respectful of our humanity, that does not negate the emotional side of our lives, and does not separate out the emotions from reason or the mind from the body' (2006, p. 2) – might be realized where frames converge, where individual and organizational understandings of passion find some common ground. It is to this part of her analysis that we now turn to complete this discussion of passion, work and management. These convergences are represented in Figure 1 below.

|  | Intrinsic (Organization) Passion driven | Extrinsic (Organization) Passion advocating |
|---|---|---|
| Intrinsic (Individuals) Meaningfulness | Passion as *creative* | Passion as *co-opted* |
| Extrinsic (Individuals) Competitive advantage | Passion as a *conduit* | Passion as a *skill* |

*Figure 4.1*   Framing Passion (based on King, 2006, pp. 5–6)

We are interested at this stage in where individual and organizational frames of passion come together. In the first instance we want to focus on the convergence where passion is *extrinsic*; where, for King (2006, pp. 7–8), passion emerges as a *skill*. As a skill, passion is understood as a state that can be learned or developed to enhance individual and organizational competitiveness and performance. Here, the *appearance* of being passionate – passion as a surface effect – is important as this can lead to the development of 'emotional competencies and high levels of energy' that can be directed to identifiable, desirable outcomes. For King, the *performance of passion*, as either authentic or simulated, is important because a simulated passion is more appropriately understood as a 'form of emotional labour with the potential for dissonance and emotional exhaustion'.

Where passion is *intrinsic* for both organizations and individuals, then passion, suggests King (2006, pp. 6–7), is *creative*. Passion in this space is authentic, not simulated. It is something to be 'discovered or uncovered', and it is intimately connected to individual and organizational identity. In this type of intrinsic convergence: 'Organisations put their members first, creating a culture and work environment that is driven by collective passion.' Moreover, this convergence can produce a type of *psychic income*, a state of *feeling good* about the work, the practices, the products of organizational activity/life.

In a claim that has some resonances with the discussion of passion in *Jamie's Kitchen* that follows, King (2006, p. 6) argues that: 'Where the objects of passion also converge, it is possible to conceptualise this mode of being in an organisation within the framework of work feelings – spontaneous, emergent and meaning centred.' Here, the variety of 'emotional competencies associated with passion can be supported by the organisation and encouraged to develop in the knowledge that they will be used to enhance the mutually desirable objects of meaning'. We will return to some of these understandings when we position and discuss passion – for food, for work, for transforming the self – as a technology/technique that holds out the promise of enabling the marginalized young people targeted by the Fifteen Foundation to secure their salvation as entrepreneurial passionate workers.

## Passion, food and technologies of the self

In *Heat* Bill Buford (2006) powerfully, and whimsically, taps into the sorts of passions that certain understandings and uses of food can provoke: passions that provide the sometimes explicit, sometimes implicit, energies that drive our hungers and tastes:

> I found myself thinking of Mrs Waters's seduction of Tom Jones, in the Henry Fielding novel. Actually, I see the movie version with the young Albert Finney, where 'passions and appetites' blur and Mrs Waters's soft sighs commingle with Tom's energetic consumption of a vast piece of roast beef. Food has always had erotic associations, and I suspect that cooking with love is an inversion of a different principle: cooking to *be* loved. The premise of a romantic meal is that by stimulating and satisfying one appetite another will be analogously stimulated as well. How exactly does Tom Jones's appetite for a rib medium rare stimulate a craving for Mrs Waters? Fresh pasta cooked in butter, Mario once told me, illustrating how these things seem to conjoin, 'swells like a woman aroused'. Marjoram, he said on another occasion, has the oily perfume of a woman's body: 'It is the sexiest of the herbs.' Lidia, Joe Bastianich's mother was more explicit. 'What else do you put in another person's body?' she asked me rhetorically when I met her for lunch one day. 'Do you understand'?
>
> (2006, p. 33)

We have suggested that passion, and its intimate relationship to food that is produced, prepared and presented in particular ways, can be understood as a *technology of the self*. In his later work Foucault developed and introduced certain concepts to open up the field of historical analysis of the forms that the self, power and knowledge assumed at particular moments. In this section we want to think about passion by using a number of these tools. In the first instance we want to make explicit what Foucault meant by technologies of the self. In analysing the forms that the self, that self-knowledge, and the interdictions, incitements and encouragements to know the self in certain ways have taken at different times, Foucault (2000b, pp. 87–8) argued that 'neither a recourse to an original experience nor the study of the philosophical theories of the soul, the passions, or the body' could be the principal interest. Rather, the sorts of studies that he undertook were guided by the concept of *technologies of the self*: those 'procedures, which no doubt exist in every civilization, suggested or prescribed to individuals in order to determine their identity, maintain it, or transform it in terms of a certain number of ends, through relations of mastery or self knowledge'. The self, in this frame, has no originary or ultimate essence, but takes, instead, a number of forms that emerge in particular ways, in particular contexts, in relation to particular purposes. For Foucault, an analysis of these forms, practices and technologies of the self could be guided by questions of the following type: 'What should one do with oneself? What work should be carried out on the self? How should one 'govern oneself' by performing actions in which one is oneself the objective of those actions, the domain in which they are brought to bear, the instrument they employ, and the subject that acts?' (2000b, pp. 87–8)

It follows from these orientations, argued Foucault (2000b, p. 88), that histories of the care of the self would be histories of subjectivity, but they would be histories that did not take as their objects: 'the divisions between the mad and the nonmad, the sick and the nonsick, delinquents and nondelinquents'. Nor would such histories be concerned, principally, with the 'constitution of fields of scientific objectivity giving a place to the living, speaking, labouring subject'. Rather they would be concerned with the 'putting in place, and the transformations in our culture, of 'relations with oneself', with their technical armature and their knowledge effects'. Within this sort of analytical project the question of governmentality would become one in which the central concern would be: 'the government of the self by oneself in its articulation with relations with others (such as one finds in pedagogy, behavior counselling, spiritual direction, the prescription for models of living and so on)'. From this perspective we can analyse passion, and the characteristics it assumes in *Jamie's Kitchen* and in the training of marginalized young people, as a powerful technology of self-transformation. In this setting passion is analysable along the three axes which follow.

First, passion emerges from and frames particular forms of knowledge and ways of knowing – the self, vocational training, paid work, the restaurant industry, food. So, marginalized young people are understood in certain ways (*What is right with these young people?*), and as requiring certain processes and practices to be put in place to enable a passion to emerge or develop from an initial sense of self that is anything but passionate (at least in relation to the ends that the training programme has in mind). In the time and spaces spanned by the original series, the emergence of a vision to develop Fifteen as a global social enterprise brand, and the Australian series, knowledges (*truths*) about how to achieve this vision have been reflexively reformulated to produce, for example, different ways of understanding the entering behaviours of these young people, and of the practices, processes and relationships that might facilitate processes of self-transformation – with lower attrition rates and less focus on individual failings/lacks. Early in the first series we get a sense that trainees ought to enter the programme with evident, pre-existing and substantial levels of passion. Passion in this time/space is largely seen as intrinsic, it is something you bring with you.

> *Ruth Watson:* What do you want? What kind of people are you looking for?
>
> *Jamie Oliver:* I just want people that are observing what is happening. If the food is burning I want them to take it off. We are looking for an inner instinctiveness about food. They don't have to be able to cook. They just have to feel it. Do you know what I mean? ... All I know is that they're not employed and not in education. But I'm not sure I need to know too much about them really – I think this is about spending quality time and a bit of inspiration and encouragement really.
>
> (*Jamie's Kitchen*, Episode One, Broadcast in Australia on Channel 10, 21 July 2003)

Late in the *Jamie's Kitchen Australia* series there is evidence of a different, not unproblematic, understanding of why some trainees might struggle with the demands and expectations of the programme, why some of the trainees might not appear as passionate as they should.

> *Jamie Oliver:* I came from a very middle class background where everything was perfect and nothing went wrong. Most of the students we have haven't got fathers so it is mainly single families. The stability at home is very questionable ... if there is any at all. I've never been through any of that so who am I to judge really?
>
> (*Jamie's Kitchen Australia*, Episode Four, Broadcast in Australia on Channel 10, 5 October 2006)

Knowledge here also has as its objects the sorts of understandings of food that Jamie Oliver is famous for. Food, understood in these ways, is something to get passionate about. It can excite the passions. It can be produced, prepared, presented and consumed with passion. Because food is understood in these ways, the work that goes on in a restaurant kitchen is also something to be passionate about. Unfortunately, not all the training and regimentation, the rule learning and obeying, and the skill development that is a necessary precursor, and developmental stage, to becoming a cook or a chef is all that passion-provoking. Indeed, the menial and mundane nature of many of these practices of the self can dampen passion, can make you bored. Michael Pizzey, a trainee from the original series whom we introduced in some detail in Chapter 1, illustrates all too well the often ephemeral nature of passion in a work and training context.

> *Michael Pizzey:* I love every second of it. Do it again and again and again. Brilliant. The way you have to make everything perfect and on time. It is undescribable how I feel. I am so chuffed with myself
> (*Jamie's Kitchen*, Episode One, Broadcast in Australia, Channel 10, 21 July 2003)

> [The following scene is an exchange between Michael Pizzey and Jamie Oliver in the living room of Michael Pizzey's house.]
>
> *Jamie:* So what's going on then?
>
> *Michael Pizzey:* I'm just totally ... I'm just bored at the moment.
>
> *Jamie:* Bored?
>
> *Michael Pizzey:* Yeah, because nothing really exciting is happening
>
> *Jamie:* Right, what do you mean by that?
>
> *Michael Pizzey:* Well, my colleagues were cooking and enjoying it, and some of the staff [inaudible] doing it all over again, but when it comes to Mondays and all we do is parcel these boxes upstairs ... It's just not really exciting me much.
>
> *Jamie:* Unfortunately, the start is always the most boring.
> (*Jamie's Kitchen*, Episode Three, Broadcast in Australia on Channel 10, 5 August 2003)

Second, passion is produced, regulated and managed within relations of power – sovereignty, discipline and government – that emerge from and give structure/shape to particular fields of possibilities. In the context of this training programme – undertaken in various spaces including training colleges and restaurant kitchens – sovereignty represents the relationship of power which locates authority in the hierarchy of chefs, cooks, assistants that characterizes the restaurant kitchen. In these spaces military metaphors are often used to identify *command and control* structures that are understood as being vital to the task of preparing and presenting substantial amounts of food, *to order,* and on time. Sovereignty resides in the capacity to order someone to do something – Now! Yes, Chef! – and to the required consistency and quality. Throughout both series, in kitchens, in off-the-job training spaces, we witness the exercise of sovereignty by Head Chefs, trainers and teachers, at the same time as we witness trainees resisting, or choosing to conform, to these demands. The aim of the exercise of sovereignty is to establish the field, and its limits, in which appropriate forms of passion might emerge. Sovereign power can't *will* passion into existence, but it might establish the conditions in which it emerges or is uncovered.

In this training environment disciplinary power takes a form that requires trainees to submit to the often menial, mundane tasks of cleaning, of maintaining a work place/space and utensils such as pots, pans, knives. It also involves learning, repeating, mastering the mechanics of food preparation. At one level this cleaning, sweeping, tidying, dicing, slicing treadmill seeks to develop essential skills. At another it also promises to develop new forms of self-awareness and self-knowledge: as someone who can discipline themselves; can conform to the demands of rationalized clock time, workplace practices and behaviours; can situate and understand their membership of a crew or team which is more than the sum of its individual parts; can become passionate about doing these things well through a sense that they have a purpose, and that this purpose contributes to a larger project which can deliver feelings and understandings of self-worth, competence, ability. Again, discipline cannot *will* passion into existence, but these forms and relations of power promise to produce a skill, knowledge, attitude base from which passion might be uncovered or emerge.

Finally, governmental, pastoral forms of power seek to develop a form of well-regulated autonomy, a capacity for passionate, self-regulation, via an encouragement to develop new forms of self-knowledge and self-awareness. These new ways of knowing the self – as passionate, as skilled, as capable, as self-governing – will, so the programmes promise, emerge as a consequence of developing skills, capacities, behaviours and dispositions from fields in which the self has submitted to the demands and discipline of others such as Jamie Oliver, Toby Puttock, trainers, work-placement chefs.

Third, passion seeks to produce certain practices of the self. In addition, these practices promise to energize the development and performance of an entrepreneurial, passionate self. These practices take their shape from the field of possibilities structured by the relationships between knowledge and relations of power outlined above. In *Jamie's Kitchen* and in the Fifteen programme these practices of the self include such things as: attendance requirements at both college and in work placements; the mundane, menial tasks of cleaning work benches, ovens, grills and hotplates, floors and utensils; learning how to dice, slice and generally prepare and present ingredients correctly so that dishes can be cooked, assembled and presented for consumption – the seemingly endless practice of diverse skills and techniques that are vital to food preparation in the hectic, frenzied, chaotic context of commercial kitchens; tasting and testing of foods in ways that develop new vocabularies, understandings and orientations to food and its possibilities; shopping and sourcing expeditions to develop and practise skills necessary to knowing food as having different origins, different qualities, different possibilities in terms of preparation and as ingredients for particular dishes; team-building excursions to test the limits of the self, to locate the self in different fields where different understandings of the self, and of others, and of a team might be encouraged to form and emerge.

> *Jamie Oliver:* I think the thing is that we've learnt about the kids you know those few days that you take them away to try to get to know them you know doing team building and stuff like that. You want to get a sense of whether they're team players. Whether they're lazy people ... The truth is we've picked students in the past that have been in jail for fraud right. They're fantastic liars and they'll come to an interview and they'll impress everyone in there. They'll tell you just what you want to hear. Take them on a team-building day for 2 days and you'll start seeing – even though two days is only a little bit – and every year now we take [past] students with us to choose the new students. And it's fantastic because you have a united front of chefs, people working in the foundation looking after kids and students going: 'He's bullshit. Like, he's never going to make the year. He's just telling us what we want to hear.'
> (*Jamie's Kitchen Australia*, Episode Two, Broadcast in Australia on Channel 10, 21 September 2006)

A major interest for us in this discussion of passion is to situate and analyse the relationships between, and differences in, approaches to food, and to work-related entrepreneurial dispositions that are evident at various times in *Jamie's Kitchen*. Put simply, Jamie Oliver and his colleagues understand food, and work, differently to the trainees – at least at the beginning of the journeys of self-transformation that these young people undertake. And these differences are made known, fundamentally, through the *idea* of passion. Are these differences – following King (2005, 2006) – intrinsic or extrinsic? Are these differences understandable in terms of social class positions? To return to a question we raised in an earlier chapter, is Jamie Oliver a *middle-class tosser* telling the working classes how to think, act, behave – particularly in terms of food and work? Are these differences understandable in terms of gender relations and positions? Or, is it appropriate to think of these differences in terms of the rationalization, industrialization and globalization of food production, processing, distribution? Whatever the answers to these questions, we think that they are important in terms of the training activities, and the processes of self-transformation, that are core business for the Fifteen Foundation. As a social enterprise the Foundation is confronted with dilemmas of passion in ways that other for-profit enterprises can avoid (*So Bill isn't passionate about that task? Move him on!*).

Jamie Oliver's particular *passionate* disposition to food is well documented in the introductions to his numerous cookbooks, in his unauthorized biography, in his various television series, especially *Jamie's School Dinners*, and in a range of other media. His passion for food, particularly food that is fresh, regional and seasonal is reiterated time and time again in these spaces.

> It wasn't until I went to work at Chateau Tilques in France that I learnt that quality, real care, love and individual flair have to go into every stage of food preparation. This was where my passion for food was conceived; surrounded by people who were so much more talented than I was, whose enthusiasm was highly contagious and very inspiring.
>
> (Jamie Oliver, 1999, *Jamie Oliver: The Naked Chef*, p. 4)

Oliver's passion led him into fully fledged food activism through the *School Dinners* series. In an illustration of the processes of rationalization, industrialization and globalization that we think are central to this problem of passion for food, Gilly Smith (2006, p. 182) notes that 'Italian children might be able to tell the difference between an aubergine and an artichoke', but their British counterparts 'couldn't even tell a stick of rhubarb from a stick of celery'.

> I've also learnt on my journey round Italy that the word regional, when it comes to cooking, is the tip of the iceberg. They are far more parochial than that. There should be a word invented for it like 'villagional', because these guys, rightly or wrongly, will argue that their own village makes a certain thing in the most perfect way and will look down on another village's method with utter contempt! It's this passion, which is reflected in their food.
>
> (Jamie Oliver, 2005, *Jamie Oliver: Jamie's Italy*, p. viii)

Smith's biography of Oliver locates the origins of what she terms the *School Dinner Revolution* in the activism of people such as Jeanette Orrey, 'an unusually imaginative dinner lady' from Nottinghamshire, and Peter Melchett, policy director of the British Soil Association (Smith, 2006, pp. 197–200). Although these and other activists had been working for some time to change the nature of school dinners, it was Oliver's mixture of celebrity profile and social conscience – his social entrepreneurship – which gave this *revolution* the exposure it needed to succeed in England. As one food journalist noted, 'You only have to say "Jamie" in a food context and everyone knows who you're talking about' (Lumby and Probyn, 2003b, p. 128).

Smith (2006, p. 210) recounts the ways in which Oliver's campaign involved: 'Shaming the government, storming into the school kitchens, embarrassing parents into realising just how they were killing their kids with a diet of junk food and attitude based on sloth, Jamie was our culinary crusader'. The drama of much of the *School Dinners* series resided in the resistance that Oliver's *gung-ho* approach produced and encountered – from school dinner ladies who objected to the intensification of their work, and from groups of parents who objected to being told what they should feed their children. For many commentators this resistance represented a form of class warfare that was also gendered, as the *resisters* were overwhelmingly female and from working-class or underprivileged backgrounds.

Despite Jamie's high profile, and his ability to influence and sometimes initiate change, it is important to remember that he is only one player among many in a global movement focusing on food quality (or lack of it), and a push for a more sustainable approach to growing, preparing and eating food. We want to suggest that this focus on food in the context of its rationalization, industrialization and globalization is not only historically specific, but it is also classed and gendered.

At one level of analysis those who have a similar, *passionate,* orientation and disposition to food to Jamie Oliver are largely of the middle and upper classes – at least in locations such as the UK, US and Australia. It is probably harder to sustain such a claim in some southern European/Mediterranean contexts where Oliver, for example, finds inspiration in working-class/peasant understandings of food (often with a regional flavour). And those that the middle and upper classes pass judgement on for feeding their children (and themselves) processed, fast, industrialized food – for being less passionate, and de-skilled in terms of food production, preparation and presentation – are below them on the social ladder.

In 1825 the famous French gastronome Jean Anthelme Brillat-Savarin, in a book entitled *The Physiology of Taste*, declared, 'Tell me what you eat and I will tell you what you are'. What was true then, may indeed be true now. Elspeth Probyn (2003, p. 119), for example, argues that food – and the diverse processes and practices that accompany its production, distribution, processing, preparation and, ultimately, consumption – is a lifestyle issue: 'if we understand life-style in the deepest sense of the term. What and how we decide to eat affects us – in obvious physical ways – just as it always connects to families, relationships, health, as well as local and global environmental concerns.' In this sense food is a vehicle, a technology for knowing, and understanding, and acting – both on ourselves, and in relation to others. It is a technology that structures and emerges from a variety of fields in which social class, gender, ethnicity, age and a number of other relations (religious, for example) shape our understandings of ourselves and others, and the choices, chances and opportunities we imagine – or are denied.

Deborah Lupton (1996, pp. 15–16), drawing on Foucault's concepts of technologies of the self, argues that 'food habits and preferences are central practices of the self, directed at self-care via the continuing nourishment of the body with foods that are culturally deemed appropriate'. They not only 'constitute a source of pleasure' but they act 'symbolically as commodities to present a persona to oneself and others'. At a time where bodies are considered 'highly amenable to change', one way of doing this is to take control over what you eat. Such practices of the self can demonstrate – depending on context and fields – such things as self-discipline, self-awareness, and an aesthetics of the self grounded in consumption and choice (*My slim/fat/fit/unhealthy body and the food I eat tells you something about me, and the choices that I can make!*). As Clive Chappell (2003, p. 27) has argued, contemporary 'social identities are constructed as much through patterns of consumption as through patterns of production'. Recent media commentary about the pursuit of *gourmet* food for children helps to illustrate and situate our focus here on the class dimensions of the problem of passion.

> As Kylie Minogue's *Step Back in time* blasts from the kitchen of a Malvern shop, birthday girl Aimee Clark, 9, greets nine of her closest friends ... the girls are soon kneading colourful balls of biscuit dough ... and so begins another 90 minute cooking party extravaganza at Gourmet Kids, where Aimee and her friends will cook, eat and play games before taking their edible art home. Welcome to the world of children's cooking ... The coupling of food and children is big business, and there's now a smorgasbord of cooking classes around that are tailored for children. Cooking instructors say the demand for children's classes has increased enormously in the past couple of years. The reasons are varied. It's come at a time when well-known chefs, here and abroad, are championing the good-food cause in schools and at home ... There is a move to broaden children's perception of food and their relationship with it.
>
> (Liz Cincotta, 2007, *Small Fry*, p. 4)

The focus on children in these sorts of programmes and commentaries echoes the emphasis accorded to childhood and pre-adult nutrition and diet in Jamie Oliver's *School Dinners* initiative (see, also, Chater, 2007). These activities, and developing understandings of food, are designed to make up individuals who have a reflexive orientation to particular types of food. These technologies, which in particular configurations of time/space/place have a character that is marked by social class and gender relations and divisions, are being introduced to younger and younger audiences, some as young as kindergarten-aged. At the same time other groups and individuals maintain orientations to food, and to the self, that are understood as being less passionate: many of Fifteen's trainees fit this category.

In developing her arguments about the relationships between food as a technology of the self, and the ways in which these technologies produce particular bodies, and diverse understandings of what particular bodies *mean* – what they say about us and our social locations and capacities for choice and consumption – Lupton (1996, p. 19) highlights what she calls the 'routinely drawn' distinctions between 'civilised' and 'grotesque' bodies. Civilized bodies (and their owners/producers/consumers) signify bodies that are 'self-contained', that are 'highly socially managed', and which conform to 'dominant norms of behaviour and appearance'. The grotesque body by contrast is 'uncontained, unruly, less controlled by notions of propriety and good manners and is therefore regarded as more "animalistic"'. The distinctions between 'civilised' and 'grotesque' bodies are evident between Jamie Oliver and many of his trainees. Although not explicitly referred to, these distinctions are evident in Jamie's constant declaration of his middle-class status and his avowed interest in helping only those who are more disadvantaged, marginalized than he is.

> *Jamie Oliver:* We're interested in dealing with the kids that most governments are really shit at dealing with. The ones that have probably grown up in tough families, drugs, drink, physical abuse, sexual abuse, problems with the law, problems with school, possibly came out with no exams. That represents what Fifteen students are in general.
>
> (*Jamie's Kitchen Australia*, Episode One, Broadcast in Australia on Channel 10, 14 September 2006)

Social class matters in this context because Jamie Oliver makes it matter. In the UK, where he has lived most of his life, and where he continues to exercise his passion and tries to understand and make sense of marginalization, social class is a key referent. Class makes things knowable in ways that make sense, that appear as *truthful*. At this point we would not question Oliver's motives in deploying his considerable resources to help these young people – indeed his motivation is largely inconsequential, and is probably beyond the scope of the analysis we are developing here. What we can argue though, is that Oliver is passionate, about food – in the ways that he understands it – and about the work of preparing and presenting it in a commercial kitchen. We can also see, often quite clearly in the drama of *Jamie's Kitchen*, that his trainees don't share this passion – at least, initially. The lived experiences of Fifteen's trainees: their family histories and their socio-economic status, impact directly on the knowledge and dispositions (including their passion for food or their lack of it) that the trainees bring to working in *Jamie's Kitchen*. All have an impact on the success or otherwise of the technologies employed by Jamie, his trainers and other Fifteen Foundation employees in an effort to make up the type of worker required in *Jamie's Kitchen* – and in the individualized labour markets of a globalized risk society.

McLeod and Yates (2006, pp. 152–61), drawing on data from their longitudinal study of subjectivity, schooling and social change in Australia, argue that even in England 'class is not a category [that] young people themselves think with'. They raise questions, as others have done (Connell *et al.*, 1982, Teese and Polesel, 2003) about 'the utility of a concept built from nineteenth century industrial England and Germany'. Despite its status as a problematic category – 'hard to pin down and define' in the new economy – McLeod and Yates argue that this concept is still useful when trying to account for the 'differentiated achievement and self-belief' evident in the lived experiences of young people, and which are identifiable in the 'databases about retention, participation in higher education and the labor market'. In this view, the utilization and mobilization of a concept such as class enable the social sciences to continue to 'address issues of social distinction, hierarchy, power in individual identities and in the patterns of social relationships between individuals'. Moreover, an analytical frame that pays proper attention to the material realities and consequences of social relations that continue to be marked by difference and hierarchies, can also attend to such things as: 'the relationships between individual formation and subjectivity, especially in the context of family and schooling, and to patterns of work, including the form of work and of different jobs; the structure of what types of jobs people from different backgrounds enter'.

While Jamie Oliver makes various matters knowable and understandable in terms of social class, it is not evident that his trainees do. However, the sorts of family backgrounds, patterns of schooling and work, and power relationships evident between trainees and Oliver can be understood as fields of possibilities that are given structure, in part, by class relations. In this sense, we can argue that class is a series of forces, of relationships, of locations, of self/other understandings and knowledges, that work to structure and give form to the fields of possibilities in which we must practise our freedom, make choices, develop a sense of self and of opportunities and possibilities. These class dimensions to passion, to food as a technology of self-transformation, impact directly on the effectiveness of the practices and processes deployed in a range of environments where self-formation and transformation might occur.

## Passion, training and self-transformation

Our discussion and analysis of the role of passion in *Jamie's Kitchen* allows us to connect to the passion/pleasure dimensions of learning, of self-formation, and of self-transformation that are rarely discussed in a vocational education and training environment driven largely by modules, competencies and outcomes (Ball, 2003a, 2003b; Biemans *et al.*, 2004; Hager and Smith, 2004). The place and practice of education and training is an important ingredient in our discussion at a number of levels. Much of the training in *Jamie's Kitchen* occurs off-the-job in the training spaces such as Westminster Kingsway College (WKC) London in the first series, and Box Hill Institute of Technical and Further Education (TAFE) Melbourne in the second series. The difficulties that many trainees encounter in these institutionalized spaces provide much of the drama in both series. Whether on-the-job, or off-the-job, training and development processes, particularly with marginalized young people who have experienced sustained failure in other educational contexts, is a field of possibilities in which passion might be ignited. On the other hand it can, more often than not, be a process in which passion is dampened. Indeed, training and development processes in many organizational contexts attract concerns about the outcomes they envisage, the outcomes they deliver, and the gap that often exists between the ideal and the actual.

In this section we want to identify and discuss the ways in which much contemporary vocational education and training is shaped by the sense that knowledge is a product; is a commodity; is quantifiable and measurable against a series of pre-defined and determined outcomes and competencies. Here knowledge is understood less in conceptual terms, and more in terms of being skills based. This view of knowledge shapes the field, in sometimes contradictory ways, in which passion might emerge or be uncovered – particularly when the end or purpose of this training is to develop an entrepreneurial, passionate form of selfhood. The training and labour markets that Fifteen positions its trainees in have come to demand measurable, quantifiable skills and competencies, and transferable credentials. To deny these qualifications to trainees would limit their chances and choices in these markets. However, the practices of the self that emerge in these environments may, indeed, stifle the passion, or limit the chances of marginalized young people being judged as competent/skilled. Moreover, these views of knowledge and of the self – both in terms of entering behaviours, and in terms of the ends/purposes of this training – are given a particular shape by the exercise of disciplinary relations of power. The emphasis on skills and competencies as quantifiable and measurable outcomes requires that trainees be disciplined by those more skilful, and that this discipline also aims to produce certain orientations to the self that will lead, it is promised, to the development of a well-regulated, autonomous, passionate self.

Carolyn Williams' (2005, pp. 33–8) analysis of the forms of worker identities that are embedded in a number of key documents on competencies in the vocational education and training sector in Australia provides a useful frame to commence this discussion. She suggests that a 'nature/nurture dichotomy haunts past and present discussions about the personal attributes of learner-workers'. Williams argues that the focus in contemporary education and training is on the 'construction of the competent learner-worker' and that discourses of generic skills constitute 'a normative-regulatory ideal'. For Williams, key policy documents such as that generated by the Mayer Committee (1992) deploy a *nature* versus *nurture* dualism, which produces distinct and separate 'domains of "innate predispositions" and learnable competencies'. This dualism plays out across a range of policy documents in arguments about whether attitudes and values are learnable or innate. Despite evident disagreement on this, there is a consensus that personal attributes need to be included in any reformulation of key workplace competencies. The personal attributes listed in these reports include: 'loyalty, commitment, honesty and integrity, enthusiasm, reliability, personal presentation, commonsense, positive self-esteem, sense of humour, balanced attitude to work and home life, ability to deal with pressure, motivation and adaptability'.

These attributes characterize a particular *ideal* learner-worker in the new economy; an identity that many of Jamie's trainees struggle to exhibit – at least initially. In *Jamie's Kitchen* there are tensions and contradictions between a view of passion as an innate quality on the one hand, and a view that passion can be developed, incited, or learned on the other. Our discussion of *the passion of Jamie*, and of his trainees, gives some weight to a range of issues raised by Williams – questions that make problematic the development of a passionate, entrepreneurial ethics of the self that would facilitate the transition of young people into work: 'What of learner-workers assessed as "not yet competent" against benchmarks of acceptable performance of personal attributes when these attributes are understood as innate? If personal attributes are not understood as learnable, how are those learner-workers to become competent?' (Williams, 2005, p. 47).

Clive Chappell (2003, pp. 21–4) charts the reform of Vocational Education and Training (VET) around the world, noting that one of the more remarkable features of this reform is its similarity across countries as diverse as the UK, New Zealand, Canada, Thailand Mexico, Singapore and China. A consistent feature of these reforms has been the turn to Competency Based Training (CBT) as part of the *New Vocationalism* in which economic discourses dominate educational policy formation (see also, Foster, 2001). These transformations have been designed explicitly to bring about a closer alignment of education and training systems with economic imperatives. These reforms have been energized by 'the emergence of new forms of work and work organization' that also appear to 'go hand in hand with new more complex social, cultural and economic configurations'. For Chappell (2001, p. 7) this articulation of new vocationalism with neo-liberalism or economic rationalism: 'promotes the view that government should withdraw from many of its traditional social responsibilities and promote market style environments and commercial business practices within state services including education'. Narratives of *enterprise* and *entrepreneurialism* are features of these policy transformations.

Chappell (2001, pp. 8–9) has argued that the new meaning making practices that neo-liberal and new vocational discourses introduce into institutionalized training spaces, such as TAFE, trouble the discourses of industrial skill development, liberal education and public service which have historically 'supported the construction of TAFE teachers as particular types of teacher'. Although the focus on the skills needs of business and industry appears to complement the industrial skills development discourse, TAFE teachers find themselves continually measured against the constantly changing skills needs of industry and their 'credibility as "industry expert" is always open to question'. This situation is compounded by their location in an educational institution rather than in an industrial setting. This positioning has always created tensions. However, the privileging of 'industry relevance and workplace learning over other learning goals' that is evident in the new vocationalism has resulted in increased tensions when the learner-centred practices and humanist goals of liberal education also compete for position and relevance in training spaces.

High rates of youth unemployment in OECD countries such as Australia have meant that the age profile of training institutions has changed quite markedly in recent years. More 15–19-year-old young people now attend these institutions, and teacher identification with certain principles of adult education – which has historically marked training institutions as different to schools – is becoming increasingly problematic. Particular assumptions about prior experiential learning, basic literacy and numeracy skills and the ability to work independently may no longer necessarily hold. This is certainly an issue for the marginalized young people, and their trainers/mentors in *Jamie's Kitchen*.

> *Andrew Sankey:* It's not like high school here. We're going to treat you like adults and you are going to behave like responsible adults.
>
> *To camera:* It's rather a daunting process to see so many sometimes damaged people. And it's not my job to straighten out their heads but it is my job to give them something else. Yes it's a challenge … a huge challenge but I'm really looking forward to it.
>
> (*Jamie's Kitchen Australia*, Episode Three, Broadcast in Australia on Channel 10, 28 September 2000)

Assumptions about entering behaviours, skills and attitudes become particularly problematic when trainers and teachers are faced with students (and their damaged learner identities) such as those in *Jamie's Kitchen*. The current focus on life-long learning – in which learners are seen as effective and able to 'understand their learning processes' – is also problematic in this context (James, 2002, p. 370). Fifteen trainees/students do not often see themselves as effective learners:

> *Dovid (Fifteen trainee) to camera after being given a pep talk by Glen Flood, Training and Development Chef, Fifteen Melbourne, following a series of kitchen disasters:* It just seems that they can see more in me than I can actually see in myself. You know they can see that I can do this but really you know what I mean. Like put yourself in my shoes. I don't think I'm doing a real perfect job.
>
> (*Jamie's Kitchen Australia*, Episode Five, Broadcast in Australia on Channel 10, 12 October 2006)

CBT is characterized by 'pre-specified training and assessment outcomes and standards based on industry requirements within a system of credentials'. The discourses and practices of CBT privilege procedural technical knowledge, standardization and adaptability. The discourse of CBT also stresses the need for 'knowledge workers and innovators', although what these mean here are heavily circumscribed and related to furthering the needs of industry (James, 2002, p. 369).

> *Andrew Sankey (chef/trainer) to Harry, one of the trainees, when Harry says he thinks he has missed an instruction:* It's one of those things mate where we have to go at a certain speed. I'm not helping you do things at your speed.

> *Toby Puttock:* You know at the end of the day we can get them mentoring, we can get them aids, we can hold their hand all the way through this and we can let people help them and turn a blind eye to it but in reality we're just helping them get a piece of paper really and that piece of paper isn't going to mean a whole lot if they can't follow through. I mean the whole aim of this thing is to turn these guys into chefs.
>
> *(Jamie's Kitchen Australia*, Episode Three, Broadcast in Australia on Channel 10, 28 September 2006)

Vocational education and training researchers have noted that the instrumental focus in CBT that sees concerns with meeting pre-specified industry-driven outcomes has both positive and negative consequences. On the plus side CBT can develop identities as 'competent learners' because of its hands-on, practical orientation and the requirement for trainees to be able to replicate learned skills. This type of training can 'develop identities of competence for those for whom studies at school were disempowering' (James, 2002, p. 383). All of the trainees in *Jamie's Kitchen* fall into this category for various reasons. However, as Pauline James (2001, p. 307) has noted: 'CBT seems to rely for much of its success, if real proficiency is to be achieved within a reasonable time-frame, on prior experiential learning through informal training.'

Training time-frames are severely contracted in *Jamie's Kitchen*, making 'reasonable' time problematic even for the best of students. In addition, very few of the trainees have any form of experiential learning that would be useful in the kitchen. As James (2001, p. 308) points out, *applied learning* 'seems to rely upon trainees bringing a body of knowledge and skill to the situation in order that learning can be maximised – it requires both experiential and conceptual knowledge'. Despite the promise CBT holds to facilitate learning in educationally disempowered young people, it is these very same young people whose lack of prior experiential learning restricts their abilities to meet this promise. In turn, this limits their capacity to identify, uncover or develop passion towards food, work, and training that align with the more instrumentally focused organizational passion required of the workers in Jamie's Kitchen and other hospitality workplaces. Buford (2006) describes well the sorts of issues that we are touching on here:

> From the start of the day to the end, the place was frenzied. In fact, without my fully realizing it, there was an education in the frenzy, because in the frenzy there was always repetition. Over and over

again, I'd pick up a smell, as a task was being completed, until finally I came to identify not only what the food was but where it was in its preparation. The next day, it would be the same. (By then, I was somehow managing to put in extra days in the prep kitchen, even though I was technically employed elsewhere.) I was reminded of something Andy had told me. 'You don't learn knife skills at cooking school, because they give you only six onions, and no matter how hard you focus on those six onions there are only six, and you're not going to learn as much as when you cut up a hundred.'

(2006, p. 67)

Pedagogically, CBT has been associated with 'self-paced learning' and 'facilitation' and this orientation is aligned with 'humanist discourses' which promise 'self-fulfilment' while at the same time demanding 'greater individual responsibility' (James, 2001, p. 318). Whilst promising flexibility and allowing trainees to work at their own pace, these pedagogical devices also subtly blame the victim if they fail to do so (Usher and Edwards, 1994). Indeed, one of Oliver's trainers in the first series, German chef Herr Bosey, produces a victim-blaming response in situations where the trainees who fail to meet the standards he sets are constructed as not trying hard enough.

*Herr Bosey (talking to the trainees):* Our standards are high and if I show you now a certain kind of standard that I expect you to repeat. There is no middle way, there are no short cuts. There is only one way, the way I've been showing you.

*Voice over:* The chef does not mince his words with Michael Pizzey either: There is no such thing as 'Oh chef I no can do it. You can do it'. But you need your head screwed on and your brain going.

(*Jamie's Kitchen*, Episode Two, Broadcast in Australia on Channel 10, 29 July 2003)

In these instances there is no mention of passion. For Herr Bosey this is about technical skills and the one right way. Because of the compressed time-frame of the Fifteen training programme this is necessarily fast and furious stuff and if you can't keep up then you are at risk of being cut. James (2002, p. 375) points out that real proficiency is not only about knowing the rules and following them but also being able to 'modify them judiciously'. She argues, however, that within a CBT regime there is often a failure to 'recognize the time required for skill development, particularly when workers are inexperienced and unprepared'.

Yet, in *Jamie's Kitchen* not all of the trainers take this approach. Later on in this same episode Michael Pizzey is talking to Jamie's former college tutor Peter Richards.

> *Michael:* Some of the stuff you say and do I just don't understand.
>
> *Peter Richards (chef/trainer):* Just come down the front with me. Stand next to me. What I don't want to do is single you out but at the same time I want to give you as much support as I can.
>
> > (*Jamie's Kitchen*, Episode Two, Broadcast in Australia on Channel 10, 29 July 2003)

Peter Richards' response to Michael is of a different sort, akin to a master/apprentice model of pedagogy. In addition it is more in line with the features of a liberal education discourse, and one that acknowledges that Michael is struggling to keep up. The dilemma Peter faces in *singling* Michael out is the classic dilemma of difference faced by teachers, trainers and mentors the world over: 'when does treating people differently emphasize their differences and stigmatize or hinder them on that basis? And when does treating people the same become insensitive to their difference and likely to stigmatize or hinder them on *that* basis?' (Minnow, 1990, cited in D.Kelly, 2000, p. 92).

The focus in CBT on instrumental knowledge and technical skills in the service of industry does not often allow space for this ethic of care. As James (2002, p. 370) suggests, 'focussing exclusively on the requirements of individual and company competitiveness' is 'likely to be socially and personally detrimental'. The increased focus on social support evident in *Jamie's Kitchen Australia* in comparison to the first UK series suggests that Oliver and the Fifteen Foundation have recognized these tensions and dilemmas. However, even the changed emphases, and the efforts of a team of support people, was not enough to get some of the trainees through. In these circumstances it would seem that some level of attrition is inevitable.

Wenger (1998, cited in James, 2002, pp. 370–2) makes a distinction between education, which he sees as transformative, and training, which he characterizes as formative. Wenger has argued that transformative learning opens up 'new dimensions for negotiation of the self'. James suggests that this argument is problematic when applied to industry workers because many of them, for whatever reasons, 'abandoned formal education early in their lives' and therefore their 'capacities for such learning cannot be assumed'. The processes of self-transformation envisaged in many training and education discourses depend in part on the fields of possibilities that are given form by these discourses, and by the location of student/trainees and trainers in various fields of possibility. Some of the sovereign, disciplinary and governmental practices employed in different training and education settings produce understandings of the self that serve to mark trainees out as failures. However, other technologies of the self encourage trainees to see themselves as successful learners. Wenger has argued that 'our identities form in this kind of tension between our investment in various forms of belonging and our ability to negotiate the meanings that matter in those contexts'. Michael Pizzey, for example, has a strong investment in belonging in Jamie's Kitchen but his ability to negotiate the 'meanings that matter' are severely curtailed by his learning difficulties and his past experiences of failure in structured learning environments.

## Conclusion

The ideas about passion that circulate in contemporary management discourses, and which suggest – as Debra King's (2006) analysis indicates – that passion is a vital ingredient in understanding and promoting performance, productivity, and motivation, should be approached and analysed as being problematic, as being particular truths that in certain contexts seek to produce particular outcomes. Passion can energize the self, can give direction or purpose or meaning to a life. It can be creative, it can be a skill. The evidence from *Jamie's Kitchen* and from the Fifteen programme is that passion has the capacity to transform the self, to be a vital ingredient in processes of salvation (however precarious these may be). Marginalized young people may not appear as passionate, may not approach a variety of tasks, activities and skill development processes with much passion – at least not initially. Indeed they may be passionate, but not about the things that work organizations and labour markets demand, and not in ways that their trainers, mentors, supervisors and bosses consider appropriate. Passion, as a vital ingredient in processes of salvation, needs to be disciplined and exercised by a self capable of exercising a well-regulated, self-governing, autonomy. The self here needs to be *made* passionate via a variety of practices of the self.

There is evidence that the Fifteen Foundation, as a social enterprise that has an explicit focus on producing passionate chefs, has developed processes which are successful in terms of these ends. Not all these practices produce the desired outcomes. Some practices, as we have demonstrated, may, in fact, stifle the energy, creativity and passion that they seek to promote. But it is possible that there are some lessons in the Fifteen model that can inform training and development practices in other contexts. Especially in terms of the Foundation's capacity to recognize and manage difference and diversity in ways that have potentially productive outcomes for both the marginalized young people they train, and the organizations that they work for.

Much of what is called training – either on-the-job or off-the-job – does little to generate, create or provoke practices of the self that might enable a passionate or entrepreneurial self to develop. The practice of much Competency Based Training may lead, by design or by practice, to *conformity*, to 'rule following rather than understanding', 'benchmarking rather than innovation', 'singular ways of performing rather than acknowledgement of differences' (James, 2002, p. 376). This does not mean that training or skills development should be understood as a necessarily impoverished version of what education and training can contribute to processes of person formation and self-transformation. Indeed, Erica McWilliam (1999), in her book *Pedagogical Pleasures*, wants to recapture the notion of *good training* as part of *proper* pleasurable pedagogy. She argues, in the context of schools-based education and training, that the word training has been rendered problematic by its modern association with processes of technical skills development stripped of context. Training, here, is positioned as the poor cousin of liberal humanist education that seeks the fullest development of human potential.

The possibilities of good training, of pleasurable pedagogy may, indeed, be limited when, as Bauman (2004, p. 6) argues, the 'totality of human production and consumption has become money and market mediated, and the processes of the commodification, commercialization and monetarization of human livelihoods have penetrated every nook and cranny of the globe'. In these spaces – where salvation is precarious and uncertain, where trimming the fat and rationalization, reorganization, and re-engineering conspire to produce human waste, and where marginalized young people may, indeed, be condemned to the material and social oblivion that Bauman and Beck identify – then the training and development processes of social enterprises such as the Fifteen Foundation offer possibilities for young people to develop and practise passionate forms of selfhood: forms of selfhood that might enable them to imagine and secure a different future (that is something no one can be sure of). These practices of the self are not unproblematic. They emerge in fields of possibilities that have certain limits and certain relationships to other fields. But they do offer these young people a different set of options, choices, futures to the fields they currently practise their freedom in. For someone like Dovid this training, this transformation of the self, enabled him to imagine a future that was not characterized by homelessness, failure, loneliness, lack of a sense of worth. Passion, in this sense, is a vital ingredient in salvation.

> *Dovid:* I guess I've started to come out of my shell a bit and started to socialise with people. Try to do my best with things. Thought I couldn't do it and had doubts. I passed my training and stuff really doing all this. And I just think if I stop doubting myself there's no reason why I can't do it.
> (*Jamie's Kitchen Australia*, Episode Nine, Broadcast in Australia on Channel 10, 9 November 2006)

# 5
## 'Because She's Pretty?' Gender Relations and Young Workers

### Introduction

As we have illustrated throughout this book, much of Jamie Oliver's appeal as a celebrity chef and social entrepreneur can be attributed to his *laddishness* – contrived, manufactured, authentic or otherwise. This laddishness is, by definition, gendered. *He's a lad*! His apparent (to some) boyish charms, his appeal, his brand is gendered. The trainees we see in both series of *Jamie's Kitchen* are also gendered, as are the trainees in additional, ongoing intakes. In many accounts of the restaurant and hospitality industries the largely male celebrity chefs provide accounts of an industry that is also gendered and intensely hierarchical. Often this results in female employees occupying lower ranks in the *food chain*, and in bullying and harassment by macho male chefs further up the food chain. In this chapter we will discuss the complexity of gender relations, young workers, training and this industry. As we indicated in the Introduction to this book, this discussion has its origins in the following exchange from the very first episode of the original *Jamie's Kitchen*.

*Jamie:* I was a bit upset about Elisa [Roche]. I think she's quite sharp and I think she loves food. And I had a good time with her when we were doing the recipe cooking.

*Ruth:* Because she's pretty?

*Gennaro:* They're all pretty.

*Ruth:* She was asking far too many questions. Because they were questions you had already answered. I think it's great to ask questions if you don't know about something or whatever. But actually it was as if she had no instruction from you whatever at any stage. I feel for myself that in a kitchen situation she would be very flakey. She's too distracted.

[Jamie Oliver and colleagues/mentors discussing the merits of particular trainees in the midst of the selection process.]

*(Jamie's Kitchen*, Episode One, Broadcast on Channel 10 Melbourne, 21 July 2003)

In hinting, however fleetingly, at the possibilities, and problems, of attraction, flirtation and desire in the workplace this exchange brings into the spotlight issues of gender relations and sexuality that are integral elements of the fabric of all organizational life. Oftentimes, however, attempts to understand and analyse this fabric tend to ignore or discount the ways in which gender relations and sexuality shape, and emerge from, organizational life. It is almost as if gender and sexuality are unexceptional elements of organizations: elements that do not make their way into, or give form to discussions, processes and practices that determine work processes; training and development endeavours; opportunities for advancement and promotion; the ways in which practices, processes, environments (*cultures*) enhance or limit opportunity, performance and effectiveness.

Contrary to this sense of gender and sexuality being unexceptional in, and to, various dimensions of organizational life, we want to suggest, with the support of the findings and claims of much research, that gender and sexuality should be central elements of the story we are telling here. A story that is concerned with the possibilities and limits of the Fifteen Foundation's attempts to facilitate processes of self-transformation that promise to secure salvation for marginalized young people. In other words – in the words of the literatures on the reflexive self, and the care of the self – we want to suggest that the reflexive self is a gendered self: that knowledges of the self are always gendered; that processes of self-transformation are gendered; that processes of self-transformation and the promise of salvation are gendered; that the fields of possibilities in which we are positioned, and in which we contrive to fashion a self are gendered.

While these relations, processes of reflexivity, practices of freedom, fields of possibility and forms of selfhood are gendered, the nature of what some have called gender systems, structures, relations – and their consequences – are not always readily apparent, predictable or amenable to agreement. Indeed, we can suggest that some of the difficulties associated with thinking about gender – with making gender relations and sexuality *exceptional* – in studies framed by concepts of reflexivity and the care of the self, is that gender, much like social class, ethnic background, age, is very much a mid-level (*mezzo*-level) unit of analysis. Gender, class, ethnicity, and similar concepts/*realities*, mediate, in many important ways between *macro*- and *micro*-level processes, forces and practices. Foucault's metaphor of *fields of possibility* helps illustrate the point we make here. Fields of possibility can, potentially, occupy a number of different levels. For example, a *labour market* for young people in the hospitality industry can usefully be understood as a *field of possibilities* that is shaped by myriad processes, forces and relations. And, as we will see in the following section, this field can be readily and appropriately characterized by the gender divisions that shape it. Within the hospitality industry particular workplaces, commercial kitchens, training colleges, classrooms can be imagined as distinct *fields of possibilities* – that are, at the same time, always connected to and shaped by other fields (adjoining *and* separated by time and space). At this micro-level, in these smaller fields, can we discern similar patterns of gender divisions and relations as evidenced in larger fields, at a more macro-level? Or are there different patterns, different forces, and different possibilities in terms of gender relations in these spaces – including *Jamie's Kitchen*?

While the field of globalization studies is a burgeoning one, traversing a number of theoretical and disciplinary orientations (see Kenway *et al.*, 2006, for a good overview of these) one key set of ideas is concerned with 'what can be understood as new, and what is rather a continuation of the recent or distant past'. Much is made, particularly in popular cultural contexts, of what might be termed the 'disappearance' of gender, or at least its significant diminution as an 'anchor of identity'; and particularly as a Category that signifies the uneven distribution of power and resources (practically, materially and psychologically) in new global economies. The category of gender is replaced, in part, by a form of hyper-individualism that tells us that we all have the same chances in life and that success or failure is dependent on individual effort. This movement away from 'traditional institutional formations' is often described as a process of de-traditionalization (Kenway *et al.*, 2006, p. 14). However, many theorists are beginning to question how far processes of globalization are able to break down traditional gender relations and ways of being. As Giddens (1999) has emphasized, processes of globalization do not have only one point of origin and their effects are always contingent and uncertain. Not only is globalization imposed on us from above but also 'by our everyday acts we help to shape the global' (Giddens,

1999). This means that gender re-traditionalization can also emerge from and shape various fields of possibility. These processes of gender de- and re-traditionalization provide the focus for the three narratives we present in this chapter. The first is drawn from the original series of *Jamie's Kitchen* and the other two from *Jamie's Kitchen Australia*. These stories, of single motherhood, sexual harassment, and issues around gender and sexuality in the Fifteen training environment, continue to apply some of the key concepts in the reflexive self and the care-of-the-self literatures that we have canvassed previously. In relation to the *gendered* self these can be summarized as:

- Knowing, understanding and acting on oneself and in relations with others in ways that are gendered.
- Knowing and performing appropriate forms of masculinity and femininity in particular settings – such as in commercial kitchens, training venues.
- Understanding oneself in ways that are situated in, and constitute gender as a shifting, sometimes stable, often times restricted field of possibilities in particular settings.
- The ways in which fields of possibility encourage, direct, compel us to act and think in certain ways, but which also enable us to act otherwise. We can always find examples of the exceptional individual who acts otherwise but nonetheless if enough people think and act otherwise this can result in the transformation of a field of possibilities. Likewise relationships with another field can transform a particular field.
- The capacity to know oneself as a self who should have, or is able to develop, a reflexive disposition to questions/problems associated with the various ways one can exercise, practise masculinity/femininity.

The stories serve to illustrate the dilemmas some of the trainees face as they practice their freedom in different and shifting fields of possibility. Before moving on to this micro-level analysis in our stories, however, we first address the gendered nature of the hospitality industry more broadly via a discussion of some *warts and all* accounts of work practices and gender relations in commercial kitchens (Bourdain, 2000; Buford, 2006; Cadwalladr, 2007).

## Gender and the hospitality industry

### Heat (and balls)

From all accounts commercial kitchens are places where *heat* is generated. In this context *heat* can signify – literally and metaphorically – a number of things that are important to understanding gender relations in these settings. Quite literally, as Bill Buford (2006, p. 81) suggests, kitchens – grill stations in particular – are hot, exhausting, frenetic, frenzied places in which to think about, prepare and present food: 'The grill station is hell. You stand at it for five minutes and you think: so this is what Dante had in mind. It is in a dark, hot corner – hotter than any other spot in the kitchen; hotter than anywhere else in your life'. The energy and frenzy of a busy restaurant kitchen generate another form of heat – a heat that is made knowable through that old saying: *If you can't stand the heat get out of the kitchen.*

The immediacy, urgency and timeliness that characterizes busy restaurants (whatever happened to *slow* food?) creates a range of pressures and demands on those who work front-of-house, and for those who work in the heat of the kitchen back-of-house. In many accounts of the nature and characteristics of this hot-house environment this heat, this urgency, this frenzy is given some order and made manageable within hierarchical structures that allocate specific and particular tasks to certain individuals, teams or sections. The ability to manage this heat successfully and profitably is dependent, so it seems, on expectations that these tasks will be done properly and quickly; and that the hierarchies that facilitate these task/job allocations and their management will be maintained with those at the top exercising a form of sovereignty over the activities in these domains/fields. Of course, as Foucault's formulation would suggest, the exercise of this sovereignty should be understood as a power relation, not an act of domination. As a power relation those *kitchen slaves* who sweat, toil and labour in the heat of the kitchen can, in the *normal* course of events, choose not to do as directed; they can walk out or stay away; or they can remain and do the job because they may have few choices/options to do otherwise.

In this sense the restaurant kitchen is a field of possibilities in which it is assumed that you need to be a certain *type* of person to survive. You need to have developed and be able to exercise certain behaviours and dispositions to *stand the heat*. What we want to suggest in this chapter is that many accounts of this environment suggest that you need *balls* to survive and thrive. You need *balls* because the heat of the restaurant kitchen is energized (so to speak) by what some would call a testosterone-fuelled, masculinist, misogynist culture that judges a person's worth by the size of *his* balls; which must, you would think, make it difficult for women to succeed in this industry.

In a chapter entitled 'Who Cooks?', Anthony Bourdain (2000) raises what seems, at second glance, to be a pretty obvious question: *Who is cooking the food that you eat in a restaurant?* The question becomes obvious because it is highly unlikely, at least in the world of *starred* chefs, that the celebrity chef is the actual person who has prepared and cooked the food which appears on your plate not long, hopefully, after you have ordered it. Bourdain poses the question as a means to identify the *type* of person he looks for to staff the lines and stations in his kitchen. Line cooking, what Bourdain calls the *real business* of food preparation in the restaurant industry, is about 'consistency, about mindless, unvarying repetition, the same series of tasks performed over and over and over again in exactly the same way'. This well-disciplined, regimented, hierarchical monotony is not where you want to be confronted by an 'innovator, somebody with ideas of their own who is going to mess around with the chef's recipes and presentations'. Chefs, suggests Bourdain, 'require blind near fanatical loyalty, a strong back and an automaton-like consistency of execution under battlefield conditions' (2000, pp. 55–6).

In this telling of the story of what goes on in the heat of the kitchen back-of-house – a telling which is often repeated elsewhere – cooks are a 'dysfunctional, mercenary lot, fringe-dwellers motivated by money, the peculiar lifestyle of cooking and a grim pride'. In the US where Bourdain works these *types* are not usually embodied in the 'born in the USA, possibly school-trained, culinarily sophisticated types': types who are *type cast* by Bourdain as 'a lazy, undisciplined and, worst of all, high-maintenance lot, annoyingly opinionated, possessed of egos requiring constant stroking and tune ups, and as members of a privileged and wealthy population, unused to the kind of "disrespect" a busy chef is inclined to dish out'. No, in this context Ecuadorian, Mexican, Dominican and Salvadorian cooks know best the 'American dream of hard work leading to material rewards': better than 'some bed-wetting white boy whose mom brought him up thinking the world owed him a living, and who thinks he actually knows a few things' (2000, pp. 55–7).

One reading of Bourdain's account might dismiss these views as those of an arrogant bully, someone who might, indeed, personify the traits of the white boys he dismisses – except he occupies a position (chef) at the top of a hierarchy that looks down on those at lower levels of the food chain. After all he himself suggests that: 'Ultimately I want a salute and a "Yes sir!". If I want an opinion from my line cooks, *I*'ll provide one'. At this point though, we don't intend to make this judgement (or maybe we have!). Rather, the purpose of this discussion is to introduce Bourdain's view of the *type* of women who might survive and thrive in this environment. It is worth producing at length, and in its entirety, his characterization of what women might bring to this environment, and what type of person a woman needs to be to survive in it. Those readers who are easily offended might choose to skip this part!

> Women line cooks, however rare they might be in the testosterone-heavy, male dominated world of restaurant kitchens, are a particular delight. To have a rough-as-nails, foul mouthed, trash-talking female line cook on your team can be a true joy – and a civilizing factor in a unit where conversation tends to center around who's got the bigger balls and who takes it in the ass.
>
> I've been fortunate enough to work with some really studly women line cooks – no weak reeds these. One woman, Sharon, managed to hold down a busy sauté station while seven months pregnant – and still find time to provide advice and comfort to a romantically unhappy broiler man. A long-time associate, Beth, who likes to refer to herself as the 'Grill Bitch', excelled at putting loudmouths and fools into their proper place. She refused to behave any differently than her male co-workers: she'd change in the same locker area, dropping her pants right alongside them. She was as sexually aggressive, and as vocal about it, as her fellow cooks, but unlikely to suffer behavior she found demeaning. One sorry Moroccan cook who pinched her ass found himself suddenly bent over a cutting board with Beth dry-humping him from behind, saying, 'How do *you* like it, bitch.' The guy almost died of shame – and never repeated that mistake again.
>
> Another female line cook I had the pleasure of working with arrived at work one morning to find that the Ecuadorian pasta cook had decorated her station with some particularly hard-core pornography of pimply assed women getting penetrated in every orifice by pot-bellied guys with prison tattoos and back hair. She didn't react at all, but a little later, while passing through the pasta man's station, casually remarked. 'Jose, I see you brought in some photos of the family. Mom looks good for her age.'
>
> (Anthony Bourdain, 2000, *Kitchen Confidential*, pp. 57–8)

A theme emerges here. Kitchens, as frenetic, hierarchical, macho, misogynistic spaces are male spaces. If, as a female, you want to work in one you need to be foul-mouthed, 'studly' (butch), trash-talking, sexually aggressive, *one of the boys*. It also helps if you can be sharing and caring if the need be.

The idea that to be successful in this industry a woman has to be more of *a lad than the lads* is discussed in Carole Cadwalladr's (2007) profile, in *The Observer Food Monthly* magazine, of Angela Hartnett who is described as 'perhaps the leading female chef in Britain today'. Hartnett's list of achievements include: a Michelin star in the first year of her restaurant being open; an MBE for services to the hospitality industry; a soon-to-be-released first cook book; and a lead role in a TV show called *Kitchen Criminals*. The most telling and significant theme in this profile – at least for our purposes – is that Angela Hartnett is a success in the industry in spite of (possibly as a consequence of) her apprenticeship in what are described as the 'brutal, war-torn kitchens of Gordon Ramsay'. Ramsay – himself a multi-starred Michelin chef – is notorious for being angry, loud and foul-mouthed (his latest [2007] TV show is called *The F-word* after his propensity to use it), and for being an arrogant, macho, misogynistic, even bullying head chef. This is certainly a characterization easily and appropriately made from his various representations on TV and in a number of biographies. He, and others, might disagree.

As Cadwalladr puts it, there might be a number of more macho spaces than a restaurant kitchen: 'An oil-rig, perhaps. A coalmine. On the editorial staff at *Nuts* magazine. But not all that many'. Apparently the order of machismo is of a different, heightened, magnitude in Gordon Ramsay's kitchens: 'When Angela Hartnett went to work for Gordon Ramsay in 1994 – before anyone had ever heard of him and the staff turnover was so high it was more like a body count – nine out of 10 employees simply did a runner'. In this environment, Hartnett, as a matter of course, worked 17 hour days, 6 days a week in 'conditions that she describes, in an offhand way, as "psychological warfare". Chefs in other restaurants simply referred to the place as "Vietnam"' (p. 49). Hartnett's achievements in this environment are many and exceptional, not the least being that she has continued to work for Ramsay for 17 years, and because she is a *she*. Ramsay is notorious for his low opinion of women as chefs (not necessarily of women as cooks). Indeed, Cadwalladr quotes Hartnett as saying that Ramsay believes that 'women can only work three weeks out of four'. This is a view supported by Marcus Wareing, a colleague of Hartnett's from Ramsay's restaurants in the 1990s, and now a chef-patron at Petrus, another Ramsay restaurant. According to Cadwalladr, Wareing is full of 'admiration and respect' for Hartnett: 'but you can tell when Angela Hartnett is [in] a bad mood. It's written all over her face. And it happens every bloody month!' Cadwalladr responds: 'What? You're saying you could tell if she was pre-menstrual?' To which Wareing says: 'Too bloody right. I worked with her for five years. And if she denies it, she's a liar' (2007, p. 51).

Some might say that at this time (of the month) Hartnett is only acting the way that the likes of Ramsay, Wareing, and Bourdain act all the time. But that is not the point we are exploring here. Rather, what seems apparent is that women in the restaurant industry are cast as a certain type: a type that has been recast and transformed in many other organizational settings at the start of the twenty-first century (even though in these settings the type may retain tracings of earlier types). We will return to Cadwalladr's views on this shortly. Back in Ramsay's world, Hartnett, who embodies the exceptional female – the exception that proves the rule that the restaurant industry is overwhelmingly a male space – has had to, in order to survive and thrive, exercise her freedom in a field of possibilities that is powerfully shaped by (archaic) gender norms and expectations. She has, indeed, had to become one of the boys: 'Every kitchen she's ever worked in has been dominated by men and she's had to compete with them on their terms.' Moreover, her capacities, skills, performance, success – her personhood – is rendered knowable and understandable largely in masculine terms. Apparently the greatest compliment that the likes of Gordon Ramsay can pay the likes of Angela Hartnett is to suggest that she has '*bigger bollocks than most men*' (p. 51).

In many of the OECD economies the hospitality industry (broadly defined, but including areas such as accommodation, cafes and restaurants) is a significant employer of young people, and a sector of the economy that is identified as promising significant employment growth in the next decade (Ball *et al.*, 2000; Baum, 2002; Australian Bureau of Statistics (ABS), 2005). At the same time it is a labour market that is characterized by low wage rates, casualized, temporary and part-time forms of employment, and a gendered structure that appears to limit female participation to lower levels in many occupational categories. As Baum (2002, p. 347) argues, the industry has a number of characteristics that impact on young male and female workers in the industry, but which also contribute to significant gender differences in employment. These include:

- The tendency to low wages, except where skills shortages act to counter this.
- The prevalence of unsocial hours and family-unfriendly shift patterns.
- The rare incidence of equal opportunity policies and male domination of higher-level, better-paid work.
- Poor or non-existent career structures.
- Informal recruitment practices.

- Failure to adopt formalized 'good practice' models of human resource management and development.
- Lack of any significant trade union presence.
- High levels of labour turnover.
- Difficulties in recruitment and retention.

In Australia, for example, the hospitality industry is 'the third strongest industry for projected employment growth to 2011–12' with projections concluding 'that food, hospitality and tourism will provide 8 per cent of new jobs to 2011–12'. Forty-eight per cent of the workforce is either part-time or casual, with 91 per cent of all restaurants and cafes employing people under 20. Indeed, the proportion of casual workers is substantially more than the all-industry average of approximately 26 per cent (Restaurant and Catering Australia, 2007, pp. 6–13).

Because of its size and projected growth the gendered nature of the hospitality industry workforce is of some significance. Although 55 per cent of the workforce is female they only make up 33 per cent of the full-time population compared to the male full-time population of 58 per cent (Restaurant and Catering Australia, 2007). ABS (2005, p. 127) figures for August 2003 indicate that 58.7 per cent of those employed in accommodation, cafes and restaurants were female. These figures are confounded by the large percentage of students who work in hospitality while they are studying and are not really looking for full-time employment and women with families who 'choose' to work part-time. Apprenticeships and traineeships, as the primary forms of entry into many of the occupations that characterize this industry, chefs for example, have traditionally been dominated by males. Many education, training and employment policy initiatives of the last two decades or so have attempted to promote female participation in traineeships and apprenticeships. These initiatives aim to encourage diversity in the industry, but also to establish viable and promising career pathways for young women into growth areas of employment. According to the Australian Bureau of Statistics (ABS) apprenticeships have traditionally been the pathway of choice into work for many young men as an alternative to staying on at school after the age of 15 (ABS, 2000). As a consequence they dominated VET courses until the introduction of traineeships in 1985. Traineeships are an option that appear to be more attractive to females and the gender gap has been slowly narrowing with women 'making up 38 per cent of VET students aged 15–19 and 47 per cent of those aged 20–24 in 1999' (ABS, 2000, p. 94). By 2003, female

VET students made up 48.6 per cent of the total VET students (ABS, 2005, p. 88).

A number of the issues here will be discussed in more detail, and with reference to the drama of *Jamie's Kitchen*, in later sections of this chapter. Of particular relevance then will be concerns about sexual harassment, sexuality, and the de- and re-traditionalization of gender roles in fields such as the restaurant industry. When we discuss these we will not be suggesting that what we see in *Jamie's Kitchen* in terms of gender relations and sexuality is of the order apparent here and in Bourdain's writing. But what these accounts highlight is that the training which the Fifteen Foundation provides for marginalized young men and women is designed to provide entry into an industry that has a history, and a reputation, for being radically masculinist, heterosexual and disrespectful, even antagonistic to other forms of being a person. For Cadwalladr *all of this* is *depressing*: 'Not Angela, she's warm and charming and open and engaging as well as being successful.' No, what is depressing is that the restaurant industry is 'still an industry that discriminates against women reaching the top because they self-select out'. In Cadwalladr's reckoning the difficult choices that women face in many organizational settings are 'exaggerated in the restaurant trade'. Being a chef is 'still not a job for women because if a male chef wants a family, he can have one. Just so long as he has a wife who's happy to stay at home and look after them' (2007, p. 52). As Cadwalladr argues, this is not a matter or question of biology, of men being inherently better cooks than women. Indeed, in Buford's (2006, p. 59) account of kitchen life, he quotes chef Mario Batali's claim that women make the best cooks: *'I know it doesn't make sense, and I don't understand it. But it is consistently the case: women are better cooks. They approach food differently.'* Rather, it is about often archaic work practices, gender norms and expectations, and the capacity or willingness to conform to these, or to be able to exercise your freedom as a woman in ways that mark you as *one of the boys*.

## The enterprising worker and the de- and re-traditionalization of gender

McLeod and Yates (2006, p. 189) argue, in relation to debates about gender de-traditionalization, that 'many theoretical accounts tend to overstate the extent of such processes, neglect the ways in which new forms of gender traditionalism are being reinscribed, and fail to adequately acknowledge the unevenness and social differentiation of such change'.

They draw on Harriet Bjerrum Nielsen's concept of 'unacknowledged gender' in their analysis. For Nielson:

> gendered subjectivity is the gendered 'being in the world' which consists of unacknowledged and to some extent unconscious gender (unconscious images/discourses and feelings attached to gender). Unacknowledged gender is the way gender is present as background when one reflects on something else, for example what kind of person one is, what kind of desires one has, what kind of feelings one experiences having.
>
> (1996, p. 11, cited in McLeod and Yates, 2006, p. 191)

McLeod and Yates (2006, p. 196) argue the significance of these attitudes to gender 'in the context of changed economies, labour markets, and changing social and interpersonal expectations'. Their research found that masculinity was commonly regarded as innate and therefore not 'influenced by social norms and changes', whereas 'femininity and girls were seen as open to change and needing to undergo some reshaping as we enter a different social and economic period'. They argue that many of the current debates about boys and schooling presume that masculinity is set and that it is schooling that needs to change to accommodate this (see also McWilliam and Brannock, 2001). This presumption is evident in the 'what about the boys?' debates in schools where ameliorative programmes for boys who are failing are promoted. There are traces of these views about young women and young men to be found in the stories we tell later in this chapter.

One of the many interesting findings in McLeod and Yates' (2006, p. 199) study is the gendered and classed nature of modern processes of reflexivity. The strategies of self-making that comprise an enterprising subjectivity – 'flexibility, knowingness about oneself and the impression one needs to make' – were taken on much more readily by young women in their study as opposed to young men, although class (and particular school and life experiences) appeared to be a factor in particular young men's willingness/ability to take on an enterprising subjectivity. Working-class males, for example, were less likely to engage with this form of subjectivity. While this opened up 'new possibilities for autonomy' for young women, it also presented some 'dangers in the potential for punitive self-scrutiny and feelings of never being the "good enough" woman' (p. 200). The processes of self-transformation in *Jamie's Kitchen*, facilitated by the variety of technologies of the self that gave form to processes of training in kitchens and classrooms, required marginalized young men and women to problematize themselves. It can be argued that at one level these demands to problematize the self in the pursuit of self-transformation open these young people to the possibility of the punitive self-scrutiny McLeod and Yates describe. The processes themselves are integral to the drama of these shows, and are powerful reasons for large numbers of us to continue to watch.

McLeod and Yates (2006, p. 208) have called for an analysis of the production of knowledges and subjectivities that is more nuanced and situated than that offered by 'big picture' theorists, who have examined the ways in which 'psychological knowledges and techniques structure the way in which we understand and know ourselves'. They suggest that such analyses do not pay enough attention to:

> the particular ways in which these new forms of the self are either gendered or enacted by situated, embodied individuals. In cultures saturated with knowledge of gender difference, particularly the feminization of affect and relationships and the masculine connotations of the norm of autonomy, such therapeutic techniques of the self are going to resonate differently for girls and boys.
>
> (2006, p. 208)

Similarly, Judy Wacjman, in her book *Managing Like a Man* (1999), has examined gender relations in management. She describes the uphill battle women faced in achieving equal status with men and identifies different forms of masculinity in different professions – a 'warrior ethic' of 'heroic masculinity' in engineering; a 'cult of toughness and "hard" masculinity' in the manufacturing industry, and a form of masculinity that involves 'mastery of technology and the control of other people' in technology industries. These different forms of masculinity, in different fields of possibility, are located in relation to what Wacjman identifies as a 'new corporate masculinity'; where the norms and behaviours of managers are understood in masculine terms and femininity is seen as in need of amelioration. As such, because of women's minority status, Wacjman argues that successful women become symbols of 'how-women-can-do, stand-ins for all women' (1999, p. 110). This process is typical of what happens in a range of marginalized groups where a lack of success is often seen as a problem inherent in individuals rather than structures.

## The single mum in Jamie's Kitchen: limiting the field of possibilities?

24-year-old Michelle Cooper from south-west London, like Erin Zonneveld in the Australian series, is a single mother. At the time the first series was televised in 2002 her daughter was 6 years old. Michelle was a talented pianist and clarinet player but 'found it difficult to get into the classical world'. Although the information about her is sketchy, before she joined the training programme she had worked in supermarkets and shops, supplementing this with some private piano tuition. She had completed some initial qualifications in health and social care but 'didn't really know what to do next' (Channel 4, 2007).

Research into teenage parenting indicates that they are much more likely to experience economic hardship and family disruption in later life than those who bear and rear children when older. Teenage parenting does not, in itself, confirm a life of poverty and welfare dependence but prior disadvantage, combined with limited academic ability and aspirations, increases the odds of hardship for teenage parents and their children. Research in Britain has indicated that teenage mothers are less likely to find secure paid employment and, as such, are more likely to become reliant on welfare and to suffer poverty (Angwin *et al.*, 2005). Given these possible outcomes it is clear that Michelle was already operating within a particularly limited field of possibility when she entered her traineeship and had a lot invested in being successful in *Jamie's Kitchen*. Her story examines some of the issues/problems faced by Michelle when she tried to negotiate movement between two different fields of possibility and where she was expected to meet the particular demands of the professional kitchen despite her personal circumstances.

Michelle was outspoken and clashed with Jamie several times during the first series. In an interview in response to the question: 'What is the most important thing you have learned on this course?' Michelle replied:

> I've learnt to keep my mouth shut, which is difficult when you're argumentative like me. I've learnt that the chef is always right and although I might not agree with that completely, I've learnt to keep my thoughts to myself.
> (*Return to Jamie's Kitchen: Meet the Trainees*, 2007, Channel 4)

Most of these clashes were because of perceptions that Michelle lacked commitment to the course. Michelle had a different view.

> *Voice Over:* While the others finish putting the tents up, single mum Michelle is on the phone to her six-year-old daughter.
>
> *Michelle Cooper:* Hello, I told you I went camping didn't I with your favourite Jamie. Listen I've got to go anyway. OK, goodnight, Do you love me? I love you too. See you later. Bye bye.
>
> (*Jamie's Kitchen*, Episode Three, Broadcast on Channel 10 Melbourne, 5 August 2003)

In terms of what we, the audience, and possibly the Fifteen (Cheeky Chops) personnel know of Michelle, her status/position as a single mother is not problematic until the drama that surrounds her failure to pass exams, and to attend classes and work-placements.

> *Voice Over:* Most of the trainees are starting to look more like potential chefs but two still haven't passed all their exams. While the others tuck in, Jamie takes aside Nicola Andronicou and Michelle Cooper to have a heart to heart about their future.
>
> *Jamie (Jamie, Nicola Andronicou and Michelle Cooper sitting on a bench, framed by a large window looking out onto fields):* We've now got to the, sort of the end of the part of the course and you haven't done enough NVQ sort of test work to be able to qualify for the NVQ1. From my point of view I didn't really imagine sort of taking any students into the kitchen without it and I just wondered what you thought and what you would do if I was you?
>
> *Michelle Cooper:* I can't stay if you don't want me there, that's cool but what can I do?
>
> *Jamie:* I suppose what I'm trying to say is, we set up this course, I mean it's quite basic work and what I thought I'd be going through into a professional ....
>
> [At this point Michelle gets up crying [trying to hide it] and walks off camera and through the door. Jamie looks really uncomfortable, waits a while then follows, followed by camera.]
>
> *Michelle Cooper:* Everybody knew I had childcare problems and nothing was done and I needed help and there was no help. Now it's come to the end and everyone's getting their qualification and I'm not getting it, it's like 'OK Michelle we'll help you now'. I just find that a bit weird to be honest.

*Jamie (with lots of difficulty in articulating his thoughts, and dealing with Michelle's distress. This doesn't come through in just a transcript of his words):* Don't worry about not getting the qualifications, you'll get them in September. What's two and a half months? You know, quite frankly your kids are much more important than this bloody project. But also, I think you know becoming a parent is really finding your balance in life and you're young and you need to give yourself opportunities and you're single which makes it ten times worse quite frankly. Just because you're a single mother doesn't mean you haven't got the right to be educated and learn a trade. And I suppose what I wanted to say to you was, we're not here to make things tougher you know, but we want to help, you know I want to help, let's look at all the options for now and maybe we'll have a talk next week.

*(Jamie's Kitchen*, Episode Three, Broadcast on Channel 10 Melbourne, 5 August 2003)

In this exchange it is clear that when Jamie became aware of the problems that Michelle faced as a single mother he was sympathetic. But for Michelle this recognition was too little too late. Some concrete help should have accompanied an awareness and acknowledgement of how her personal life was impinging on her ability to meet course requirements. Failure to do this meant that Michelle was forced to work within a diminished field of possibilities, in effect being forced to choose between attending training and looking after her child. Her difficulties in meeting workplace demands to adhere to rationalized clock time also spilled over into her work-experience placement.

[Shot of Michelle arriving at Smith's of Smithfield (work experience restaurant).]

*Voice over:* Day two of Michelle and Dwayne's work placement. Michelle's late and Dwayne is nowhere to be seen.

*Michelle (at her locker at Smith's):* I hate it already [laughs]. I hate being late, the tube was packed [inaudible] traffic [inaudible] so I'm a bit late, a bit, it's not my fault.

[Balcony of unidentified building with Jamie addressing off-camera interviewer.]

> *Jamie Oliver:* I've got lots of people putting pressure on me to get rid of her because of the bad attendance and quite frankly, y'know, she needs help. So what I've done is taken a sort of a executive decision as in: No she's staying on the course. Darling you shouldn't feel like you're behind because we'll catch you up. Your work experience is a great opportunity for you to shine, just go out there and make me proud, y'know, for yourself, go and learn. But I will be watching her closely 'cos … cos I don't know yet if she really means it.
> [Inside quiet room addressing off camera interviewer.]

> *Michelle:* I'm having my doubts to be honest, it's not that I don't like it, I just don't know if it's … if it's me, if it's Michelle Cooper. If it's, y'know, if that's what I'm meant to be. I dunno.
> *Tony Morse:* Dwayne only worked for two days. He disappeared and we didn't hear from him again. And Michelle, I haven't got a clue about Michelle. She worked the first week, she did two and half days in the second week and then we didn't see her. They've let Jamie Oliver down something chronic, to be quite honest.
> (*Jamie's Kitchen*, Episode Four, Broadcast on Channel 10 Melbourne, 12 August 2003)

Michelle arrived late on the first day of her work-placement but despite declaring 'it's not my fault' towards the end of this excerpt she is rationalizing her failures by focusing inward and questioning whether or not she is suited to the job. Earlier in the chapter we referred to how successful women come to stand in for all women, for 'women who can do'. The flip-side is how young mothers like Michelle come to stand in for all those who *can* but don't try hard enough or take the opportunities given to them or refuse to 'shine'. While Jamie acknowledged yet again that the trainees do not start out on a level playing field and that Michelle's starting point was way behind the rest, he talked about 'catching her up' and 'watching her closely', not convinced that 'she really means it'. He was unclear about what kind of help it was that she actually needed and, taken with his expressed concerns, the responsibility fell back onto Michelle to lift her game. It is clear that the options open to her in the field of possibilities circumscribed by her status as a single mum are at odds with those expected and required in the world of work.

In this final example Jamie was very annoyed that Michelle had to leave early to take care of her daughter. In this episode the trainees had to prepare and cook for paying customers as part of their training. But the drama of the episode – of having to prepare, cook and present food to order, on time, under pressure – was revealed as a sham, as make-believe. Oliver and his team pretended that there were customers, pretended there were orders and pretended that there were difficulties: all in order to see how the trainees dealt with the pressure (and of course it made good television). During this episode Jamie and Michelle repeatedly clashed and the arguments between the two made for compelling viewing. The question though is what influence Michelle's parenting status had on how the situation unfolded.

*Jamie:* So, 'right, let's go and have a drink. Michelle you've obviously got to get home. Say goodbye to the team.

[Michelle leaves without saying goodbye.]

*Jamie to remaining trainees:* Can I just give you a word of advice, right? I'm not talking behind Michelle's back because she wanted to go because her daughter has left a phone call for her or something. That is not the attitude I want from you. If you've got that inside you might as well piss off home now. I'm not saying it because she's gone. If she keeps doing that … she hasn't even said goodbye to you lot, right? Do you think you want to work with someone that argues like that in the kitchen? If you think you've got that aggression inside you to answer back to chefs, forget it. Forget it. No pay cheque. P45 time mate.

*Michelle (being interviewed away from the restaurant):* I don't think I'm going to get on with him at all. I think I'm always going to clash with him. Because it's not fair … [inaudible] … second time and he winds me up, quite frankly, he winds me up. He gets on my nerves.

*Jamie to camera:* I very, very much doubt that … er … Michelle is gunna last. I'm sure she hates my guts and she thinks the whole thing's a farce and this whole set up, this whole make-shift dinner party that we did. But I got to see her weakness and so did she, and if she doesn't deal with that, she can't be in the group, because we can't have hot heads in the group, right? I'm really glad that they felt being in the shit. It's important, because so far these guys, it's all been lovely. It's lovely. College is lovely. I'm a cook. I'm a chef. I'm working at the River Café. I'm working at the Capital with

Eric Chavot. It's all sweet, and we go see, up to see Pete and we see lovely pigs and baby pigs. It's all lovely, it's all good, but do you know what? Cooking in the real world, when the shit hits the fan, is horrible! I can't think of anywhere worse! It scares me and I'm glad it scared them and they might not like me but I wasn't even a bastard tonight! You wait until there's *real* customers and we've got [inaudible] there and they get a bit of dried old pasta like that. 'Mmm very nice', that's what I mean. They're goin' to ruin me. I've got a 1.3 million pound restaurant being built for these guys to be cooking in and they're crap.

*(Jamie's Kitchen*, Episode Four, Broadcast in Australia on Channel 10 Melbourne, 12 August 2003)

*Jamie:* Michelle, right? We've had our little … we've had our ups and downs, right? And you've given me a bit of shit, and you know, for whatever reason and you've had good reasons right? As I probably would say, control your temper, OK? No-one wants to work with a hot head, right? [Shows flashback to incident in episode 4.] But you did it yesterday and technically you were doing what you were told yesterday, so thank you for that.

*(Jamie's Kitchen*, Episode Five, Broadcast on Channel 10 Melbourne, 19 August 2003)

In Jamie's voice to camera above he had finally had enough. He implied here that it was Michelle's inclination to fly off the handle that had made her unsuitable for the job ahead. Not only did she not attend frequently enough and on time but she also caused problems because she answered back.

*Q:* **What has been the worst point?**

I've had arguments with Jamie and I've ended up feeling depressed and fed-up. I got chucked off the course because they thought I had a lack of commitment. I cried all the way home on the tube. It seemed so unfair; I was having trouble with childcare and I felt I was being unfairly treated. I couldn't stop crying and couldn't sleep at night for a weekend. Then I decided I didn't want to give up. I had a heart-to-heart with Jamie and we agreed I could carry on. I'm really glad I did.

*(Return to Jamie's Kitchen: Meet the Trainees*, 2007, Channel 4)

Her profile update on the *Jamie's Kitchen* website informs us 'Pressures of the job coupled with problems at home led to Michelle taking some time off. Though she has come off the project for the time being, it is hoped that she will rejoin the course at some point in the future' (Channel 4, 2007).

The processes described here are just some of the ways in which structural issues such as a lack of adequate childcare and family-unfriendly working hours and expectations come to be translated into personal pathologies such as lack of *commitment* and *hot-headedness*, effectively shifting the blame for Michelle's lack of success back on to her.

Diane Reay (2001; 2002; 2004, p. 71) has argued that processes of individualization have been 'uneven and uneasy' for women and that these processes are both complex and conflictual 'as contemporary notions of 'living your own life' clash with conventional expectations of 'being there for others'. We can read this complexity and conflict off from Michelle's frustrations and volatile responses and her sense of being treated unfairly. With the right kinds of support Michelle could well be the right person for the job. If equity and catering for diversity are to be taken seriously, and the Fifteen Foundation as a social enterprise certainly shows evidence of wanting to do so then we need to ask: *What allowances can be made in the rationalised world of work for young women like Michelle?* And: *How flexible can organisations such as this be?*

## Negotiating different fields of possibility: sexual harassment in Jamie's Kitchen

Masculinities are configurations of practice that are accomplished in social action and, therefore, can differ according to the gender relations in a particular social setting.

(Connell and Messerschmidt, 2005, p. 836)

The above quote is from a recent paper in which Connell and Messerschmidt (2005, pp. 836–40) attempt to rethink the concept of 'hegemonic masculinity' and to counter charges of essentialism both in the concept itself and in researchers' use of it. They adopt a relational approach to gender in order to prevent dichotomizing the experiences of men and women. They argue that there has been a great deal of essentializing of masculinity in 'pop psychology', 'the mythopoetic men's movement' and in 'journalistic interpretations' where 'the invention of new character types is endemic (the alpha male, the sensitive new-age guy, the hairy man, the new lad, the 'rat boy', etc.)' and, as we saw in a previous chapter, Jamie himself is not immune to these inventions. Their focus on social actions in particular settings is an attempt to account for different practices and processes in different places and spaces, in different fields of possibility.

Connell and Messerschmidt (2005, p. 838), however, do not want to throw the baby out with the bathwater, arguing that even though 'hegemonic masculinities can be constructed that do not correspond closely to the lives of any actual men' they 'do in various ways, express widespread ideals, fantasies and desires' and as such 'they articulate loosely with the practical constitution of masculinities as ways of living in everyday local circumstances'. They cite studies by Roper and Wacjman who identified 'well defined patterns of managerial masculinity in ... British corporations' as evidence.

Connell and Messerschmidt (2005, p. 840) argue that 'because the concept of hegemonic masculinity is based on practice that permits men's collective dominance over women to continue' it is not surprising that in some contexts men do engage in 'toxic practices' that work to 'stabilize gender dominance in a particular setting'. One such toxic practice is sexual harassment and the following narrative examines one example of this and attempts to capture some of the complexity of gender relations in a space such as *Jamie's Kitchen*. We again use Foucault's notion of fields of possibility and the different technologies used in the training environment to 'make up' the ideal young male worker in *Jamie's Kitchen*. This ideal worker is at odds with the hyper-masculine worker idealized in the kitchens of Gordon Ramsay and Anthony Bourdain. Many of the young men in *Jamie's Kitchen* are more familiar with those ways of doing masculinity described by Buford and Bourdain. Negotiating the rules and expected behaviours between these two different fields of possibility, such as training colleges, work-placements, commercial kitchens, and peer cultures, proves more difficult for some than others.

We introduced AJ (aka Amos and Alan) in Chapter 1. He appears again in this chapter because he became the central player in an incident of sexual harassment perpetrated against Lauren Tyler, one of the young female trainees in the *Jamie's Kitchen Australia* series. If you remember back to this chapter, AJ had problems relating to authority figures and had a particularly problematic relationship with Andrew Sankey chef and trainer at Box Hill TAFE.

**Being one of the boys**

> *Andrew Sankey:* Yeah I think the boys thing overall. They need maybe a psychologist to give them a program of things to work through so that they can see that they are a pain in the arse to work with.
>
> *Voice Over:* Over the last few weeks a boy's club culture has developed within the group with several of the male trainees interrupting the class with their juvenile antics.
>
> *Toby Puttock:* They need way more adult contact. It's like summer camp you know. They're all 16 years-old, they're all 18 and they're not growing up out of it so once they're in the kitchen with people that are all 30 years old and even older ...
>
> *Andrew Sankey:* Work is not like playing games as a 16 year old. It's work.
>
> (*Jamie's Kitchen Australia*, Episode Five, Broadcast on Channel 10 Melbourne, 12 October 2006)

The boys' culture described briefly here will be familiar to most. It is characterized by joking, pranks and disruptive behaviours and can be found in any number of school, training and workplace settings (and is not always or even necessarily confined to the young). McDowell (2000, pp. 404–6) has described these behaviours using the term 'laddish masculinity' in which macho values such as 'physical strength, courage and toughness' appear hegemonic among young working-class men. In McDowell's study, processes of both gender de- and re-traditionalization were evident. Young working-class men might deny sexist attitudes in themselves, while at the same time operating within 'a simplistic narrative of binary difference' between males and females: girls go into childcare and boys into IT. While we do not subscribe to an essentializing view of this form of masculinity we do agree with Connell and Messerschmidt (2005, p. 838) that these characteristics 'articulate loosely' with many of these young men's ways of living 'in everyday local circumstances'.

McDowell (2000, p. 396) has argued that with the increasing domination of service sector employment in current labour markets there is also increasing emphasis on 'personal interactions' in the notion of 'good service' and that such things as 'bodily presentation and personal attitudes (deference, politeness, cleanliness) are of overwhelming significance in the opportunity to gain and hold employment'. McWilliam and Brannock (2001, pp. 8–14) made a similar argument when they examined the 'What about the boys?' debate in the field of education, relating this to a shifting focus over time to a consideration of boys' feelings as well as their behaviours. They trace this to a trickle-down effect, claiming that 'the importance of reclaiming boys' hearts (not simply their minds) is precisely in tune with current thinking about the sorts of capacities that are increasingly being regarded as necessary to enterprising workers in corporate settings'. Communication and interpersonal skills are seen as necessary for 'looking after the emotional health of the workplace', leading to a focus on 'emotional literacy' as a generic attribute that can be 'evaluated, taught and learned'.

In their examination of the new management literature McWilliam and Brannock (2001, p. 8) have discerned a blurring of 'the emotional/logical and the personal/public', which they argue 'is producing new identities that are more closely aligned with enterprise culture'. In particular they refer to 'the domain of therapeutic expertise' (psychologists, counsellors, teachers, mentors) and 'its techniques for managing the happiness of employees', which is mobilized to 'collapse the personal and the economic'. It is interesting to note that Andrew Sankey's response is to psychologize the boys' behaviour while Toby Puttock alludes to the need for mentors. Both, usually in combination, are common strategies in sites where boys behave badly.

Jamie Oliver himself (a self-confessed, one-time 'at risk' student) is one example of this blurring of the emotional/logical and the personal/public, combining cool and rational business acumen with public displays of emotion. We see these therapeutic techniques for managing happiness, which were given much less emphasis in the original *Jamie's Kitchen*, employed and reported on quite deliberately in *Jamie's Kitchen Australia*. These technologies sought to better manage the turbulent personal lives of the trainees in order to reduce any negative impact on their training. McWilliam and Brannock (p. 8) argue that: 'It is not sufficient in a culture of enterprise that service providers provide a good service – they must also *feel like doing so* (original emphasis). In so doing, they are self-regulating and self-sustaining as motivated and productive workers.'

According to McDowell (2000, p. 390) the type of *laddish masculinity* displayed by the boys has come to be seen as 'a disadvantage rather than an advantage in labour market entry'. The concerns expressed by Toby and Andrew in the excerpt above can be read as a common concern for boys and their antisocial behaviours. However, when read against the backdrop of the service industry and its project to make up enterprising individuals with the necessary affective attributes, these young men's ability to successfully negotiate a different field of possibility becomes of primary importance.

It is not long before the boys' fun and games that have caused concern for the trainers take a distinctly more serious turn.

---

*Voice Over:* ... and it's come to chef's attention that the issue is much more serious.

*Andrew Sankey:* Especially as last week it came about that some of the girls were getting touched. Having spoken to a couple of the fellas, and I don't know who actually did it, but um I hope that message got across. They can't move into a regular work situation with this mind-set and think it's okay because it's just not okay.

*Voice Over:* It's at the end of tonight's cooking class that a line is finally crossed when Amos strikes the backside of Lauren who has been on the receiving end of such behaviour one too many times.

*Lauren:* Seriously that's not on. That's one fucking boundary you don't cross.

*Andrew Sankey:* What's going on?

*Lauren:* He hit me on the fucking arse [throws cloth down and walks out].

(*Jamie's Kitchen Australia*, Episode Five, Broadcast on
Channel 10 Melbourne, 12 October 2006)

---

It is clear that this message did not get across. As we noted in our introduction, gender is always relational and these relations take on different configurations and meanings in different places and spaces and over time. Connell and Messerschmidt (2005, p. 848) have argued that 'women are central in many of the processes constructing masculinities' and that 'gender hierarchies are also affected by new configurations of women's identity and practice, especially among younger women'. Lauren, although extremely upset, was able to indicate that she would not put up with any form of harassment from the boys. The problem is that in other spaces and places, like the commercial kitchens run by Ramsay and Bourdain, this type of behaviour is tolerated, even celebrated. Clair Feig, a successful Melbourne chef, in a recent newspaper article (Lallo, 2007) commented on her success in the industry:

> Clair Feig has some advice for girls who want to be the next Nigella Lawson. 'I don't consider her to be a real chef,' says the chef and management trainee at Richmond Hill Café & Larder. 'She has lovely little books that you can flip through and bake a cake from – and I own some of those books. But being a serious chef is not about baking fairy cakes on a Sunday or biscuits for the football team. You've got to love getting dirty and love the long hours. You've got to be strong and fit, and not mind the dirty jokes and swearing. You've got to be tough and give as good as you get. And you've got to work your arse off.'
>
> (2007, p. 9)

Here Fieg introduces binaries between chefs/cooks, real/not real, serious/not serious, and feminine/masculine. In this representation 'real' chefs are 'tough' and 'give as good as they get', in other words they act more like men. Although the hospitality industry has regulations in place designed to prevent and deal with sexual harassment and other forms of discrimination, the course of action Lauren followed is never mentioned as an option. This is not the case in the highly regulated environments of large institutions such as Box Hill TAFE.

> *Andrew Sankey:* You've been warned about shit like that. That's instant ... you're out.
>
> *AJ:* So you want me out then?
>
> *Andrew Sankey:* Yes. You're not allowed to do it. See you later. Go. That's it.
>
> *Amos:* [packing his things] We've just been mucking around, whipping each other and shit. Whatever. I whipped someone on the wrong day. I fucked up. Who cares?
>
> *Andrew Sankey:* It's over.
>
> (*Jamie's Kitchen Australia*, Episode Five, Broadcast on Channel 10 Melbourne, 12 October 2006)

Ashley, one of the other male trainees, tried to question Andrew Sankey's actions but was told that it was none of his business. Punishment for AJ was swift despite Ashley's attempts to intervene and Lauren at this stage was unrepentant.

*Voice Over:* After throwing Amos off the course for his behaviour towards Lauren, teacher Andrew Sankey has a stern warning for the rest of the trainees.

*Andrew Sankey:* Stop where you are. Okay are we listening? I mean really listening. Amos will not be joining the group okay. He crossed the line. He's been told and you guys have all been told as a group that you do not touch the girls. You do not make sexist comments and you do not make any derogatory comment about any person regardless of what their sex is, their sexuality or their behaviour. The college does not accept that kind of behaviour at all and I mean in the tiniest degree. This is your only warning. I cannot be more serious. If I have one person come to me and say that person over there said or did or slapped or touched me that person will be off the college premises straight away. I cannot stress this enough and guys that means you, you, you, you, you, you, you, you and you – right everybody. Across the board.

*Ashley:* That goes for females as well.

*Andrew Sankey:* There is to be no more swearing.

*Ashley:* Pointing to all the boys and talking.

*Andrew Sankey:* Shut up. I am so serious.

*Ashley:* But don't just point to all the boys.

*Andrew Sankey:* [going right up to him] It's because of the boys that we have this problem.

[Ashley shaking his head]

*Andrew Sankey:* Do not talk back to me right now when I'm being this serious otherwise you can see the door and that would make me so upset because I have a great deal of faith in you. Do not backchat me right now. We are going to toe the line and the next person that

> steps over it is out. I'm furious. I never want to see this behaviour again or hear about it. Get on with it.
>
> (*Jamie's Kitchen Australia*, Episode Five, Broadcast on Channel 10 Melbourne, 12 October 2006)

Sankey, with his TAFE hat on, attempted to articulate the limits of the field when he outlined these unacceptable behaviours. We can gather by previous comments that this is not the first time he had done this but until this incident the limits of the field had not been readily apparent to these young men. Ashley was the most vocal in testing these limits. He became defensive and attempted to deflect blame away from the boys and back on to the girls, seeming to imply that they were *equal* partners in this behaviour. But Lauren is small and slight. As well, the ratio of males to females is almost three to one and this recruitment strategy produced unequal power relations in *Jamie's Kitchen Australia* from the beginning.

> *Amos (to camera):* I don't know. I can only really blame myself for it. I've seen it happen. I could have stopped it or I could have told them to stop it or I just couldn't have done it you know. I can only really blame myself. [Starts crying] Now I'm tearing fucking now. [Looks totally dejected] Way to throw it all away huh.
>
> (*Jamie's Kitchen Australia*, Episode Five, Broadcast on Channel 10 Melbourne, 12 October 2006)

The levels of reflexivity encouraged by Fifteen and provoked by the *voice to camera* techniques and the other forms of therapeutic expertise deployed encouraged this form of punitive self-scrutiny in AJ and the defensive attempts at deflection by Ashley. However, these practices and processes did not work to uncover the institutional limits to behaviours in this setting. Shutting down discussion may well have given the illusion of compliance and may even have changed their behaviours. However, it is unclear whether this action would have altered their attitudes towards women and/or prevent such behaviours occurring in other fields.

AJ apologized to Lauren but was still suspended. When it became clear that there were still divisions in the group over this, not surprisingly mostly along gender lines, a group meeting was called. AJ apologized once again but qualified this by indicating that others were guilty of worse behaviour – he was just the one that got caught. Toby echoed Andrew Sankey when he outlined the institutionally imposed limits of the field.

*Toby Puttock to Amos:* It's basically about growing up a bit and taking responsibility for your own future you know. We can open the doors as much as we want and unclog the entrance to let you in as early as possible and we're fucking doing everything we can but it's like the end of the day you guys have got to walk through it you know.

*Voice Over:* Amos's bad attitude has led to poor marks and even without this latest issue passing TAFE was always going to be touch and go.

[A meeting is held with trainees and Toby to heal divisions in the group.]

*Amos:* first off sorry to all of youse if anything affected you in any way whatsoever. Lauren mostly. I'm not pushing the blame but I wasn't the only one doing it you know. I've seen people do it. I've seen people do worse [Lauren nodding]. I was the one that happened to have got pulled up at the time and look that was dumb, that was stupid. I learnt from it so. Learn from that.

*Toby Puttock:* What has to be understood is that this is the same in any job. It's not tolerated whether you slap somebody on the arse and they're not offended someone else might get offended and go and complain to the boss.

*Voice Over:* Toby's words are falling on deaf ears with some of the boys still unhappy with Amos's punishment.

*Ashley:* Is it a sackable offence though? Because he's basically getting sacked for something that's been accepted by the victim.

*Lauren:* I didn't accept it at the time ...

*Ashley:* But since then he's apologised and you said you accepted the apology.

*Lauren:* But I don't think it should be responsible on the person it happened to. I think that act in itself is so degrading that it should never be accepted in a work place.

*Toby Puttock:* Ash if I can jump in. It's not tolerated, won't be tolerated, won't be tolerated at Fifteen and ... [AJ – having trouble keeping his emotions in check]. It's certainly not tolerated here. And there's

> a process for dealing with all this kind of stuff. Yeah and the process
> is they've put an investigation and this is how they deal with it. Until
> he's cleared on the investigation he can't come here.
>
> > (*Jamie's Kitchen Australia*, Episode Six, Broadcast on
> > Channel 10 Melbourne, 19 October 2006)

Lauren demonstrated a sophisticated understanding of the dynamics
of sexual harassment – an ever-present possibility in women's fields of
possibility – and the limits and imperatives of the role she was unwill-
ingly forced into: you must not be silent; you have a right to be upset and
there is no one 'right way' to demonstrate this; it is not your fault, you
do not blame the victim. Some of the boys obviously found it difficult
to be reflexive about the institutionally sanctioned modes of performing
masculinity and femininity. Shifting between fields, and the different
forms of gender relations that emerge from these different fields, requires
levels of self-knowledge and awareness that are not evident, or able to
be mobilized by, some of these young men.

> *Toby Puttock:* Rod?
>
> *Rodney:* But isn't that not accepting cultural diversity. Like if that
> was the culture ... [girls' voices raised] just listen. If that was the
> culture of a group of three or four mates where it was funny and
> quite acceptable ...
>
> *Toby Puttock:* Not in the work place.
>
> [Lauren visibly upset again and leaves the room.]
>
> *Rodney:* If it's part of your culture?
>
> *Toby Puttock:* So you're saying pinching people's arses is part of a
> culture? When you go to work you come to work. When you come
> to school you're there to study and ... [Chris follows Lauren saying
> something like 'You're an arse' and Erin stands up. AJ follows them.]
>
> *Ashley:* People make mistakes and they deserve a second chance.
>
> *Erin:* That's right. That's right but youse are all going on like it's not
> a big deal and it is. It's a big deal to Lauren and that's the point. If it
> was happening to you Ash ...
>
> *Toby Puttock:* How many girls are in this room right now is what
> you've got to look at right now as well. I think – there's five or six of
> you and 20 guys.

> *Chris (who has come back into the room):* I'm a male and I've made official complaints about guys in this group because of sexual harassment because I've seen plenty of males do stuff to females in this class. I've seen guys grab a female and not even apologise to her.
>
> *Lauren to Chris in corridor outside (visibly upset):* I know those comments weren't even that big but knowing what they were coming from. The deep seated things they were coming from. I've got to work with those people. That's just a bit hard to comprehend at this point in time. [Chris hugs her.] There are a few goodies out there.
>
> *(Jamie's Kitchen Australia*, Episode Six, Broadcast on Channel 10 Melbourne, 19 October 2006)

Rodney attempted to test the limits of the field by drawing on discourses of cultural diversity and the celebration of difference to justify their behaviour. His position represents the unfortunate flip-side of this discourse and is commonly used to promote the view that there is no *wrong* as long as you adhere to the, often unspoken or poorly articulated, rules of a particular 'culture'. However, Chris challenged this view, demonstrating knowledge of the rules that structure this field and practising the forms of emotional literacy required of the entrepreneurial self.

Connell and Messerschmidt (2005, pp. 849–50) have argued that hegemonic masculinity 'operates in the cultural domain as on-hand material to be actualised, altered, or challenged through practice in a range of different local circumstances' and is 'constituted in men's interaction with women'. This story of sexual harassment provides instances of all of these and demonstrates the unevenness of some of the processes and practices at a local level that contribute to the de- and re-traditionalization of gender relations.

## Hospitality doesn't do well with visible tattoos': on the limits of doing sexuality and gender differently in *Jamie's Kitchen*

> I think they see me as a thug. You know what I mean? Like someone who's just street all over.
>
> *(Jamie's Kitchen Australia*, Episode One, Broadcast in Australia on Channel 10, 14 August 2006)

> We come from violent pasts. We're not the normal Christian, or whatever, society like ...
>
> > (*Jamie's Kitchen Australia*, Episode Five, Broadcast on
> > Channel 10 Melbourne, 12 October 2006)

This is the audience's introduction to 24-year-old Kate (known as CJ) in the Australian series of *Jamie's Kitchen*. CJ's perception of the judgement of those selecting trainees comes from an awareness that she does not 'fit' with the 'female' norms of acceptable appearance and deportment. She has extensive and visible tattoos, her hair is short, she has a chunky build, she is loud and aggressive in voicing her opinions and she is a lesbian. At 24 she is also at the upper end of the age range for trainees.

> For the last two years I have been trying to get into hospitality but because I've got like the tattoo on the neck [a large gecko] ... hospitality doesn't do well with visible tattoos. Like I've got one there [pointing to wrist] and a big one on my arm. I get an overwhelming sense of depression because I really don't feel like I can fit into society because people don't allow me to and that's probably my biggest downfall.
>
> > (*Jamie's Kitchen Australia*, Episode One, Broadcast in
> > Australia on Channel 10 Melbourne, 14 August 2006)
>
> The way I speak isn't so elegant and the way I look isn't so ladylike.
> > (*Jamie's Kitchen Australia*, Episode Eight, Broadcast
> > on Channel 10 Melbourne, 2 November 2006)

Connell and Messerschmidt (2005, p. 851) have argued that 'Bodies participate in social action by delineating courses of social conduct' and as such they are 'both objects of social practice and agents of social practice'. While these claims are familiar, and well rehearsed in branches of sociology and feminist studies concerned with *bodies that matter*, CJ demonstrated an awareness of herself as an *object* of social practice born from bitter experience.

In our previous story on sexual harassment we quoted Clair Feig on what it takes, in her opinion, to be a successful female chef. This quote appeared in a recent article in the Melbourne *Age* entitled 'Making the cut', and the subheading stated 'It's hot, sweaty and you'll be judged just like the next man. Meet three female chefs who *can* stand the heat' (Lallo, 2007). In this short sentence we can discern that the norms and behaviours of successful chefs are masculine and success for women is judged in reference to these. However, there are contradictions evident here. A full-page photo of Feig appears under the bi-line and she is described in the article as looking 'like a supermodel' – 'Her appearance is striking: Amazonian physique, flawless complexion and spiky blonde hair' (p. 9). The photographer has posed her crouched down with legs apart like a frog preparing to jump, holding a very large cook's knife dangling between her legs, looking straight at the camera – looking straight at us. The challenge and the phallic symbolism are not hard to read off this image. The female chefs who are the subject of this article *can* stand the heat; the author's emphasis implying that there are plenty of others who can't. If, following Foucault (1985), we examine the ethical practices that govern the self, what is evident in these examples is that the 'ethical substance' of a successful chef is characterized by reference to particular hegemonic male dispositions (Connell and Messerschmidt, 2005). At the same time mediascapes rely on hyper-sexualized images to represent these women (Appadurai, 1996). You may well have to act like a man but you also need to look like an attractive woman.

When we meet her, CJ has been homeless for nine years and is currently living in supported accommodation provided by the Melbourne City Mission, an outreach service offered by Melbourne churches that provides welfare and education assistance to a range of marginalized people. Her father died of AIDS when she was six. CJ was expelled from four different schools between Years 7 and 10 and during this time she came under the supervision of the Department of Human Services and was made a ward of the state when she was 15 years old. She started using heroin around this time and has been clean for two and a half years. In Episode Eight she tells Jamie that she 'used to eat out of bins to stay alive' (*Jamie's Kitchen Australia*, Broadcast in Australia on Channel 10, 2 November 2006).

CJ makes it through the initial selection process but it is not long before she is making waves with the other trainees. In Episode Two the final 30 young people attend a camp on the Murray River in Victoria as part of the selection process and CJ decides she does not want to participate in a team-building exercise: 'What are we proving to ourselves? That we can go through rope?' – leaving her team one person down. Her attitude puts her offside with the rest of her team.

*Georgie:* She gave up. It was not a cool thing to do. She was sitting down and she was saying you know ... 'Why are you still going.'

> You know, what is the point of that? We are trying to get our team
> through and you're sitting on your arse and fucking pissing on us.
> (*Jamie's Kitchen Australia*, Episode Two, Broadcast
> on Channel 10 Melbourne, 21 September 2006)

Later at dinner CJ had heated words with Chris who was ahead of her in the line and apparently 'looked at her funny'. Later that night, and as part of her *rehabilitation*, CJ apologized to her team-mates: an example of reflexivity provoked by the need to conform to the demands of this field.

> I think these guys did a really, really, really good effort … like I actu-
> ally did crack the absolute wobblies and I got up and walked off and
> thought no this is a challenge that you can finish by yourselves and
> they did. Which I'm proud of you guys and I've said my apologies
> for cracking the shits because it's not really appropriate in the team
> effort. And today for now I think maybe I should practice more of
> my patience because I found that it wasn't there because I had no
> team spirit really but now we're just got to work together [applause
> from the rest of the trainees follows].
> (*Jamie's Kitchen Australia*, Episode Two, Broadcast
> on Channel 10 Melbourne, 21 September 2006)

CJ's volatility is an issue that surfaces at various times during the series despite Lauren Oliver's assertion that CJ is '100% committed' to managing 'some of that volatility and anger'.

> [Someone takes CJ's knife in the kitchen and she loses her cool. Toby
> Puttock has to talk to her.]
>
> *Voice Over:* CJ was placed in the streamers group on the condition
> that she work on managing some anger issues and right now she is
> finding it hard to control her temper.
>
> *CJ (sitting outside in the corridor – head in hands):* Just being around
> the smell and herbs and the food makes me feel sick.
> (*Jamie's Kitchen Australia*, Episode Three, Broadcast
> on Channel 10 Melbourne, 28 September 2006)

As well as anger management problems, CJ experienced problems attending classes and other commitments on a regular basis.

> *Judy Sanford (TAFE OH&S Teacher):* Kate rang in today to say she wouldn't be in class at all so ... It's only day 3 so I thought they would be all keen and eager.
>
> > *(Jamie's Kitchen Australia*, Episode Three, Broadcast in Australia on Channel 10, 28 September 2006)
>
> *Lauren Oliver (Director, Fifteen Australia):* It does worry me that she has a history of deciding ... she's very decisive about it. She tends to say, 'Look I'm sick I'm not coming in'. You can say 'Oh mate have you been to a doctor?' 'Oh I'm not going to make it to a doctor today'. She makes it sound like she's completely justified in doing that. She's made the decision and there's no discussion.
>
> > *(Jamie's Kitchen Australia*, Episode Ten, Broadcast on Channel 10 Melbourne, 16 November 2006)

When the trainees were assigned to Melbourne restaurants for two weeks' work experience CJ only managed to turn up for one full shift.

> *Jonathan Alston (head chef Scusa Mi Melbourne):* Unfortunately CJ has missed most of her placement here at Scusa Mi through what seems to be one drama or another drama. I think she hasn't come to the party. Hasn't absorbed herself in what we've offered her here.
>
> *Toby Puttock:* She's very smart CJ and she's telling him what he wants to hear but she ain't following through with the goods and mate this has happened and that's happened and it's all shocking but at the end of the day she's not doing it. She's not going there. And it comes from a woman who fucking screamed at me and said she's going to do this with my help or without my help and she's going to be a chef whether we like it or not type thing.
>
> > *(Jamie's Kitchen Australia*, Episode Eight, Broadcast on Channel 10 Melbourne, 2 November 2006)

As late as Episode Nine the team was still trying to handle this situation. In this episode Jamie was in Australia checking on operations and getting to know the trainees. He took the group to visit well-known Australian chef Stephanie Alexander and some of the students involved in her Collingwood Kitchen Garden Foundation but CJ failed to turn up. Jamie was told by one of the other trainees that she had hurt her fist punching something.

---

*Chris:* We got kicked off the last train and we had no way of getting home. She ended up losing it and punching a sign a couple of times.

*Voice Over:* CJ's aggression has been an issue throughout the course.

*Jamie:* So every time she gets a bit angry she punches something?

*Chris:* It's the first time I've seen it.

*Jamie:* What happens when we get in a busy kitchen? Hot oil and loads of stress?

[And later when she does not show for a media launch organized to publicise Fifteen Melbourne.]

*Jamie:* She's an intelligent girl but she's fucking self-destructive some-times. It's such a shame. I thought I was going to get to really bond with her while I was here cos on the first day it was incredible. She was amazing. Such an intelligent lovely girl.

*Voice Over:* After so many non-appearances CJ could be cut from the group. Fifteen Melbourne would consider that a failure. They want her to turn up.

(*Jamie's Kitchen Australia*, Episode Nine, Broadcast on Channel 10 Melbourne, 9 November 2006)

---

After Jamie talked to her on the phone she turned up to the launch after the meal, late and out of uniform.

There are hints throughout the series that CJ has a less than ideal existence outside the training environment. She has a young girlfriend whom she described as innocent and not used to the 'wild life' and we can only guess about her struggle with drugs. After blowing up yet again in the final episode after one of the younger trainees teased her about the camera, she confides to Glenn Flood (Training and Development chef) after he has taken her into the cool room for a chat in an effort to diffuse the situation.

---

*CJ:* There's a lot of things just going on outside the restaurant and there's fuck all I can do about it because I've got to be here.

> *CJ (later, voice to camera in a wry tone):* I'd like to make my fuse a little
> bit longer so it's not so short. The wicks not so short to explode. I
> think that I'd also like to improve in just social skills.
> > (*Jamie's Kitchen Australia*, Episode Ten, Broadcast on
> > Channel 10 Melbourne, 16 November 2006)

Much has been written about 'compulsory' heterosexuality (Rich, 1994) or the assumption of heterosexuality and the sexual binary system that constructs/produces homosexuality as the *dark side* of heterosexuality. As Quinlivan (2004) points out:

> The homosexual/heterosexual binary legitimates and normalises het-
> erosexuality, rendering same sex desire as abnormal. Binaries structure
> our ideas about sexuality and our expectations of sexual experience.
> The heterosexual part of the binary consists of taken for granted ideas
> and practices around sexuality, while homosexuality represents ideas
> and practices considered abnormal or 'special cases'.
> > (2004, p. 89)

While CJ's lesbianism is not marked as 'abnormal' by Jamie Oliver, the trainers or the other trainees (at least not on camera), it is produced as such by the very fact that we know her as 'the lesbian' in the series. The sexual identity of the other trainees goes un-remarked and therefore, without evidence to the contrary, the assumption is that they are hetero-sexual. This of course is not in and of itself a 'problem' but it becomes so in CJ's case because she does her gender differently.

Judith Butler (1990, pp. 3–24), in her theorization of sex/gender/desire, has questioned the distinctions between sex and gender arguing that, 'Gender ought not to be conceived merely as the cultural inscription of meaning on a pregiven sex; gender must also designate the very appar-atus of production whereby the sexes themselves are established.' She has also pointed out that race, class, ethnicity, sexuality and geograph-ical location intersect with gender ensuring that 'gender is not always constituted coherently or consistently in different historical contexts'. For Butler, although 'gender is not a noun' it is also not 'a set of free float-ing attributes' because the 'substantive effect of gender is performatively produced and compelled by the regulatory practices of gender coher-ence'. It is these regulatory practices that act as a limit experience for CJ in this context. Her choice to practise her freedom by performing her sex/gender outside the accepted norms of heterosexuality reduces and limits her options in the field of possibilities that is this highly regulated training environment.

Yet CJ seems to fit the representation of the ideal worker in commercial kitchens such as Ramsey and Bourdain's described earlier. She is not 'culinarily sophisticated'. She is loud, aggressive, opinionated, 'ballsy' and one of the 'boys' in the way she performs her gender. She is neither elegant, nor ladylike and the aggression she displays is not unlike that of the likes of Gordon Ramsay who has built his reputation and success on such behaviour. In Episode Six, however, CJ got the message that this was not behaviour that would see her experience success in *Jamie's Kitchen*. Given the kinds of interventions that the staff had organized for her before this, they are surprised that she had not picked up on it previously.

> *CJ:* I can't improve anymore. Like seriously ... So ... to hear this when there's no actual evidence ... Like what? My voice is loud. So what? In a kitchen don't you need to be loud? What am I meant to go? [whispers] 'Hot pot ... Hot pot'. What am I meant to do?
>
> *Lauren:* I'm sorry CJ I didn't expect the information to be unexpected. I thought you would look at it and say 'OK, maybe this has happened'.
>
> *CJ:* It is unexpected.
>
> (*Jamie's Kitchen Australia,* Episode Six, Broadcast in Australia on Channel 10, 9 October 2006)

For CJ the fact that she had tried was 'good enough' but also it should be pointed out that the messages she received were ambiguous. She was told that her forthright behaviour 'is great when you are a head chef' (Toby Puttock, Episode Six, *Jamie's Kitchen Australia*, Broadcast on Channel 10 Melbourne, 9 October 2006), but not when you are a trainee. This ambiguity is overlaid by the regulatory practices in service industries such as hospitality that work to produce workers of a particular type. Despite interventions in the training environment that encourage her to do certain work on herself (team-building in training camps, anger management sessions, time out, etc.) in order to fit the idea of the new enterprising/entrepreneurial worker, CJ failed to live up to expectations. She may have fitted well in the field of possibilities that is the macho work environment in commercial kitchens. But in the new service training environment where males are expected to be more like females (a form of de-traditionalization?) in terms of their motivations, behaviours, and emotions – something that the male trainees also struggled with – women who perform their gender in similar ways to those in Bourdain's kitchen, but are unable or unwilling to achieve a feminine appearance may be out of place.

Liz Egan, another female chef interviewed for Lallo's (2007, pp. 9–10) article, is convinced that 'If you work hard and treat people well, they'll respect you. It's as simple as that. It doesn't matter what your gender is.' Catriona Freeman, the third female chef interviewed, was quoted as saying, 'I don't even think of things in terms of being a boy or a girl. And I don't think many other people do these days', although 'she says not enough women consider becoming chefs'. Gender disadvantage is not something these female chefs think with (McLeod and Yates, 2006) because they have been successful in what is acknowledged as a male-dominated profession. In this sense they come to be examples of 'how-women-can-do' and therefore 'stand-ins for all women' (Wacjman, 1999, p. 110).

CJ's story highlights the fact that the achievement of normalized conformity is necessary to participate in globalized labour markets. These labour markets, and workplaces such as restaurant kitchens, are fields of possibility in which entrepreneurial forms of self are encouraged/compelled to take particular forms. These forms, we have argued, are gendered and in many instances are characterized by powerful, enduring traditional gender practices/norms (McLeod and Yates, 2006).

## Conclusion

The three stories we have represented on single motherhood, sexual harassment and gender/sexuality have been used to exemplify issues around diversity and difference in the service industry. The particular life histories of the trainees recruited for this social enterprise project make these issues more acute but they are nonetheless illustrative of issues faced by employers more generally.

The achievement of conformity in these fields holds out the promise of a precarious form of salvation in rationalized, globalized modernity. As our three narratives indicate, choosing not to conform, or failing to be able to conform can condemn the individual to marginalization, to *material* and *social oblivion* (Beck 1992). In these rationalized spaces the difference, in terms of consequences, is largely immaterial. The responsibility for conforming increasingly resides in the individual – with more and more aspects of the life course open to possible choice and risk, then responsibility for choosing, or not, to conform becomes individualized. Individualization processes increasingly locate the self as the space/site in which the paradoxes of globalized, rationalized capitalism are to be managed- or not. What fates, we might ask, await those who can't *make the cut*?

# 6

# Don't be a Smart Arse': (Neo)liberalism, Generation Y and the Achievement of Conformity

## Introduction

> *Peter Richards:* Don't be a smart arse. Because I know my work. I know my work because I know it's good. You know your work because at the moment it's crap. You're going to be doing this for real. You're going to be sending this out to somebody to eat and pay for and I wouldn't be prepared to pay for that.
>
> [Peter Richards, chef/lecturer, disciplining Dwayne Montford when he tried to substitute Peter's work example for his own, inferior, example.]
>
> (*Jamie's Kitchen*, Episode Two, Broadcast in Australia on Channel 10, 29 July 2003)

In Chapter 2 of this book we spent a significant amount of space examining, analysing and problematizing the ways in which young people are made known within a variety of spaces (policy, academic, community); in relation to a variety of purposes and ends (education, training, work); by a variety of individuals, organizations, agencies (Jamie Oliver, Fifteen Foundation, Education departments, employment agencies, NGOs). Much of that discussion was framed by the intent of locating the Fifteen Foundation training programme in particular historical, social, economic and technological contexts; and in the sorts of problematizations that make contemporary populations of young people knowable, manageable, governable in these contexts.

Indeed, the Foundation's own desire to re-problematize young people (*What's Right with these Young People*) speaks directly to the material and discursive possibilities, limitations and consequences (intended or otherwise) of rendering populations of young people knowable in particular ways.

In this chapter we want to return to the question/problem of young people in ways that connect to the contemporary *fetishization* of young people under 24 as belonging to Generation Y. A large part of these *fantasies* of generation (Walkerdine, 1997) are bound up with identifying, characterizing and describing the different behaviours and dispositions that are, apparently, evident in the latest generation to enter labour markets.

The Master's Apprentices belong to Generation Y. Jamie Oliver is a member of Generation X. So too are many of his colleagues. Interestingly, if we are to fetishize generation/age, most of Jamie Oliver's mentors and heroes are much older and of a different generation. Gennaro Contaldo, Ruth Rogers and Rose Gray, for example, are Baby Boomers through and through.

Our concerns in the discussion that follows are with the consequences that emerge when we fetishize age in our characterizations of populations, when we discount, or ignore completely, a range of other institutional structuring processes and forces that shape the fields of possibilities in which individuals and groups of particular ages (generations) live and lead their lives, make choices, practise their freedom, seek some sort of salvation. So, while we don't discount, entirely, the possibilities that emerge when we understand a population in generational terms we approach the following discussion with a sense of needing to explore the limits and possibilities of the concept of Generation Y.

In this context we will review characterizations of Generation Y, and explore suggestions that Generation Y's orientations to paid work, its purposes, the roles it plays in a lifecourse, the meanings that attach to it, mark this generation as being significantly different to prior generations. Apparently, Generation Y lacks a good old-fashioned work ethic. This lack, it is claimed, is evidenced by the demands from Generation Y that work has meaning and purpose, is interesting and fun. And if it isn't, if it is boring, menial or there seems to be little reason to do it, then Generation Y, so the argument goes, will not perform, will question – even confront – managers and supervisors, will walk away. As the Master's Apprentices begin their training there is some evidence that these members of Generation Y may indeed lack such a work ethic: although, as our discussion has suggested, a lack of opportunity, support, and choice may be bigger deficits in these young people's lives.

Following this discussion we want to locate Generation Y (the trainees) in particular historical, cultural and social settings. Again, the possibilities here are diverse, and could take any number of orientations. Continuing the themes introduced via our engagements with Foucault's understandings of power/knowledge/subjects and government we will draw on governmentality studies of (Neo)Liberalism (or advanced liberalism) to suggest that across diverse global, national, local, organizational and institutional settings/spaces particular understandings of the *individual as enterprise* shape a variety of programmes, practices, processes that seek to regulate and provoke a variety of human behaviours and dispositions.

We will give a particular structure to this discussion through the idea that conformity – *Don't be a smartarse!* – is an achievement. By this we mean that we are all subject to various demands, pressures, encouragements to develop a self that is employable, that can provide us with the means to secure salvation – however tenuously – in the individualized, globalized labour markets of the twenty-first century. Given these expectations we are interested in examining the capacity of a self to conform to these expectations, to develop a sense of self, and forms of self-understanding and self-regulation that enable this conformity to occur, to appear as natural.

It can be argued that it is only when large numbers of people do not conform – willingly, or because of an incapacity to do so – that we become aware that conformity is an achievement, is, indeed, a choice, is a consequence of the ongoing practice of freedom in more or less limited fields of possibilities. Within (Neo)Liberal governmentalities the responsibility for conforming increasingly resides in the individual. With more and more aspects of the lifecourse – the DIY project of the self – open to a variety of possible choices and risks, then responsibility for choosing, or not, to conform becomes individualized. Importantly, we will suggest that individualization processes increasingly locate the self as the space/site in which the tensions, risks, contradictions, and paradoxes of globalized, rationalized capitalism are to be resolved and managed – or not.

## Don't be a smart arse: conforming in Jamie's Kitchen

*Jamie:* But the reality is I am going to inherit them very shortly and I've got to open up a first class London restaurant open to all the press who are going to have their knives out and I'm still going to have to worry about is Pizzey going to season that salad just right? When they're filleting a 100lb piece of fish are they not going to care

> and just slip or have they got a blunt knife. There are so many things that can go wrong so to say that I'm nervous is a complete under statement. This has always been about training unemployed people to a really professional level. I want them to be employable. I'm not doing them any favours by laying down the red carpet and giving them an easy ride. You know if there is dead wood in the group holding it back you know I have to deal with it.
>
> [Jamie Oliver talking about the risks he faces as a social entrepreneur in attempting to train young people who possess, or display few of the dispositions and skills the industry/job demands.]
>
> (*Jamie's Kitchen*, Episode Two, Broadcast in Australia on Channel 10, 29 July 2003)

As we have suggested throughout this book much of the drama that made *Jamie's Kitchen* and *Jamie's Kitchen Australia* such compelling viewing for many millions of viewers around the globe centred on the apparent inability of many of the trainees to conform to the demands and expectations of Oliver, his colleagues and institutions such as vocational education and training colleges. Again, we have been at pains to point out an acute awareness that much of this drama is manufactured, is a selective representation designed to encourage us to watch, and to establish a relationship with key figures/characters in this drama. We are meant to care for the likes of Dovid, Kat, Dwayne and Michael. We are meant to wonder why they appear to be not making the most of the opportunities they are being presented with. If we care then we will watch.

Given the manufactured nature of these relationships and representations, we have indicated that what we witness in these shows does, indeed, *ring true* at a variety of levels when our concern is with identifying and analysing the forms of work-related personhood we are all expected to develop and cultivate; and the difficulties many have with producing, sustaining, and performing these versions of the self.

Within different fields of possibility diverse technologies and practices of the self require us to practise our freedom – make choices – in ways that conform to the variety of expectations, suggestions, demands that emerge from and give shape to these fields. These demands to conform often have a range of consequences for both those who can or are willing to conform, and for those who can't or won't. Often, too, we may not be aware, at a rational, cognitive level, of what these consequences might be; though processes of individualization and reflexivity in these settings will locate responsibility for knowing these risks, these consequences, in the individual. We may have a fair idea that there are consequences, but not all of these are readily identified or managed. In continuing to choose to act in ways that others might identify as being risky or *asking for trouble* we can appear as foolhardy, or as not being concerned with what the consequences might be. Again, as we have discussed in previous chapters, these choices, these practices of the self often exist in tension with changing expectations that emerge as we shift, or move within and between different fields of possibility in the ongoing conduct of our lives.

The point here is that conformity is an active accomplishment or achievement, and the range of positive and/or negative consequences that flow from conformity are not, themselves, self-evident. These too need to be learned. These too are outcomes of developing forms of self-understanding and reflexivity in relation to the character of different fields of possibility in which we are situated or find ourselves.

In both series of *Jamie's Kitchen* there are many episodes and instances in which this apparent unwillingness or inability to conform to the demands and expectations of work and training spaces places young trainees in situations and relations that put their ongoing participation at risk. As viewers, we can see this; it is pretty self-evident. Yet, in many of these instances the young trainees apparently don't get that their behaviours will have consequences which they might not actually want. Dwayne, for example, continues to *take the piss out* of trainers and fellow trainees. He appears to not be capable of taking the situation and its expectations seriously. He has an inkling of a range of possible consequences, but he does not seem to be willing or able to conform to the expectations and demands that give shape to institutionalized training and workspaces.

> *Peter Richards:* I have doubts about Dwayne. I was bloody angry because he was taking the piss out of me. Now he doesn't need to do that [Dwayne pokes his hand into the chef's hat when he is judging his food]. Now he doesn't need to do that. I give him far more than he gives me. All I expect him to give me is commitment and I've told him this.
>
> *Dwayne:* When I started, I started off crap cos I was messing about, mucking around. Doing things I shouldn't be doing and then I had this big talk with chef and he told me I had to pick up or I'm coming

> off the course. Sometimes I go too far on the funny side ... If I got kicked off the course I would never be able to live with myself.
>
> *Voice Over:* What would you end up doing?
>
> *Dwayne:* I don't know. It would make me think that I am shit so I would end up doing something shit like working in a crappy restaurant. It would bring me down basically.
>
> > (*Jamie's Kitchen*, Episode Two, Broadcast in Australia on Channel 10, 29 July 2003)

In the previous chapter we discussed in some detail AJ's apparent inability to *pull his head in*, to conform to the expectations of Andrew Sankey, or Toby Puttock, or to the regulations of training institutions in relation to proper modes of conduct towards fellow trainees – the female trainees in particular. Indeed, AJ was vocal in his assertions that he would not change, even if it meant he would not succeed on the terms demanded by Fifteen and the training institution. And, of course, he didn't conform and he didn't succeed.

> *AJ:* So I have to change to suit your needs?
>
> *Andrew Sankey:* No. You have to change to fit into everybody else's needs. Otherwise all of your life you're going to be an aggressive little punk in a society that doesn't want you there like that. It doesn't work that way in a kitchen. There's no room for behaviour where you think 'Fuck you all, I'm out of here'.
>
> *AJ:* You can't change five or six years of my life in what ... two weeks.
>
> *Andrew Sankey:* I'm not asking you to change now in the next five seconds. I'm asking you to take this on board and over the next six weeks you do have to change otherwise I won't pass you.
>
> *AJ:* That's your choice.
>
> *Andrew Sankey:* No it's your choice. I'm asking you to develop as a person. As a human.
>
> *AJ:* I'm telling you right now I am not going to change just for something like that so then it's your choice whether you pass me or not.
>
> > (*Jamie's Kitchen Australia*, Episode Four, Broadcast in Australia on Channel 10, 5 October 2006)

In that chapter we also discussed another *problem child*: CJ and her loud, aggressive, sometime violent performances of self in work and training spaces that, quite rightly, cannot allow these sorts of behaviours and dispositions. Again, our discussion there pointed to forms of self-understanding on CJ's part that positioned her in conflict or tension with the demands of these different fields of possibility. And this reflexivity seemed more or less developed at different points. In one instance a public apology and reflection on her behaviours was a condition imposed on her by the organization to enable her to continue in the programme.

> *CJ:* I think these guys did a really, really, really good effort ... like I actually did crack the absolute wobblies and I got up and walked off and thought no this is a challenge that you can finish by yourselves and they did. Which I'm proud of you guys and I've said my apologies for cracking the shits because it's not really appropriate in the team effort. And today for now I think maybe I should practice more of my patience because I found that it wasn't there because I had no team spirit really but now we're just got to work together [applause from the rest of the trainees follows].
> *(Jamie's Kitchen Australia,* Episode Two, Broadcast in Australia on Channel 10, 21 August 2006)

Yet, on another occasion CJ's self-awareness and understanding appeared to be lacking as Fifteen cut her from the main group of trainees on account of her limited capacity to transform herself, and her anger and aggressiveness.

> *CJ:* I can't improve anymore. Like seriously ... So ... to hear this when there's no actual evidence ... Like what? My voice is loud. So what? In a kitchen don't you need to be loud? What am I meant to go? [whispers] 'Hot pot ... Hot pot'. What am I meant to do?
> *Lauren:* I'm sorry CJ I didn't expect the information to be unexpected. I thought you would look at it and say 'OK, maybe this has happened'.
> *CJ:* It is unexpected.
> *(Jamie's Kitchen Australia,* Episode Six, Broadcast in Australia on Channel 10, 9 October 2006)

There are any number of other examples and instances that we might discuss here. Not all would necessarily focus on those trainees who fail to conform in aggressive, loud, confrontational ways. Indeed, someone like Dovid appears unable to conform to expectations not because he is loud, aggressive, confrontational, but because he lacks a sense of his abilities or capacities to the extent that he is unable or unwilling to put himself on the line in these training and work environments. His sense of self does not allow him to perform the tasks and the forms of self that these spaces demand.

> *Dovid speaking to camera:* I'm trying my best but something keeps holding me back. You know what I mean? You can just tell. People get frustrated you know. They show you something that's so easy you know. Something a five year old can do this guy here can't even do something a five year old can do. So fuck ...
>
> *Head Chef Adrian Richardson to camera:* It seems like he's kicking himself. He doesn't want to fail. He's scared that people might think he's an idiot.
>
> (*Jamie's Kitchen Australia*, Episode Seven, Broadcast in Australia on Channel 10, 26 October 2006)

As we witnessed in *Jamie's Kitchen Australia*, Dovid's journey of self-transformation developed forms of self-understanding that eventually allowed him to make the choices that work and training spaces expect. He developed a self that has the capacity to choose to conform. And he chooses to conform because conformity in these contexts holds out the promise that he will develop meaning and purpose in a life that, until this point, seemed to have little purpose beyond precarious and uncertain survival on the margins, on the rubbish heaps, of rationalized, globalized modernity.

Our purpose in revisiting a number of these incidents in the context of this present discussion is to question whether, as some commentators on Generation Y have suggested, this apparent unwillingness to conform to various expectations and demands of work and training environments is a generational characteristic of 16–24-year-olds – that cohort of the population who are the most recent entrants into the labour markets of twenty-first-century, flexible capitalism. Much of this commentary appears to suggest that Generation Y understand themselves, understand work, understand other dimensions of their lives in ways that are both different to prior generations, and have some generalizable coherence that emerges from the shared experience of being born between 1978 and 1994.

## Thinking about Generation Y: problematizing youth at the turn of the millennium

In Chapter 1 we discussed, in some detail, Michael Pizzey's difficulties in maintaining his commitment and passion for the training he was expected to do in *Jamie's Kitchen* – difficulties that translated into a number of interventions by Jamie Oliver and/or his colleagues and teachers in the training institution. At the time of one of these interventions Michael confessed to Oliver that the mundane, routine, repetitive nature of much of his training was making him bored. As the following exchange indicates this attitude left Oliver mystified.

[The following scene is an exchange between Michael Pizzey and Jamie Oliver in the living room of Michael Pizzey's house.]

*Jamie:* So what's going on then?

*Michael Pizzey:* I'm just totally … I'm just bored at the moment.

*Jamie:* Bored?

*Michael Pizzey:* Yeah, because nothing really exciting is happening.

*Jamie:* Right, what do you mean by that?

*Michael Pizzey:* Well, my colleagues were cooking and enjoying it, and some of the staff [inaudible] doing it all over again, but when it comes to Mondays and all we do is parcel these boxes upstairs … It's just not really exciting me much.

*Jamie:* Unfortunately, the start is always the most boring. We're only two months away from opening the restaurant. Our restaurant. You know what I mean, I just think it's a real, I mean, at the end of the day I'd be really disappointed in myself if we lost you at this point, because we haven't started cooking yet. You know sometimes things in life are a bit boring …

*Michael Pizzey:* I know that, if I do basically quit, I've just wasted three months … And I'm going to disappoint a lot of people.

*Jamie (in car, to camera):* I don't know what to say really, I'm quite shocked, I thought he was going to give me a whole load of reasons why he didn't want to do the course. But I was bombarded with the one thing, which is, 'I was bored.' I like the boy, I want him to do well, that's why I came all the way out here to sort him out. He's being a fucking baby.

(*Jamie's Kitchen*, Episode 3, Broadcast in Australia on Channel 10, 5 August 2003)

Peter Sheahan is a Generation Y'er. He has also made a significant, commercially profitable name for himself as an Australian-based management consultant who specializes in advice on the nature and characteristics of Generation Y. The jacket notes for Sheahan's *Generation Y: Thriving and Surviving with Generation Y at Work* (2005) offer glowing testimonials from business leaders and academics to the *compelling, engaging, accessible* insights that he offers into the 'secrets to hiring, inspiring and most importantly retaining this emerging generation'. For example, James Millar (CEO, Ernst and Young) suggests that Sheahan's accounting of/for the generation born between 1978 and 1994 'provides practical, commonsense advice and solutions to winning the war for young talent; addressing head-on the challenges of attracting, managing and holding on to this new breed of talent'. Moreover, claims Millar, the book 'provides a refreshingly honest and eye-opening read for those of us who may be grappling to understand the mindset of this unique post-modern generation'. For Margaret Beerworth (Director, CPA Australia), Sheahan's insights provide a 'toolbox' of 'tips to make life less complicated when dealing with and understanding the younger generation. For my mind, this is critical stuff if you want to be an employer of choice for Generation Y.' Lest we think that we can easily dismiss these various reviews as marketing *fluff* from business figures who deal in surface impressions and effects as legitimate currency on a daily basis, Professor John Worthington of the School of Architecture, University of Sheffield claims that Sheahan, 'in a fast, direct, iconoclastic style, defines the expectations and actions of his generation': a generation that is more than a 'cohort of the population born between 1978 and 1994 – it represents an attitude of mind which will increasingly pervade all generations as E information and communications technologies become ubiquitous.'

These testimonials and recommendations are as effusive as any author would want as their book went to market. In some respects they create – if we can take them at least a little seriously – a series of expectations in prospective readers that might be difficult to deliver on. For some, the book will deliver on expectations – those looking for *tips*, for a *tool box*, for certain understandings given particular purposes may very well find them in the pages of Sheahan's book. And we can readily agree that there are many individuals, groups and organizations that have many and varied interests in the cohort identified as Generation Y. Indeed, in July 2007, if you 'Googled' Generation Y you would have returned approximately 118,000,000 hits in 0.12 seconds. If that number means anything at all in a global environment characterized by information overload it is, at the least, indicative of interest in the term, the population, and the values, beliefs, and ideas that the cohort brings with it to education, training, work, consumption, relationships, cultural production. In terms of what that volume of hits might mean, we 'Googled' Paris Hilton to test for interest in a particular figure that could reasonably be expected to attract interest in cyberspace. Paris, the embodiment, the personification of celebrity, of being famous for being famous, and, hence, likely to figure prominently in the often banal, superficial virtual firmament of the World Wide Web, *only* returned 67,600,000 hits. Gen Y trumps Paris! Except that Paris is Gen Y, and Gen Y has an apparently insatiable appetite to consume Paris!

In the Introduction to his text Sheahan tells a story about the experience of his first real job: a story that is meant to indicate that he knows Generation Y and what this generation thinks about work – especially work or training or induction/orientation programmes that are routine, mundane, boring.

> It's unlike me to fall asleep in anything, least of all the orientation program for my first 'real' job (whatever that's supposed to mean). But there I was, sound asleep, awoken only by a sharp pain in my ribs. It was the elbow of my fellow recruit sitting next to me.
> 'Wake up, the speaker's looking at you.'
> I'd begun to snore ever so slightly. Why? I was bored. I'd dozed off thinking that in the interview they'd assured me their accounting firm was a vibrant and energetic place to work. Clearly, the orientation program did not match the promise. After just 24 hours I was tempted to make a career change, but I decided that just because the orientation program was boring, it didn't mean the job would be.
> (Peter Sheahan, 2005, *Generation Y: Thriving and Surviving with Generation Y at Work*, p. vii)

This initial experience of what was supposed to be a challenging, exciting, passion-provoking job in a successful, professional environment failed to stimulate Sheahan. This lack of stimulation resulted in what Sheahan goes on to claim is characteristic of the engagement/relation between many Generation Y workers and work organizations – bored Gen Yers have a tendency to walk!

> So I persevered. For eight days. That was it. I couldn't stand another minute. The final straw was when an accountant in my division

handed me about 350 numbered pages and asked me to renumber them in green.

'But they're already numbered,' I said.

'Yes, but we need them numbered in green.'

'Why? What's wrong with black?'

'Nothing. We just need them numbered in green.'

'Yeah, but why?'

'Because'.

"Because' is not an answer.'

'Listen, this is just the way we do things around here!'

And that was it. I left the papers on the desk, grabbed my meagre personal belongings and went to my manager's office. I thanked him, let him know that I appreciated the opportunity but had decided it wasn't for me.

'But you've only been here for eight days' he said. 'No-one's ever left after just eight days.'

(Peter Sheahan, 2005, *Generation Y: Thriving and Surviving with Generation Y at Work*, pp. vii–viii)

Peter Sheahan claims to be emblematic of what he identifies as *talented* Generation Y'ers. Michael Pizzey is a Gen Y'er too. But for Sheahan, Michael would be representative of what he calls *labour* – although at this stage Michael isn't even labour. As Sheahan (2005, pp. 2–6) argues, his characterization is focused on that particular section of Generation Y that he suggests 'represents "talent" in the workplace'. For Sheahan there are 'plenty of other, probably less glamorous characteristics of those Generation Y'ers who are representative of what I would call "labour", not talent'. At first glance Sheahan might well be talking here about distinctions between the trainees in *Jamie's Kitchen*, and other 16–24-year-olds who are successful in education, training and work. He confirms this view by claiming that his book 'is NOT designed to give you insight into the mindset of the lowest common denominator. It is concerned with those Generation Y'ers who will be the target of professional organisations.' Indeed, in many respects this is a trend in many characterizations of Generation Y. Rebecca Huntley's *The World According to Y: Inside the New Adult Generation* (2006), for example, also over-represents the values, beliefs, behaviours and dispositions of what might be called the successful, middle-class members of this population.

The issue at this stage is what, or who, are we taking about when we discuss Generation Y, and at what level of generalization or simplification are we operating when we participate in these discussions? Christopher Scanlon (2006), in a small article entitled 'Gen X, Gen Y – it's generation con, actually', touches on a number of our concerns here. Scanlon, a research fellow at Royal Melbourne Institute of Technology (RMIT) University's Globalism Institute, wondered why so many supposedly *intelligent* journalists continue to serve up the 'marketing tosh' characteristic of so much commentary on Generation Y 'without a hint of criticism'. His argument is that we have come to know, understand and think about Generation Y largely through the findings of market researchers and the subsequent marketing campaigns of the many and varied products/service/images that see and understand Generation Y as their *natural* demographic. So, argues Scanlon, we are presented with representations of Generation Y that point out that the cohort has been nurtured in contexts 'saturated by media and technology'. As a result, by 'age eight they've consumed more images and information than any previous generation'. As a consequence of being technology and media *savvy*, of being highly educated, of living complex lives and negotiating shifting and multiple identities, Generation Y 'know the standard repertoires of the ad-men and can guess the punchline of an ad before its finished'. These media–savvy individuals, these generationally determined and defined behaviours and dispositions, so the argument goes, mean the marketing agencies 'don't know which way to jump', and if such organizations do 'manage to corner' Generation Y, they 'have their work cut keeping them'.

For Scanlon, one of the problems with this generalization of generations is that similar characterizations have been made of Generation X, and the Baby Boomers before them. So, to use Scanlon's example, Generation X has historically been classified as more tech- and media-savvy than prior generations, and more knowledgeable and critical of media culture. Sprite soft drink marketed itself in the 1990s to Generation X through the following slogan: *Image is Nothing. Thirst is Everything. Obey your Thirst.* For the Baby Boomers the 1960s and 1970s saw a host of brands vying to position themselves as hip and cool for and to a generation that was made knowable as more sophisticated, free-thinking, revolutionary, experimental than prior generations. Scanlon points to the flimsy nature of many of these generalizations and their tendency to melt away under the merest hint of a critical, sociological gaze. At one level we would heartily agree with this contention. At another level,

*Table 1.1*   Generational influences

| Influence | Baby Boomer | Generation X | Generation Y |
|---|---|---|---|
| Role models | Men of character | Men and women of character? | What is character? |
| Television | I Love Lucy | Happy Days | Jerry Springer |
| Musical icons | Elvis Presley | Madonna | Eminem |
| Music mediums | LPs and EPs | Cassettes and CDs | Digital (iPods and MP3s) |
| Computer games | Pong | Pacman | Counter Strike |
| Money | Earn it | It is not everything | Give it to me |
| Loyalty to employer | Work my way to the top | Shortcut to the top | Give me Saturday off or I'll quit |
| Respecting your elders' sex | Automatic | Is polite | Whatever! |
| | After marriage | On the backseat | Online |
| Change | Resist it | Accept it | Want it |
| Justice | Always prevails | Up to the courts | If you can afford it |
| Technology | Ignorant of it | Comfortable | Feel it in their gut |

*Source*: Based on Sheahan, 2005, p. 4.

however, we think that the fetishization of generation requires a more considered discussion and analysis.

Sheahan's (2005) ideas about generation are framed by a particular understanding of human nature. Indeed, it should be apparent that if generation is seen as a marker that is capable of characterizing attitudes, behaviours and values, then these behaviours and dispositions are understood as being largely influenced by social, historical, economic and political contexts, and not by genetic and biological differences. Generation Y is different to other generations not because of genetic mutation, but because they have developed a sense of self in environments that are markedly different from prior generations. At least that is what Sheahan (2005, pp. 3–4), and others who formulate these generalizations of generation, would insist: 'It is logical, then, that groups of people born around the same time will have similar characteristics. Why? Because certain social, cultural, economic and technological environments remain relatively consistent for pockets of time.' Sheahan argues that these pockets of time and the important processes, relations and influences in them, 'can be used to define a generation'.

For Sheahan (2005, p. 4) this characterization of the social, economic and technological transformations since the 1960s – 'the world in 1960, compared to the world today, is so far apart you could scarcely believe it was the same place' – proves that it is 'simply impossible that teenagers today are like any teenage generations that have gone before'. It is possible to agree with this statement at a number of levels – even allow-ing for the gross simplifications presented in his frame of reference. We too have suggested that labour markets, education and training, technological developments and any number of other processes have profoundly reshaped the fields of possibility in which young people grow up. However, we question the assumption that mezzo- and macro-levels of various social, economic, political, cultural and technological pro-cesses translate directly into the more or less uniform shaping of the hearts and minds of individuals of a particular age range – without any intervention or contradictory or paradoxical mediation by such things as social class relations, gender relations, the geographical spaces you are born into and grow up in, or the nature of family/caregiver settings, let alone that these large-scale processes are often more heterogeneous than homogeneous, and may, indeed, be uneven in their unfolding, their outcomes and consequences, and the experience of them in different configurations of time/space/place.

So, Sheahan glosses over the complexities and contradictions that shape any historical period to suggest that in the years between 1978 and 1994 the Western world witnessed an *echo-boom* in which large numbers of the so-called Baby Boomer generation had children. This echo-boom resulted in substantial and significant increases in birth rates. By some accounts Generation Y represents the largest generational cluster since the Baby Boomers themselves. Huntley (2006, pp. 10–12), for exam-ple, cites figures which suggest that in the US, Generation Y, comprising 70 million young people, is three times larger than Generation X. She also claims that this *super-size* generation is not as large in Australia, where, according to her sources, there are 1,119,755 young people aged between 18 and 25, compared with 2,025,351 in the 26–39-year-old age bracket that comprises Generation X. As an aside there is no hint from Huntley that she has missed the difference in age spread between X and Y, or that she doesn't count young people under 18 in calculating the size of Generation Y. Instead, she moves on from this accounting to claim that: 'this million-plus will form the bulk of the adult population within the next 20 years and may steamroll Gen-Xers in the process ... Generation Y's sheer size will make sure it makes its mark in the world in a way Generation X never did'. On the back of this sort of claim she, as many others have done, suggests that we 'will have to understand their mindset in order to navigate our own future'.

It is to this characterization of mindset that we now turn. Again, the challenge is to actually keep up with the flood of theories/models/descriptions that claim some authority to reveal and translate the nature of Generation Y's mindset. For example, in the last weeks of completing this book two more significant reports on Generation Y came across our desks: one on the educational and work pathways of members of Generation Y from low socio-economic backgrounds in Australia; the other from a multinational financial services organization on the financial attitudes, habits and practices of Generation Y (AMP, 2007; Smith Family, 2007). Given this flood of information we want to suggest that Sheahan's work is largely illustrative of the ground that is covered in many of these characterizations of the hearts and minds, behaviours and dispositions of Generation Y. In this sense it is appropriate to spend time outlining the ways that he problematizes Generation Y.

## Generation Y: street smart

Sheahan (2005, pp. 7–17) argues that Generation Y is 'mature in a way no other generation has been'. They are more enterprising, more resourceful, more educated, more instrumental/pragmatic, more street smart: 'They are not naïve', claims Linda Potter from Lion Nathan Australia. The positive dimensions to these characteristics, are, for Sheahan, self-evident, but pose challenges for business and managers to regulate these tendencies in directions that facilitate and promote organizational efficiencies and performance. Digital information and communication technologies, and the environments they have created and transformed, have played an important role in shaping this apparent energetic, pragmatic, enterprising instrumentality – information overload means that only that which is useful is valued.

## Generation Y: lifestyle centred

For Sheahan (2005, pp. 28–42) Generation Y has an orientation to work and its place in life that locates a personal, individualized style of life as most important: 'They want all the success and all the money that a career offers, but unlike the Baby Boomers, they are not prepared to give their life to get it.' For Sheahan there are two, possibly contradictory, orientations to work that are discernible in this generation. Work will largely be an instrumental means to achieve the end of fashioning a particular style of life. Or work will give a purpose, a meaning, a passion to life – if only members of the generation can find vocation, or, as Sheahan calls it, their *occupassion* (more on this in our concluding chapter).

## Generation Y: independently dependent

According to Sheahan (2005, pp. 43–8) Generation Y wants the best of both worlds: members want to be free to pick and choose and to be able to fashion the life that they desire, but they want material and emotional support while they do it: 'Generation Y want independence with strings'. We might say that *they want to work with a safety net.* 'They want to be free to have their own thoughts and views, to do their own things and make their own rules, but they want their parents to pay for their rent, their food, their education, and help them financially while they are doing it.' In the workplace, suggests Sheahan, this tendency plays out in demands from Generation Y for mentoring (not *bossing*), for emotional management (*They need stroking and nurturing* – Trish Rodley, MarcEdward Agency), for *empowerment*, for opportunities for *decision making,* and for *resourcing* to do the job.

## Generation Y: informal

Generation Y has, apparently, taken *youthful arrogance* to new levels: an arrogance that is evident in a lack of respect for rank/status; for established ways of doing things that do not appear as practical, useful, relevant; for *formality.* Sheahan (2005, pp. 49–59) argues that this generation have been encouraged to express their opinions, ideas and thoughts – considered or not. They have been raised by Baby Boomer parents who might wonder at 'just how upfront their children' have become: 'There is certainly just cause for Boomers thinking Generation Y are rude, and I suppose by traditional standards they are. However, I don't believe they are intending to be.' Rather, suggests Sheahan, 'I think it is just what they have learnt to be.' This informality, argues Sheahan, poses problems for managers at any number of levels, including customer relations, communication, appearance and non-conformity.

## Generation Y: tech savvy

Sheahan (2005, pp. 59–62) understands technology here as referring to micro-processor-based digital information and communication technologies. The myriad applications of these technologies have reshaped, transformed and constructed new material and virtual spaces. Generation Y is, apparently, at home in these spaces, and considers that technology and its application will provide solutions to any number of problems: from how to find information on something ('Google' it), to how to deal with climate change.

## Generation Y: stimulus junkies

> *I'm bored.*
> (Peter Sheahan, Generation Y management consultant/guru)
>
> *I'm bored.*
> (Michael Pizzey, Generation Y trainee (unsuccessful)
> in *Jamie's Kitchen*)

For Sheahan (2005, pp. 63–71): 'Generation Y are addicted to stimulation in the same way a drug addict is addicted to drugs. It becomes part of them. They have to have it and they go AWOL if they don't get it.' As Sheahan suggests, the 'opposite of stimulation is boredom'. This is a major issue for motivating and retaining Generation Y as many of the jobs that are available for 16–24-year-olds are, largely, 'repetitive, well-systemised ... In other words, Boring! If you can't keep Generation Y entertained, you can't keep them.' According to Sheahan the major drivers of this insatiable appetite for stimulation are electronic, digital, interactive and accessible: the www, mobile platforms (phones, games, iPods), film, TV – the entire range of options in what is effectively, for Generation Y, an *Entertainment Age*, not an *Information Age*.

## Generation Y: Sceptical

Here Sheahan (2005, pp. 72–80) describes a generation that has been immersed in an environment that has been trying to sell them something – or their parents something to do with them – since birth: 'a Generation Y Australian child is seeing 22,000 advertisements per year directed at selling to them. That is insane'. This exposure, and the inevitable failures of individuals, organizations, services, and products to deliver on what they promise has produced a 'natural inclination to question everything ... They have a built-in bullshit meter on their forehead, which rings loudly at any insincerity, ulterior motive or dishonesty.' However, if Generation Y can overcome doubt and scepticism in relation to a product, an employer, a manager, an organization then they 'will be committed, loyal and positive'. This scepticism is seen as healthy and enables them to remain an optimistic generation in the face of exposure to the foibles, failures and duplicities of role models, celebrities, idols, politicians, loved ones.

## Generation Y: impatient

> Burger flipping is not beneath your dignity. Your grandparents had a different name for it; they called it opportunity.
>
> (Bill Gates)

For Sheahan (2005, pp. 81–91) this comment, attributed to Gates but not verifiable as having been said by him, is a *great line*: a line that highlights what he sees as the impatience of Generation Y. They 'do not want to start at the bottom. They despise the very thought of it. They want to start at least in the middle.' The key factor here, suggests Sheahan, is that Generation Y has grown up in an environment in which a sense of time and speed have been transformed. We now think of ourselves as being time rich and/or poor. We have little or no time (inclination) to wait – for the computer to boot up or to process something; for the lift; for traffic lights/queues; to prepare food; for a career to develop; for anything. We place little value in the idea that something worth having might be something worth waiting for. Again, the idea of global, instant, 24/7 access to anything and everything has been, apparently, a powerful shaping influence on Generation Y's orientations to many aspects of a life.

So, what are we to make of these characterizations? At one level they may appear superficial, and as simplified generalizations. At this level the danger is that they appear as caricatures. At another level these understandings attempt to locate individuals and groups in historical, social, cultural and technological time/space. In doing so they suggest that age is the most important element in the ways in which individuals and groups are shaped by and shape these configurations of time/space. Generation X has experienced these changes, and so too the Baby Boomers and the generation that parented the Baby Boomers. But they, apparently, respond to and shape these spaces and times differently as a consequence of their differing ages. As Johanna Wyn and Dan Woodman (2006, pp. 496–8) argue, embedded in characterizations of the Baby Boomers and Generations X and Y are assumptions that individuals of a similar age group have to deal with, respond to, and shape a range of social, cultural, political and technological conditions that are different to prior and subsequent generations – in substantial and not so substantial ways: 'It is assumed that it is important to know the distinctive impact of their social context on their lives and it is implied that this experience will continue to shape their lives well into the future when they are no longer youth. Gen Y will always be Gen Y – they will not "grow out of it" – just as Baby Boomers are always Baby Boomers.' An issue here is the emphasis that is placed on early childhood/adolescent experiences. It is assumed that subsequent periods of life are determined by this experience. So, the argument goes, Baby Boomers are less adaptable/adaptive to digital technology, for example, because of their early childhood/adolescent experiences and their current age. The problem here is that on any number of levels the generalization doesn't hold. The exceptions here do not so much prove the rule as make it redundant.

In addition we want to suggest that it is dangerous to assume that these representations of generational characteristics correspond to the *real*; to real flesh and blood young people under 24 years of age. Instead, we suggest that what these characterizations do is attempt to create a correspondence between forms of representation and objects that are made knowable through these representations, and that they are made knowable in these ways because of a range of quite specific purposes. That is, how is it possible to understand this population of young people that I want to employ; that I need to manage, to train, to develop; that I want to educate – in schools, training institutions, universities; that I want to deliver a public health message to; that I want to sell a mobile phone, a car, clothes, financial services, an idea, a political message to?

This does not mean that these objects are not, indeed, flesh and blood, are not biologically, environmentally and psychologically shaped entities/bodies. This does not mean that these bodies do not think, feel, desire, believe, act. This does not mean that the world that these bodies are born into, and grow up in, does not shape the ways that they think, feel, desire, believe, act. But how are we to understand these bodies and these worlds? The plural is important here because a 16-year-old middle-class boy in London is born into, grows up in, and experiences a different world to a working-class 16-year-old girl in Frankston, Victoria, Australia.

It is at the level of generalization, representation and abstraction that *generation* – as an artefact of the activities of market researchers, management consultants, demographic statisticians, psychologists and sociologists – operates to simplify the complexity of human existence and experiences. This is a process of simplification that is energized by the diversity and multiplicity of ends and purposes we hinted at above. This simplification is not necessarily a bad thing – it serves particular purposes at particular times. But this simplification brackets and excludes complexity, diversity and alternative possibilities for creating correspondences between forms of representation and objects they might attach to, even construct.

Annemarie Mol and John Law (2002, pp. 1–22) point to some of the problems that emerge from both processes of simplification, and of attempts in the social sciences to counter this simplification with processes of *complexification* (Callon, 2002). Their Introduction to a collection entitled *Complexities: Social Studies of Knowledge Practices* points to an established scepticism and wariness, even hostility, towards simplifications, classifications and ordering processes, from social and philosophical studies of science, and from postmodern and post-structuralist discourses (especially the feminist versions of these). They suggest that this antagonism, while largely appropriate, tends often to be too easy, too *simple* a position to occupy. The 'simplifications that occur in knowledge practices' can often be productive – they can construct an order out of what appears as complex or chaotic. Classifying, ordering, simplification can be productive and purposeful. In this process, though, that which escapes ordering, classification, simplification can also be productive and purposeful: the complex, the chaotic, the difficult to classify might also be productive and have purpose. But, how are we to know?

In a startling Preface to *The Order of Things*, Michel Foucault (1994, pp. xv–xxii) cites a reference from Jorge Luis Borges (*Other Inquisitions*) to a *certain Chinese encyclopaedia* that classified/divided animals in the following way: '(a) belonging to the Emperor, (b) embalmed, (c) tame, (d) sucking pigs, (e) sirens, (f) fabulous, (g) stray dogs, (h) included in the present classification, (i) frenzied, (j) innumerable, (k) drawn with a very fine camel hair brush, (l) *et cetera*, (m) having just broken the water pitcher, (n) that from a long way off look like flies'. The *fabulous* character of such a list, argues Foucault, compels us to confront the 'ordered surfaces and all the planes with which we are accustomed to tame the wild profusion of existing things'. The *charm* of thinking in such a way, of juxtaposing and creating correspondences between these objects in these ways, is that it ought to confront us with the limits of our own systems of thought: systems that provoke us to think in particular ways and not others; systems that provoke the 'stark impossibility of thinking *that*'. Foucault's influential *archaeology of the human sciences* examined the *conditions of possibility*, the basis on which 'ideas could appear, sciences be established, experience be reflected in philosophies, rationalities be formed'. For Foucault the questions here include: 'When we establish a considered classification, when we say that a cat and a dog resemble each other less than two greyhounds do, even if they both are tame or embalmed, even if both are frenzied, even if both have just broken the water pitcher, what is the ground on which we are able to establish the validity of this classification with complete certainty?'

So, simplifications leave things out. Processes of ordering, classifying, and representing reduce complexity. They make the chaotic, the complex, knowable, governable, and manageable. Generation Y, Generation X, the Baby Boomers, as classificatory mechanisms, render complex lives knowable and understandable. *But at a cost.*

We have not suggested that the trainees in *Jamie's Kitchen* are representative of a generation. We, at most, have made some claims that they, their experiences, their behaviours and dispositions are illustrative of some of the experiences, understandings, behaviours and dispositions of young people in this population: a population that in this instance can be further represented through its marginalized, precarious situation in terms of labour market participation. We have suggested that these labour markets (the plural has always been important) can be made known at one level through their increasingly global, individualized and precarious character.

In the training and work spaces represented in *Jamie's Kitchen* we are presented with representations of young people that operate at a number of levels. In turn, we have tried to examine and analyse these representations at a number of levels. As a consequence we can claim a number of things. To start with, first impressions of these young people can often be misleading. These young people lead complex lives, and this complexity is revealed in both the unfolding drama of *Jamie's Kitchen* and the ways our frame of analysis attempts to account for this complexity. We have tried not to oversimplify this complexity, but to give due weight to understanding the fields of possibility and technologies of the self that shape the ways that these young people think, act, behave and transform themselves.

These analytical frames suggest that while young people come to these (and all) training and work spaces with histories, with values, beliefs and sets of behaviours, these fragments of self – that may have more or less coherence – are shaped, and can be remade in, a variety of fields of possibility, through a range of technologies and practices of the self. So what, at first glance, might look like a lack of a work ethic, or an unwillingness to conform to a set of demands or expectations, may be understood differently as different ways of practising freedom that are always in process, are always more or less amenable to new forms of regulation or management, and may be open to the possibility of change as a consequence of the emergence of new forms of self-knowledge and understanding.

What we understand as talent should not be self-evident. What we understand as a work ethic, a set of values, an orientation or a belief system should not be self-evident. What our discussion of *Jamie's Kitchen* has demonstrated is that these things are not only able to be understood and represented in a variety of ways, but they can also be fragments of a self that a self, itself, can understand differently, perform differently, practise differently, in different fields of possibility. But what we see in generalizations of generation are processes that seek to make these things self-evident and simplified.

Throughout this discussion we have resisted the temptation to provide a characterization of Generation Y that could be drawn from our own experience of teaching hundreds, even thousands, of them during the last decade. It would be easy – trading on our perceptions, suspicions and prejudices – to agree with or counter many of these generalizations with our own: *Generation Y is lazy; they seem to think that they are entitled to good marks because they pay their fees and turn up; they lack initiative; they do not have the critical thinking/ analytical skills of prior generations (us!); they can't write; they are instrumental and not passionate in their orientation to higher learning.* The issue of course is that we know this at the level of generalization; that there are many exceptions to these rules of classification; that the forms of the self that we witness are fragments of a self that are performed in the limited field of university-based learning; that these fields of possibility are institutionally framed and require/demand certain performances of the self; that other fields (work, family, peer cultural) compete for attention/time/commitment/passion in the lives of these young people.

## (Neo)liberal governmentalities: the emergence of the entrepreneurial self

Having problematized the ways in which the classification and generalization of Generation Y attempts to *tame the wild profusion of existing things*, we want to move to an examination of (Neo)Liberal governmentalities as systems of thought that make the unruly, the chaotic, and the real knowable and governable in ways that are largely framed by particular understandings of enterprise and the entrepreneurial self. Like all modes of ordering, this classificatory regime also includes and excludes. It does so, at the level of systems of thought, of rationalities, of mentalities of rule in relation to diverse ends in various contexts. Our argument follows that of Nikolas Rose (1996a) who suggests that (Neo)Liberalism signals a problematization of the practices of Liberal welfare governance, and as such signals a transformation in the way that government (of the State, civil society, the economy, and the self) is conceived. These transformations structure, differently, the political rhetorics mobilized in the Anglo-European parliamentary democracies, including the rhetorics mobilized by the Social Democratic Labour Parties in these settings. Indeed, Rose (1996a, p. 53) argues that 'advanced liberal' problematizations of Liberal welfare governance 'can be observed in national contexts from Finland to Australia, advocated by political regimes from left to right, and in relation to problem domains from crime control to health'. We want to suggest that the work of the Fifteen Foundation – as a social enterprise that works with marginalized, unemployed 16–24-year-olds, to produce a passionate self, to transform a marginalized self into an entrepreneurial self – can be more usefully understood in terms of (Neo)Liberal governmentalities than in terms of Generation Y. That is, these young people can be made known as belonging to Generation Y, but this classification is at too general a level to reveal the diverse ways in which various individuals, authorities, agencies, organizations attempt to train, educate, produce, and encourage forms of entrepreneurial selfhood in individuals who are increasingly imagined as being responsible for identifying and managing the risks that characterize twenty-first-century education and training systems, labour markets, relationships.

We want to argue that (Neo)Liberalism, understood not as a coherent ideological or political movement, but as a rationality of government has been successful in transforming the practices of government in Anglo-European contexts, partly due to its capacity to articulate narratives of 'personal autonomy, enterprise and choice' (Barry *et al.*, 1996, p. 10) to these transformed problematics of government. The point here is that these governmentalities distinguish between generations and populations, not on the basis of age, but on capacities to exercise a well-regulated form of entrepreneurial freedom, and on the need to produce programmes, mobilize technologies to facilitate and develop these capacities and forms of selfhood. Moreover, these narratives connect with certain experiences and/or concerns about the social transformations structured by the processes of reflexive modernization identified by Beck, Giddens and others. Here we are thinking of the tendencies within *autonomized* processes of reflexive modernization for the individual to be cast free (set adrift) from more traditional anchoring points in time, space, place and communitarian (class) relationships. Beck (1992) has identified these processes as individualization processes. Giddens (1994b) talks about the reflexive project of the self in post-traditional, social contexts. This is a DIY project in which individuals are compelled to be free; condemned to choose. Or as Rose (1990, p. 213), in a different context, has suggested: 'we are obliged to be free'.

In his later genealogies on power and the Subject, Foucault (for example, 1991, p. 96) argued that Liberalism, understood not as a philosophy or coherent theory of government, but as a series of solutions to various problems of government, emerged, partly, in relation to 'mercantilism' and the 'science of police'. Rose (1996a) argues that Liberalism 'repudiates' the 'megalomaniac and obsessive fantasy of a totally administered society' (p. 43). Instead, within this emerging art of government, the State must confront certain new realities. These seventeenth- and eighteenth-century realities can be situated in relation to the intellectual and philosophical project of the Scottish Enlightenment, the emerging institutional forms of modernity (Giddens, 1990) and revolutionary moments, and movements, in Europe and the Americas. Liberal government in these transformed material and discursive spaces is faced with subjects endowed with rights and interests that are imagined as existing outside the legitimate realm of the political. Moreover, these various realms – the social, the private, the market, civil society – cannot be governed 'by the exercise of sovereign will' because the State lacks 'the requisite knowledge and capacities' to achieve these diverse ends. Instead, within emerging Liberal governmentalities various forms and practices of regulation are reconfigured with the object of ensuring that these domains 'function to the benefit of the nation as a whole' (Rose, 1996a, p. 44).

Governmentality theorists argue that the late nineteenth century and the first half of the twentieth century witnessed various transformations in the ways in which Liberal governmentalities imagined the problems and art of government. These transformations witnessed the emergence of the notion of *social welfare* as a rationality of government that would seek to 'social-ize' aspects of individual and collective life in the hope of a greater degree of 'collective security' (Rose, 1996a, p. 48). Rose (1996a, p. 48) argues that *social insurance* is an 'inclusive' technology of government, insofar as it has as its object contested notions of 'social solidarity'. These inclusive technologies of government, such as the schooling system, child welfare practices, unemployment benefits, widows' pensions, attempt to *socialize* the management of the dangers and risks associated with competitive and uncertain labour markets, and the 'corporeal riskiness of a body subject to sickness and health'. These risks are reconfigured, within the arts of welfare government, as being, rightfully, the responsibility of a social State.

Postwar problematizations of Liberal welfare governmentality, understood here as signalling the emergence of (Neo)Liberal governmentalities, have witnessed new articulations of risk, and of the rights, roles and responsibilities that attach to a range of State agencies,

NGOs, communities and individuals for managing these risks. These problematizations have particular consequences for young people and their families, who emerge as being responsible for managing a range of risks associated with schooling, employment, sexuality, diets, and peer relations. Within Foucault's investigations of (Neo)Liberalism there is a focus on the work of the German *Ordoliberalen* and the American Chicago School of Economics. Gordon (1991, p. 41) argues that in the case of the *Ordoliberalen*, the problematization of the interventionist practices of the State ought to be situated within the historical experience of National Socialism; while Burchell (1996, p. 22) argues that for the *Ordoliberalen*, National Socialism is not 'some monstrous aberration'. Instead the *Ordoliberalen* imagine the experience of Nazism as the 'quite inevitable outcome of a series of *anti-liberal* policies'. In the historical context of the emergence of the German nation state, these policies include the experience of 'national protectionism, the welfare policies of Bismarckian State socialism, wartime economic planning and management, and Keynesian interventionism'. Postwar American (Neo)Liberalism emerges primarily from the Chicago School of Economics and the work, among others, of Milton Friedman and Friedrich von Hayek. Burchell argues that while the historical context is quite different to German postwar (Neo)Liberalism, the 'general form of the argument is quite similar. One measure of Hayek's influence in the emergence of postwar (Neo)Liberal problematizations of the practice of government is found in the jacket notes from his *The Fatal Conceit* (1988). Here Hayek is described, in part, as being the *ideological mentor for the Reagan and Thatcher revolutions*.

Rose (1996a, p. 50) argues that for Hayek, the 'logics of the interventionist State', as practised within wartime planning and regulation of the economic and the social, were 'inefficient and self defeating'. Moreover, Hayek (1944) saw in such practices the *Road to Serfdom*. That is, interventionist practices of government impel the nation state in the direction of the police state as it emerged, and would emerge, in Nazi Germany, the Soviet Union and China. Robert Heilbroner (1969, p. 272) argues that Hayek saw in National Socialism the operation of an 'internal law' which emerged at a certain level of government intervention into the market order. Once this level was reached, government 'had no alternative but to embrace the economy in a top-to-bottom rigid grip'. Heilbroner argues that Hayek was not against government regulation *per se*. Instead Hayek's concerns were directed towards forms of economic regulation or planning which were: 'characterised by a peculiar inability to call a halt to itself. Once set in motion, an *inner* necessity forced it to expand.' This logic did not stem from the intentions, or motivations of planners, bureaucrats and experts to plan *more*, but rather from the inability of plans to match the contingencies, failures and unplanned for aspects of human interaction in complex extended orders (such as modern markets). In the context of these failures, this rationality of government suggested the need for *better* planning, *more* surveillance and *greater* intervention into these complex systems.

For Hayek (1988) the origins, and the survival, of 'our civilization', as a form of the social which is able to sustain large populations and economic growth, and promote ideals of 'liberty, property and justice', is dependent on what he calls 'the extended order of human co-operation' facilitated by the 'competitive market order'. Hayek argues that this extended form of cooperative human interaction 'resulted not from human design or intention but spontaneously'. This extended form of the social becomes dominant, suggests Hayek, as a consequence of processes which 'unintentionally conform' to various:

> traditional and largely *moral* practices, many of which men [*sic*] tend to dislike, whose significance they usually fail to understand, whose validity they cannot prove, and which have none the less fairly rapidly spread by means of an evolutionary selection – the comparative increase of population and wealth – of those groups that happened to follow them. The unwitting, reluctant, and even painful adoption of these practices kept these groups together, increased their access to valuable information of all sorts, and enabled them to be 'fruitful, and multiply, and replenish the earth and subdue it' (*Genesis* 1:28). This process is perhaps the least appreciated facet of human evolution.
>
> (1988, pp. 6–7)

In articulating a view of epistemology and ethics as 'evolutionary' Hayek (1988, pp. 6–9) argues that the 'formation' of 'highly complex self maintaining orders' can be accounted for only by processes that 'transcend' our ability to 'observe all the several circumstances operating in the determination of their particular manifestations'. This way of imagining the processes that lead to the emergence and maintenance of extended forms of human interaction is situated in relation to a socialist epistemology which Hayek argues is 'wrong *about the facts*'. Socialism and Liberal welfare government, for Hayek, take, as a fundamental premise, the view that reason and rationality can be mobilized in the design and implementation of a system of human interaction in such a way as to provide a better, more productive, form of the social than the 'spontaneous' extended order of cooperative human interaction facilitated by the competitive market order. The conflict, for Hayek (1988) between the socialist welfare State and (Neo)Liberalism is one between, in essence, 'those who demand deliberate arrangement of human interaction by central authority based on collective command over available resources', and the 'advocates of the spontaneous extended human order created by a competitive market'. Hayek argues that socialism's position is both 'factually impossible to achieve or execute', and 'logically impossible'. For Hayek the important issue here is socialism's assumption that 'since people had been able to *generate* some system of rules' governing their conducts, then, logically, 'they must also be able to *design* an even better and more gratifying system'. Here, the *Fatal Conceit* of socialism is, for Hayek, set against (Neo)Liberalism's promise that:

> by following the spontaneously generated moral traditions underlying the competitive market order (traditions which do not satisfy the canons or norms of rationality embraced by most socialists), we generate and garner greater knowledge and wealth than could ever be obtained or utilised in a centrally-directed economy whose adherents claim to proceed strictly in accordance with 'reason'.
>
> (1988, p. 7)

For both the American and German (Neo)Liberals, the market is no longer imagined as a 'spontaneous (albeit historically conditioned) quasi-natural reality'. An attachment to this classical Liberal view would restrict governments to the practice of *laissez–faire*. Within emerging (Neo)Liberal problematizations of the relations between the State and the economy it becomes necessary for government 'to conduct a policy towards society such that it is possible for a market to exist and function'. In this emerging governmentality there is a sense that the central problematic of government 'is not the anti-social effects of the economic market, but the anti-competitive effects of society' (Gordon, 1991, pp. 41–2). The idea of the *death* of the social, given expression in Margaret Thatcher's mid-1980s proclamation that *there is no such thing as society*, signals an attempt within (Neo)Liberal rationalities to govern through the behaviours and dispositions of individuals, rather than society (Rose, 1996a, 1996b). Government, as it is imagined here, ought have as its object a furthering of 'the game of enterprise as a pervasive style of conduct, diffusing the enterprise-form throughout the social fabric as its generalized principle of functioning' (Gordon, 1991, p. 42). Gordon (1991, p. 42) argues that this particular way of imagining the art and ends of government 'proposes that the whole ensemble of individual life be structured as the pursuit of a range of different enterprises'. The range of these enterprises is diverse: from the number of possible relations of oneself to oneself (as a reflexive project), through to the conduct of professional, family, work and cultural relations. These relations are 'all to be given the ethos and structure of the enterprise-form'. These governmental ambitions would have as their end the development of a range of activities, programmes, projects, endeavours, and organizations that promise to produce the entrepreneurial Self.

At this time it is appropriate to re-visit the idea, and the actions of social enterprises, such as the Fifteen Foundation, as exemplifying the sorts of ambitions we find here. In the UK in 2006 the New Labour government – represented at that time by the Chancellor of the Exchequer, Gordon Brown, and Cabinet Office Ministers Hilary Armstrong and Ed Miliband – launched a so-called 'Social Enterprise Action Plan: Scaling new heights'. The action plan (Cabinet Office, 2006), accompanied by a range of documents, initiatives, and a www site, claimed: 'There are at least 55,000 social enterprises in the UK – including well known success stories like The Big Issue or Jamie Oliver's Fifteen.' Launched by the Office of the Third Sector, in the Cabinet Office – a position indicating the relative merit and importance of these ideas about enterprise (it had morphed from its beginnings in 2001 as the Social Enterprise Unit, originally located in the Department of Trade and Industry's (DTI) Small Business Service) – the action plan promised to 'drive change in four areas':

1. fostering a culture of social enterprise, embedding the change that is already underway, especially through inspiring the next generation to start thinking about the social impact of business;
2. improving business advice, information and support available to social enterprises;
3. tackling the barriers to access to finance that restrict the growth of social enterprises;
4. enabling social enterprises to work effectively with government to develop policy in the areas of expertise.

What is a social enterprise?

Social enterprises are businesses with primarily social objectives whose surpluses are principally reinvested for that purpose in the business or in the community, rather than being driven by the need to maximise profit for shareholders and owners.

Social enterprises tackle a wide range of social and environmental issues and operate in all parts of the economy. By using business solutions to achieve public good, government believes that social enterprises have a distinct and valuable role to play in helping create a strong, sustainable and socially inclusive economy.

Successful social enterprises can play an important role in helping deliver on many of government's key policy objectives by:

helping to drive up productivity and competitiveness;
contributing to socially inclusive wealth creation;
enabling individuals and communities to work towards regenerating their local neighbourhoods;
showing new ways to deliver public services; and
helping to develop an inclusive society and active citizenship.
            (Cabinet Office, 2006, Office of the Third Sector)

As Burchell (1996, p. 29) argues, (Neo)Liberal practices of government 'offer' individuals, groups and communities new opportunities to participate *actively* in various arenas of action 'to resolve the kind of issues hitherto held to be the responsibility of authorized governmental agencies'. Thus the widespread privatization of formerly *public* areas of responsibility – the management and training and encouragement of the unemployed, the management of schools, the management of health services systems, the regulation and care of the Self as an enterprise – can be conceived as constituting new forms of 'responsibilization'. Here, individuals, groups and communities are 'encouraged freely and rationally, to *conduct themselves*'. However, as Burchell argues, the 'contractual implication' of these processes is that individuals and communities 'must assume active responsibility for these activities, both for carrying them out, and of course, for their outcomes'. Furthermore, these processes of 'responsibilization', as institutionally dependent processes of *individualization* and *standardization*, incite and encourage the 'individual as enterprise' to 'conduct themselves in accordance with the appropriate (or approved) model of action'.

The *re-imagining* of the social, as a *clone* of the economic, is achieved via processes in which the 'territory of economic theory' is enlarged through a 'series of redefinitions of its object' (Gordon, 1991, p. 43). For Gordon these processes witness a movement from a neo-classical view that 'economics concerns the study of all behaviours involving the allocation of scarce resources' to diverse ends, through to a view that economics takes as its object all rational thought and action 'entailing strategic choices between alternative paths, means and promises' (1991, p. 43). This process of re-articulation promises, within (Neo)Liberal governmentalities, a way of rendering reality thinkable in a manner which addresses 'the totality of human behaviour'. Imagining human motivations, dispositions and capacities for action and thought in this manner provides (Neo)Liberalism with a 'purely economic method of programming the totality of governmental action'. Where Hayek (1988) identifies socialism's *Fatal Conceit* in diverse attempts to plan all aspects of the economic and the social rationally in order to facilitate the greatest common good, this reduction of all forms of human thought and action to the realm of economic choices by an entrepreneurial subject can be identified as (Neo)Liberalism's own *dangerous conceit*.

Gordon (1991, pp. 41–4) argues that *homo economicus*, as the subject of (Neo)Liberalism, is 'both a reactivation and a radical inversion' of the subject of Scottish Enlightenment Liberalism. This reactivation centres on imagining human behaviours and dispositions in terms of rational, choice-making *man*. For early Liberalism this male pronoun was an entirely appropriate way of constructing the Subject as a 'rational, interest-motivated economic ego', engaged in 'private, individual, atomistic, egoistic' exchange relations which emerge from a particular 'natural and historical milieu' (Burchell, 1996, p. 24). Nancy Fraser (1989), and Fraser and Linda Gordon (1994) have argued that this view of the Subject, as masculine, as rational choice-making *homo economicus* underpinned the development of Liberal welfare practices of government. Such practices most often positioned women and children in relations of dependence to this Subject. In this sense, Liberal rationalities of government took as their object, 'the *natural* private-interest-motivated conduct of free, market *exchanging* individuals', insofar as the behaviours and dispositions of such individuals were the foundation which enabled 'the market to function optimally in accordance with its nature' (Burchell, 1996, p. 23, original emphasis). The 'radical inversion' of this principle of Liberal rationalities of government takes a number of forms. Gordon (1991, pp. 43–4) argues that the subject of Liberalism originally signified a subject whose motivation 'must remain forever untouchable by government'. For (Neo)Liberalism, however, '*homo economicus* is *manipulable man'*, a subject who should be for ever open to and responsive to *signals* – from the markets, from risks and dangers, from opportunities. Within this way of imagining and constructing the subject, 'economic government joins hands with behaviourism'. This articulation works to construct a view of the subject as an 'individual producer-consumer' who, in certain quite fundamentally new ways, is 'not just an enterprise, but the entrepreneur of himself or herself'.

Again, our detailed discussion and analysis of the ways in which the Fifteen Foundation seeks to encourage, facilitate, and operationalize processes of self-transformation in *Jamie's Kitchen* makes this point concrete. Moreover, (Neo)Liberal governmentalities emerge from, and give shape and form to, diverse fields of possibility. It is in these fields that a range of technologies and practices of the self need to be invented, translated, imported, mobilized to make up this entrepreneurial self. As we have shown, these fields are able to be made known, and analysable, through the diverse and shifting relations and forms of power; forms of knowledge (about training, young people, work, food); and understandings and practices of the self.

Where the meanings of life are transformed, largely autonomously, into meanings which are structured by the market form, then the subjects of (Neo)Liberal rationalities of government emerge as 'free', 'entrepreneurial', competitive, and economically rational individuals. However, within these changed problematics of government, this 'form is not so much a given of human nature as a consciously contrived style of conduct' (Burchell, 1996, pp. 23–4). That is, this subject has to be engineered via the mobilization of diverse techniques, as the active, autonomous, responsible entrepreneur of her or his own Do-It-Yourself (DIY) project of the Self (Beck, 1992). Rose (1996a, p. 57) argues that the subject, in this sense, is conceived as an active, self-creating individual seeking to 'enterprise' herself or himself. Individual biographical projects are the result, within this rationality, of the 'maximization' of the chances for a 'good life' through 'acts of choice'. Life is accorded 'meaning and value to the extent that it can be rationalized as the outcome of choices made or choices to be made'.

In many respects age may be an important influence in understanding the capacities of a self to practise the many aspects of an entrepreneurial self. For example, Youth has long been constructed in terms of apparent ungovernability. This apparent ungovernability has a tendency to produce a range of tensions within and for Liberal governmentalities. This is so because the *ideal* subject of Liberal governmentalities is the person who has developed capacities of self-reflection, self-regulation and self-government (Hunter, 1993, 1994; Dean, 1999b; Rose 1999b). As Rose (1999b) suggests, this ideal does not have its origins in a generalizable philosophical discourse about the *nature* of Man. Rather this view of a subject capable of bearing a kind of 'regulated freedom' (Rose and Miller, 1992) has, in Liberal problematizations of the art of government, been 'articulated in a whole variety of mundane texts of social reformers, campaigners for domestic hygiene, for urban planning and the like, each of which embodied certain presuppositions' about the *nature* and *capacities* of persons to be governed in relation to these programmes (Rose, 1999b, p. 42). There is, thus, a fundamentally technical dimension to these 'technologies of the self' (Foucault, 1988).

Importantly for this discussion this capacity for the exercise of a well-regulated autonomy was, and still is in many instances, used to divide and differentiate 'the child from the adult, the man from the women [*sic*], the normal person from the lunatic, the civilized man from the primitive' (Rose, 1999b, p. 44). The *fact* that young people (Children and Youth) have not developed those capacities necessary for conducting their freedom in a well-regulated way continues to be an important element of the rationalities that structure the practices and processes of surveillance, discipline and regulation that take young people as their object – in playgrounds and classrooms in schools, in families, in shopping centres, parks and malls.

These ways that have been produced for making young people knowable as *(un)governable subjects* illuminate the 'illiberal' and 'authoritarian' governmentalities (Dean, 1999b) that continue to frame much of the practice of the government of Youth. Authoritarian and illiberal governmentalities embrace those 'practices and rationalities immanent to liberal government itself, which are applied to certain populations held to be without the attributes of responsible freedom' (Dean, 1999b, p. 100). Dean argues that the *dividing practices* (Foucault, 1983) that differentiate among the population (generally) on the basis of a capacity for well-regulated autonomy result in those groups (such as young people) deemed not to have developed these faculties to be *subjected* 'to a range of disciplinary, sovereign and other interventions' (Dean, 1999b, p. 135). Again, Fifteen's interventions into the lives of marginalized, unemployed young men and women is understandable in terms of developing in these young people a passionate, entrepreneurial form of selfhood: a form of selfhood that can enable them to govern and regulate and know themselves in ways that hold out the promise of salvation in the globalized, rationalized labour markets of the twenty-first century.

## Conclusion

The dominance and widespread articulation of the view of the self as an enterprise is not reducible to a particular political ideology, or the project of a single political movement/party. Governmentality frameworks situate these forms of thinking and ways of acting in various contexts, in diverse organizational and institutional settings, and in relation to a variety of purposes and ends. It emerges and dominates the horizons of identity not from a single point of origin, but rather from a past (near and distant) and a present in which social, political, economic and knowledge processes tend to 'profit' the 'industrial and business classes of society'; the new prophets of an 'enterprise culture' who (re)emerge as the 'keepers of the moral conscience and guardians, inter alia, of our education system' (Hall, 1988, p. 4).

Stuart Hall (1988, p. 4) is instructive in understanding the problems and limitations associated with imagining the self in the terms demanded by this ethic of enterprise. In the context of a prolonged and reflexive engagement with the Thatcherite political project, Hall argued that Thatcherism and its transformation of the problematics of government was, in some quite 'obvious and undeniable ways', structured by attempts to 'restore the prerogatives of ownership and profitability'; to produce the 'political conditions for capital to operate more effectively'; and to attempt to encourage a culture underpinned by a view that there is 'no measure of the good life other than "value for money"'. In this context Hall cites Marx on Jeremy Bentham's Utilitarianism, as a measure of the New Utilitarianism which Hall sees as dominating the culture encouraged by Thatcherism. For Marx, Bentham: 'takes the modern [19th century] shopkeeper, especially the English shopkeeper as the normal man. Whatever is useful for this queer normal man, and to his world, is absolutely useful. This yard-measure, then, he applies to past, present and future'.

From a different perspective, John Hinkson (1995) critiques Hayek's *benign, naive,* commitment to the unfettered extended order of the market, suggesting that the market order deconstructs, and de-centres more concrete, face-to-face forms of association. Moreover, argues Hinkson, the extended order becomes radicalized within contemporary techno-cultural processes producing more dangerous possibilities for (biogenetic) *social engineering* than that which Hayek critiques in the practice of socialism.

It is not that passion, enterprise, and conformity are not worthwhile human capacities. It would be difficult to imagine any form of human achievement without these characteristics. Rather, it is that within the frame of an entrepreneurial form of selfhood, as it is imagined at the start of the twenty-first century, initiative, passion, enterprise, and conformity are narrowly imagined in relation to the performance of exchange relations in the extended order of capitalist markets – of all sorts. Moreover, it is a concern that these markets – characterized always by the possibility and promise of greed, deception, monopoly, winners and losers, inequities – also, at this time, penetrate all aspects of human being in the world (reproduction, sex, organ transplants, education, health, unemployment, services for the poor, aid, life management, futures, ...) in a digitally enhanced, globalized market space. And we must all assume an entrepreneurial disposition to this life form. We fail to do so at our own risk.

In these contexts the costs of being a *smart arse* can be profound and ongoing. As we suggested at the start of this chapter, (Neo)Liberal governmentalities increasingly locate responsibility for conforming – or not – in the individual. With more and more aspects of the life course open to a variety of possible choices and risks, then responsibility for choosing to conform becomes individualized. In this sense, we all, as individual entrepreneurs of our own biographies and portfolios of choice and achievement, carry an increasingly onerous burden. Individualization processes increasingly locate the self as the space/site in which the tensions, risks, contradictions, paradoxes of globalized, rationalized capitalism are to be resolved and managed – or not. The apparent difficulties that many of the characters in *Jamie's Kitchen* had, at least initially, in conforming to the demands of these training and work environments, is, we suggest, less an indicator of a range of apparent generational characteristics, and more an indicator of the potential costs we all face if we are unable and/or unwilling to conform to the expectations and demands of globalized, rationalized labour markets.

# Conclusion: *Arbeit Macht Frei* (Work Will Set You Free)

## Introduction

> The extent to which work is part of the modern European's moral being and self-image is evident from the fact that, in Western culture, it has long been the only relevant source and the only valid measure for the evaluation of human beings and their activities ... Work has become so omnipotent that there is really no other concept opposed to it. Hence, any attempt to break out of this value-circle of work lays itself open to the accusation of cynicism ... Any vision worthy of the name must therefore cast off this spell of work, and begin by breaking the taboo on any antithesis to the work society.
>
> (Ulrich Beck, 2000, *The Brave New World of Work*, p. 10)

In Chapter 2 we introduced a number of ideas/concepts from Ulrich Beck's *Brave New World of Work*. A principal concern at that point was Beck's contention that the labour markets of the overdeveloped West are being transformed in the movement from what he identifies as the *work society* to the *risk society*. In the work society the promise of salvation, meaning and purpose was to be realized in relatively stable labour markets that were rendered governable alongside forms of social insurance, welfare and regulation. A risk society, however, is characterized by forms and understandings of uncertainty, precariousness and risk that locate responsibilities for identifying and managing risk with individuals – largely, as we have suggested, via the development of entrepreneurial forms of selfhood. In this brief final chapter we want to consider a number of the paradoxes and tensions that emerge when earthly salvation is to be found in *vocation*.

Our discussion to this point would suggest a number of things. First, unemployed, marginalized young people face the real prospect of the social and material oblivion that awaits those that the competitive, rationalized, globalized labour markets of twenty-first-century, flexible capitalism consider redundant, of no use. Second, the Fifteen Foundation and *Jamie's Kitchen* offer some of these young people the possibility of salvation if only they can develop a passionate, entrepreneurial self. A self that can practise freedom in ways encouraged, demanded by these labour markets. Third, the drama we witness in *Jamie's Kitchen* suggests that many of these young people struggle to transform themselves in ways that promise to secure this tenuous salvation. While many contemporary rationalities/mentalities of government and management locate these difficulties in a series of individual lacks or deficits, the Fifteen Foundation evidences a developing awareness that the passionate, entrepreneurial self can be made up within a variety of technologies, practices and processes. These technologies of the self are of the type that provide support, and set out to account for the differing fields of possibility in which these young people live their lives and develop forms of self-knowledge and understanding. Fourth, the difficulties, issues, problems associated with these processes of self-transformation are analysable in terms that account for the ways in which power relations, forms of knowledge and technologies and practices of the self emerge from, and, indeed, shape different fields of possibility (kitchens, classrooms, vineyards, piggeries, labour markets, families). These spaces in which we develop self-understandings, capacities, and skills are also shaped by relations, processes and understandings of gender, social class, and geography. Passion and reflexivity, we suggest, must also be understood as emerging from and shaping these gendered and classed fields.

In developing and analysing these, and other points, we are concerned that we have left the point of arrival, the *telos* of the processes of training and transformation, largely unproblematized. Developing a passionate, entrepreneurial form of selfhood in formerly marginalized, unemployed young people has, as its ends, both employment, and a sense of meaning and purpose in young people's lives. Are labour markets, and their tenuous, precarious offer of salvation from material and social oblivion the spaces in which meaning and purpose can be found? If so, is this meaning and purpose also tenuous and precarious?

Our purpose here is not, in any sense, to provide a resolution or reconciliation to these tensions. Rather, we want to open up for continuing consideration a number of complexities about the nature of our lives in a rationalized, globalized capitalism: complexities that are quarantined if the prime objective is to consider labour market participation as an end in itself.

## The question of vocation as salvation

John Carroll's *Terror: A Meditation on the Meaning of September 11* (2002) is a provocative essay that constitutes part of a recent collection of books and essays by Carroll that share a common theme: namely, that Western civilization, characterized by its humanist individualism, has no ground, no base on which it can build purpose and meaning, or at least meaning that can sustain the inhabitants of the West in an environment of excess, consumption, spectacle, life*style* and individual choice. Now there is much that many would argue with in such a proposition. At the same time there is much that many could agree with. The location of this proposition in an essay that seeks to identify and examine the *meanings* of the 11 September 2001 terror attacks in the US is also problematic. Indeed, the meanings of 9/11 have been the subject of heated, often deadly, contest since that day. And it is not our intention to make a contribution to this contest in this book.

So why introduce this essay at the end of this book? We mention the essay, not because of 9/11, but because Carroll situates his search for meaning in the *lack of meaning* that he argues confronts the denizens of the overdeveloped West on a continual basis. For Carroll the mean-inglessness that is a constant, central feature of our lives has resulted in a never-ending search for meaning: a search that has resulted in *vocation* offering many of us the *best bet* at meaningfulness in our lives, of salvation in this life.

It is this claim, and its echo of Weber's protestant work ethic thesis, that connects to our discussion of the ways in which the Fifteen Foundation sets out to give marginalized, unemployed 16–24-year-olds some purpose, some meaning in their lives, through the development of a passionate, entrepreneurial disposition to the preparation and presentation of certain styles of food in a commercial kitchen.

Globalized, rationalized modernization processes produce wasted lives on a global scale. The paid labour markets of the twenty-first century are spaces of opportunity, responsibility and obligation, regulation and discipline. They are also the competitive, often destructive (of health, well-being and relationships) spaces that offer the possibility of earth-bound salvation in the face of the prospect of a life lived on the rubbish heap. For most of us our labour is a commodity to be used, purchased, managed and, possibly, discarded. Yet the capacity to sell this commodity is all we have if we want to avoid material and social oblivion.

Carroll (2002, pp. 27–42) structures his discussion around the claim that: 'We, like the preceding four generations of our Western ancestors, have been living out *Heart of Darkness*, Joseph Conrad's nasty little tale from 1899.' For Carroll, Conrad's tale has 'held the entire twentieth century in thrall, to be retold again and again, both in the lived events and in fiction that stencilled reality to its form'. Here, the twentieth century's history of world wars, of totalitarianisms, of genocides, of revolutions, of globalized social and liberation movements, alongside a continual re-imagining and re-telling of Conrad's tale in literature, film and art (Carroll references *The Waste Land*, *Waiting for Godot*, *Apocalypse Now*, *Blade Runner*, and *Fight Club*), provide convincing evidence that we continue to grapple with the meaningless, and the quest for meaning that shapes *Heart of Darkness*.

The nature of this thrall can be understood, suggests Carroll, in the unfolding of Conrad's 'squalid three act farce'. Act One in this context is about the *Point of Departure*. In *Heart of Darkness* the point of departure is the *absurd city*. The absurd city, at the level of the novel, is London and Brussels, but at the level of representation is any/every modern metropolis. Conrad's central character Marlow has a number of telling observations about the costs of order, discipline, surveillance, normality and choice in the *absurd* city:

> I found myself back in the sepulchral city resenting the sight of people hurrying through the streets to filch a little money from each other, to devour their infamous cookery, to gulp their unwholesome beer, to dream their insignificant and silly dreams.
>
> (Conrad, 1899 [2005], pp. 33–4).

Carroll argues that in Conrad's tale the order, security and comfort afforded by the metropolis hides a heart of darkness; and when the self becomes aware of the 'absurdity of such a life – beautiful on the outside, dead within – you are compelled to flee' (2002, p. 28).

At this point we prepare for the staging of Act Two: *The Journey*. Marlow flees to the heart of Africa, a journey that takes him 'beyond the confines of civilization, up a river into the barbaric wilderness – in order to get the blood flowing, in order to live' (Carroll, 2002, p. 28). This *Journey* is both individual and collective – a journey that for Carroll may very well be *unconscious* and *forced*, but in many respects is *inescapable* for all who live in the West. This journey is exemplified in the rush to war that so characterized the twentieth century: a rush to meaning and purpose that originates in the absurd city. So, in this telling, the First World War, and its appeal to a belief and commitment to the higher ideals of God, King and Country – at the terrible cost of slaughter on a grand scale – is seen by Carroll as being as absurd a journey as Marlow's. To make this point he references T. S. Eliot's *The Waste Land* as a commentary on the devastation wrought by the Great War, a commentary which had, in its first draft, an epigraph that echoed the conclusion reached in the *Heart of Darkness*: a proposition that we are ultimately confronted with the futility and absurdity of human existence, and can only respond, '*The Horror! The Horror!*'

The metaphor, and the act, of the journey also has resonances in the idea that we all must make the transition from Childhood – with its apparent disregard (ignorance) of the possibility of a life characterized by futility – to Adulthood – where we must seek some meaning and purpose to our existence. On this transition Carroll observes that in the 'absurd city it is impossible for boys to mature. For women, with their different resources, the path is more obscure, a story remaining to be told. At issue is initiation, the rite of passage which every vital human society takes as necessary for growing its boys up to become men' (2002, p. 31). For Carroll, Marlow is 'typical of the modern Western male in that he has to design and perform his own initiation'. Significantly, in terms of much of the discussion in this book about the training (initiation) programmes of the Fifteen Foundation, Carroll suggests that Marlow's journey becomes self-destructive: 'There are no elders to guide his passage, to restrain him when he strays too close to danger, to welcome and celebrate him at the end' (p. 31). The significance here is that Fifteen provides evidence of the need to both support and structure the journeys that these young people undertake, and, at the end of an important stage in these journeys, to celebrate achievements.

> Their time with us climaxes at the graduation ceremony in July. Fifteen is packed with trainees, their families and friends, previous graduates and our allies and partners from other restaurants, welfare agencies and our business sponsors. Standing on the bar, Jamie MC's the event in his inimitable style as he calls the trainees one by one to step forward and give a little speech. To see the distance these young people have travelled in such a short time is so inspiring and, by the end, there is not a dry eye in the place.
>
> (Fifteen Foundation, 2007)

Carroll extends his meditations here to wonder if the epidemic of mental illnesses in the young, if the prevalence of youth suicide in the industrialized West, are themselves indicators of a failure to successfully navigate a journey that must result in the annihilation of the child self in order to enter a space of adult autonomy, meaning and purpose.

In this story, Act Three is *The Meeting*. In this act Marlow's journey into the heart of darkness culminates in a meeting, not with a saviour, someone to provide answers, meaning, salvation, but with the figure of Kurtz – a *soul*, as Carroll suggests, *gone mad*: 'one who has surrendered to the savagery of a human life beyond any limits'. The meeting here is with a figure who has 'kicked the world to pieces. Left with nothing above or below him, nothing to obey, Kurtz has given himself over to an orgy of rampaging bestiality – his life is one of pure excess, without check' (2002, p. 38).

The journey, in the sense that it has a goal of finding meaning and purpose, is, for many, doomed to futility because it seeks a saviour, a figure in which to invest hope and purpose and meaning. The secular, materialist, consumerist, and for Carroll (2004) the humanist West, has well and truly, as Nietzsche observed, *killed God*; and, we might add, King and Country. The danger, at this point, is that we are seen to be suggesting that God, King and Country (literally and figuratively) can provide the meaning that Carroll identifies as a lack at the heart of the West for the past few centuries. As Carroll has suggested, these figures too have exacted a horrendous toll in the form of countless millions of lives lost and destroyed, and have little capacity to provide the meaning and purpose they promise without such costs. Patriotism, nationalism and fundamentalism would appear to confirm this – particularly in the aftermath of 9/11.

All of which begs the question: in which directions, in which activities, in what purposes can meaning be found? Carroll's reading of Conrad's narrative suggests that in the West over the past few centuries *vocation* has provided the *best bet* for salvation. Marlow's journey is given temporary, fleeting purpose in his vocation as ship's captain: 'He discovers he is good at getting a ramshackle steamer up the treacherous River Congo into darkest Africa and back to the coast.' It is a fleeting salvation, suggests Carroll, because on his return to London Marlow finds himself 'back in the same old absurd city'. His journey – there and back – has, suggests Carroll, 'proved so overwhelming, so debilitating, that he has lost the desire to captain again'. Any drive, passion, energy, purpose or meaning has been left up the river, or, indeed, been dissipated on the journey (2002, pp. 39–40).

What is it in vocation, then, that gives purpose and meaning? For Carroll purpose and meaning in vocation emerges as a consequence of the ways in which vocation regulates conduct. In a Foucauldian sense it is the ways in which the job requires us to know and understand and govern ourselves in relation to something other than our own self-interest that gives some purpose and meaning. Carroll's (2002, p. 37) argument is that when the 'fork is crookedly placed, the pruning flimsy, the figures sketchy, the building at odds, the attention elsewhere, or the door jams, a law has been broken. The job has not been done justice.' When we are able to imagine and understand ourselves as having a responsibility, a duty, a desire, a passion to do the job well, then we move towards finding meaning and purpose in vocation.

Carroll suggests that as we enter the 'gate of vocation' we leave the 'lawlessness' of our egos behind. At this point we enter into a relationship in which we 'come under an obligation to something bigger' than ourselves: 'Finding a central life activity, no matter what, to which they are able to devote themselves, body and mind, heart and soul, commits them to seriousness. Taken out of the flimsy cocoon of individual being, now on higher duty, they are freed, even if only temporarily, from the absurdity and horror' (2002, pp. 37–8). *Work will set you free!*

The horrible, cruel, irony of this declaration above the gates of Nazi death camps should be obvious in this context. But there are other issues at stake here – particularly in social science domains where work can be seen, alternatively, as inherently alienating, or as offering the one sure way of provoking passion and purpose in a life. Carroll illustrates some of these tensions/issues by suggesting that in the immediate aftermath of the 9/11 attacks in New York Marlow, as *everyman*, was made flesh and blood in the figure of the New York firefighter: the individual and collective heroes who in those hours of devastation and death embodied the very idea of vocation as higher purpose beyond individual self-interest. In this context vocation is the space in which to commit, literally, body, mind and soul to something other than the self. If, as Carroll suggests, 'a sense of vocation is to command the times, surely it must speak in the hardest, most hopeless, and, thereby, most valiant circumstances?' (2002, p. 39). Confronted with the ultimate sacrifice in the performance of duty to someone/something other than the self we wonder if we could do what the hundreds of firefighters did, including the more than 330 who died as the Towers collapsed. Many of us, removed from the immediacy of the event, might answer *No*. But, then, most of us don't understand or know or govern ourselves in terms of this sense of duty or purpose as a firefighter. We know and understand and govern ourselves in relation to other purposes, and the sacrifices we might make in relation to these purposes are often intangible or unknowable until we are confronted by the need to make them.

Again, the danger here is that we romanticize (even inadvertently) the nobility of vocation, of purpose in a calling, and of a duty to the calling. This is something we have no intention of doing, because in the globalized, rationalized, hyper-competitive spaces of twenty-first-century flexible capitalism many of us are unable – even fleetingly – to find a calling, to find a *central life activity* to which we can devote body, mind and soul. Alternatively, many of us are unwilling to submit to the laws of a vocation that is, by any measure, dehumanizing, drudgery, dangerous. In this context vocation can look awfully like a *privilege*.

## The question of vocation as privilege

In a world where everything (almost) is commodified, the need for paid work has become greater (one of many reasons that families in the overdeveloped West *need* two breadwinners, or individuals *need* more than one job). At the same time the *aesthetics of consumption* (Bauman, 2005) locate happiness, desire, pleasure, fulfilment, in the *art of consumption* – in the lifestyle that is able to be fashioned and displayed by active, choice-making, capable consumers. For most, this art of consumption is fundamentally dependent on fashioning a working life that can support, on a continual basis, this style of life. Here, Continuous Quality Improvement moves out of the workspace and into the spaces of consumption, style, aesthetics, the self.

There is also a sense that work is the sexiest thing out; that a great job, with great pay and conditions, fantastic opportunities for self-achievement, self-growth, self-actualization is within reach of us all with appropriate levels and forms of skill, attitude, commitment and connection. In this view, work as toil or drudgery is little recognized, because work is *better than sex*. Helen Trinca and Catherine Fox (2005) structure a discussion of the roles that paid work plays in the lives of Generation X workers through this very theme. The title of their book says much about the argument they set out to develop: *Better than Sex: How a Whole Generation Got Hooked on Work*. Their discussion aims to illuminate the tensions generated in new work regimes that demand ever-increasing levels of commitment and performance, and which promise substantial rewards in terms of a sense of achievement, worth and of self: '[Work] cannot compete with sex for glamour, excitement and emotion, but it's close. Just as importantly it can drain people of the energy, time and desire that make sex and intimacy happen. It can push away love, deaden our interest in others and flatten our horizons – and yet still rate as the most important part of our life'. For many of us, suggest Trinca and Fox, 'worklife is more fulfilling, empowering, constant and controllable than their sex life. Better, in so many ways' (2005, p. 3).

As Bauman (2005, pp. 33–6), and others, would argue there is little new in the capacity of different types of jobs, different forms of work, to give purpose, meaning and satisfaction to individuals, teams, groups. For some *vocation is a privilege*: work is profoundly satisfying, enriching, enjoyable and meaningful (at least most of the time). In this sense 'work as self-fulfilment, work as the meaning of life, work as the core or the axis of everything that counts ... in short, work as *vocation*, has become the privilege of the few; a distinctive mark of the elite'. Some jobs, however, are understood (almost universally) as 'abject' and 'worthless', and there is no way that they are the object of 'willing, unforced choice'. You do such jobs because you have little or no choice.

In a study of low-wage work in the USA Barbara Ehrenreich (2001, pp. 208–10) was 'surprised' and 'offended' by the myriad, mundane, taken-for-granted ways in which low-wage workers are routinely required to 'surrender one's basic civil rights and – what boils down to the same thing – self respect'. Workplace rules and management practices that prohibit *gossip* or *talking*; 'little unexplained punishments' including shift and roster changes, task and job allocations and requirements; 'dismissal without explanation', all work to erode what Ehrenreich understands and expects as basic civil, economic and democratic rights as a member (on a usual basis) of the professional middle class in twenty-first-century America. Minimum-wage, insecure, physically and emotionally demanding work has consequences for the ways in which an individual knows and understands her- or himself. As Ehrenreich suggests, 'if low-wage workers do not always behave in an economically rational way, that is, as free agents within a capitalist democracy, it is because they dwell in a place that is neither free nor in any way demo-cratic'. In these fields of possibility 'you check your civil liberties at the door, leave America and all it supposedly stands for behind, and learn to zip your lip for the duration of the shift'.

What is different then in twenty-first-century work orders? Bauman argues that under the dominance of an aesthetic of consumption, work has been invested with new meanings. Where the work ethic dominates, any job can be, should be, done well and the *reward* is in the doing of it well. Where an aesthetic of consumption dominates, the work that you do signals the nature, the range, the consequences of the choices you are able to make. Work has become an aestheticized object of con-sumption/choice, and, as a consequence, a powerful signal to others, and affirmation to oneself, of the worthiness of the lifestyle one can fashion.

## In closing

As we suggested, we do not set ourselves the task of resolving these con-tradictions, tensions, paradoxes. That's a job, a purpose, which is beyond us. For any distance that we can see into the future vocation will con-tinue to offer many of us the best bet at finding meaning and purpose in our lives. In many of the stories we witness in *Jamie's Kitchen* this appears as something that has myriad individual and social benefits. At the same time this meaning and purpose remains precarious and tenuous in the competitive, rationalized, globalized labour markets of flexible capital-ism – where for far too few vocation is a privilege, and for far too many work is toil, drudgery and dangerous. In these labour markets we, as indi-viduals, as discrete, often isolated, often unsupported, often overworked, often stressed units of production are, increasingly, positioned as the site/space in which the paradoxes of flexible, rationalized capitalism are to be more or less successfully managed. Processes of individualization compel us to be free, to make choices. But we must carry the burdens as well as reap the rewards of these practices of the self that are located in, and shaped by, limited fields of possibility.

In these environments the Fifteen Foundation is a social enterprise that has as its core business the production and regulation of fields of pos-sibility in which marginalized, unemployed young people might find some form of temporary salvation; some meaning and purpose in the passionate preparation and presentation of food. Like all human endeav-ours this is a flawed enterprise: for some it may do too little to change the processes that produce human waste on an increasingly global scale. In this book we have suggested that the activities of this social enter-prise do offer small numbers of young people the chance to develop new forms of self-understanding and knowledge. These self-transformations hold out the possibility of an always precarious form of salvation. The larger challenge, and not necessarily one that the Fifteen Foundation should be judged on, is to move beyond, or imagine how we might move beyond, limited forms of self-transformation for limited numbers of young people.

We have little sense of how this might actually happen, beyond the myriad, ongoing attempts by individuals, groups, agencies and organi-zations to make problematic the powerful rationalities of competition, productivity and profit that shape the diverse, rationalized fields of possibility in which we sell our labour and seek some meanings to our lives. What we can offer is limited to an orientation to critique and to ongoing debates about the nature of work; of forms of the self and technologies of the self that labour markets and work organizations demand; and the consequences, costs and benefits for different individuals, groups and populations of conforming to these technologies in various fields of possibility. This orientation, as should be apparent by now, owes much to the contributions of Foucault, and of others who have developed and engaged with Foucault's provocations to think about the relations between knowledge, power, and subjects in the ongoing management, regulation and production of subjects. The final point we make comes from a collection – *The Politics of Truth* – that brings together a number of Foucault's later interviews and lectures (including, 'What is Critique?', 'What is Enlightenment?', 'What Our Present Is').

In an essay – 'What is Enlightenment?' – that takes its reference from Kant's (1784) essay of the same name, Foucault (2007) makes a claim to think of the Enlightenment not in terms of an historical epoch, nor as a unified, transcendent philosophy or generalized scientific or political schema appropriate to understanding and, possibly transcending, such an epoch. Rather, enlightenment, for Foucault, invokes a sense of an attitude or a disposition to the ongoing, permanent task of critique – but critique of a particular kind (this form of critique is further outlined in the other essays in the collection). Enlightenment then, which Foucault suggests consists in the conduct/practice/formulation of an *historical ontology of ourselves*:

> has to be considered not, certainly, as a theory, a doctrine, nor even as a permanent body of knowledge that is accumulating; it is to be conceived as an attitude, an ethos, a philosophical life in which the critique of what we are is at one and the same time the historical analysis of the limits that are imposed on us and an experiment with the possibility of going beyond them.
>
> (Foucault, 2007, p. 118)

The characteristics of this form of critique have shaped the discussion in this book. Our concerns, in closing, provide a sense of the unending nature of the work of critique, and of the position of our discussion as just one intervention, one interference in the problematization of paid work, and the forms of the self that are required to participate in globalized labour markets at the start of the twenty-first century. From this point of view, as Foucault (2007, p. 115) argues: 'the theoretical and practical experience that we have of our limits and of the possibility of moving beyond them is always limited and determined; thus we are always in the position of beginning again'.

# References

Abbott, K. and Kelly, P. (2005) 'Conceptualising Industrial Relations in the "Risk Society"', *Labour and Industry*, 16 (1), pp. 85–104.

Aldridge, J. (2004) 'Q. What Do a Chef and a Pizza Boy Have in Common?', *The Observer*, Sunday 16 May, <http://observer.guardian.co.uk/foodmonthly/story/0,,1214923,00.html> (accessed 13 March 2007).

Alvesson, M. and Deetz, S. (2000) *Doing Critical Management Research* (London: Sage Publications).

AMP (2007) 'Generation WhY?', *AMP.NATSEM Income and Wealth Report*, 17, July.

Angwin, J., Harrison, L., Kamp, A. and Shacklock, G. (2005) *Research Report from the Taking Your Baby to School Project* (Geelong, Victoria: Deakin University and the Smart Geelong Local Learning and Employment Network).

Appadurai, A. (1996) *Modernity at Large: Cultural Dimensions of Globalization* (Minneapolis: University of Minnesota Press).

Appadurai, A. (2000) 'Disjuncture & Difference in the Global Cultural Economy', in F.J. Leichner and J. Boli (eds), *The Globalization Reader* (Oxford: Blackwell), pp. 322–30.

Australian Bureau of Statistics (1998a) *The Youth Labour Market*, ABS Cat No 6203.0.

Australian Bureau of Statistics (1998b) *The Labour Force*, ABS Cat No 6203.0.

Australian Bureau of Statistics (2000) *Australian Social Trends,* Canberra, Australia.

Australian Bureau of Statistics (2004) *Australian Social Trends 2004*, ABS Cat No 4102.0.

Australian Bureau of Statistics (2005) *Australian Social Trends,* Canberra, Australia.

Ball, S. (2003a) 'The Teacher's Soul and the Terrors of Performativity', *Journal of Education Policy*, 18 (2), pp. 215–28.

Ball, S. (2003b) 'The Risks of Social Reproduction: The Middle-Class and Education Markets', *London Review of Education*, 1 (3), pp. 163–75.

Ball, S., Maguire, M. and Macrae, S. (2000) 'Space, Work and the New Urban Economies', *Journal of Youth Studies*, 3 (3), pp. 279–300.

Barry, A., Osborne, T. and Rose, N. (eds) (1996) *Foucault and Political Reason: Liberalism, Neo-liberalism and Rationalities of Government* (London: UCL Press).

Baum, T. (2002) 'Skills and Training for the Hospitality Sector: A Review of Issues', *Journal of Vocational Education and Training*, 54 (3), pp. 343–63.

Bauman, Z. (1997) *Postmodernity and its Discontents* (Cambridge: Polity).

Bauman, Z. (2001) *The Individualized Society* (Cambridge: Polity Press).

Bauman, Z. (2004) *Wasted Lives: Modernity and its Outcasts* (Cambridge: Polity Press).

Bauman, Z. (2005) *Work, Consumerism and the New Poor* (Maidenhead, Berkshire: Open University Press).

Beck, U. (1992) *The Risk Society* (Cambridge: Polity Press).

Beck, U. (1994a) 'The Reinvention of Politics: Towards a Theory of Reflexive Modernisation', in U. Beck, A. Giddens and S. Lash (eds), *Reflexive Modernisation: Politics, Tradition and Aesthetics in the Modern Social Order* (Cambridge: Polity Press), pp. 1–55.

Beck, U. (1994b) 'Self-Dissolution and Self-Endangerment of Industrial Society: What Does this Mean?', in U. Beck, A. Giddens and S. Lash, *Reflexive Modernization: Politics, Tradition and Aesthetics in the Modern Social Order* (Cambridge: Polity Press) pp. 175–83.

Beck, U. (2000) *The Brave New World of Work* (Cambridge: Polity Press).

Beck, U. and Beck-Gernsheim, E. (2002) *Individualization: Institutionalized Individualism and its Social and Political Consequences* (London: Sage).

Beck, U., Giddens, A. and Lash, S. (1994) *Reflexive Modernization: Politics, Tradition and Aesthetics in the Modern Social Order* (Cambridge: Polity Press).

Benjamin, A. (2006) 'Recipe for Success', *The Guardian*, Wednesday 10 May, http://society.guardian.co.uk/socialexclusion/story/0,,1770933,00.html (accessed 20 June 2006).

Benjamin, A. (2007) 'Dream Catcher', *Society Guardian*, Wednesday 18 April, p. 5.

Berta, D. (2001) 'Workforce Said to Enter a New Age with Changing Values', *Nation's Restaurant News*, 11 June p. 76.

Bessant, J. and Cook, S. (eds) (1998) *Young People and Work* (Hobart: Australian Clearing House for Youth Studies).

Bessant, J. and Watts, R. (1998) 'History, Myth Making and Young People in a Time of Change', *Family Matters*, 49, pp. 5–10.

Biemans, H., Nieuwenhuis, L., Poell, R., Mulder, M. and Wesselink, R. (2004) 'Competence-Based VET in the Netherlands: Background and Pitfalls', *Journal of Vocational Education and Training*, 56 (4), pp. 523–38.

Blair, T. (2006) 'People Need Persuasion to Lead Healthier Lives', *Speech Two: Our Nation's Future series*, 26 July, http://www.number-10.gov.uk/output/Page10015.asp (accessed 4 June 2007).

Borman, K. and Reisman, J. (eds) (1986) *Becoming a Worker* (Norwood, NJ: Ablex Publishing).

Bourdain, A. (2000) *Kitchen Confidential: Adventures in the Culinary Underbelly* (London: Bloomsbury Publishing).

Buford, B. (2006) *Heat* (London: Jonathan Cape, Random House).

Bunting, M. (2004) *Willing Slaves: How the Overwork Culture is Ruling our Lives* (London: Harper Collins).

Burchell, G. (1996) 'Liberal Government and Techniques of the Self', in A. Barry, T. Osborne and N. Rose (eds), *Foucault and Political Reason: Liberalism, Neoliberalism and Rationalities of Government* (London: UCL Press), pp. 19–36.

Burrell, G. (2000) 'Modernism, Postmodernism and Organizational Analysis: The Contribution of Michel Foucault', in A. McKinlay and K. Starkey (eds), *Foucault, Management and Organization Theory* (London: Sage), pp. 14–28.

Butler, J. (1990) *Gender Trouble: Feminism and the Subversion of Identity* (New York: Routledge, Chapman & Hall).

Cabinet Office (2006) *Social Enterprise Action Plan: Scaling New Heights*, http://www.cabinetoffice.gov.uk/third_sector/social_enterprise/ (accessed 7 April 2007).

Cadwalladr, C. (2007) 'Ramsay's Kitchen Queen', *The Observer Food Monthly*, Sunday 29 April, http://observer.guardian.co.uk/foodmonthly/story/0,,2065123,co.html (accessed 3 June 2007).

Callon, M. (2002) 'Writing and (Re)writing Devices as Tools for Managing Complexity', in J. Law and A. Mol (eds), *Complexities: Social Studies of Knowledge Practices* (Durham, NC: Duke University Press), pp. 1–22.

Campbell, I. (2004) 'Casual Work and Casualisation: How Does Australia Compare?', Paper presented to conference on 'Work Interrupted: Casual and Insecure Employment in Australia', August (Melbourne: University of Melbourne).

Carroll, J. (2002) *Terror: A Meditation on the Meaning of September 11* (Melbourne: Scribe Publications).

Carroll, J. (2004) *The Wreck of Western Culture: Humanism Revisited* (Melbourne: Scribe Publications).

Cashmore, E. (2004) *Beckham* (Cambridge: Polity Press).

Castel, R. (1991) 'From Dangerousness to Risk', in G. Burchell, C. Gordon, and P. Miller (eds), *The Foucault Effect: Studies in Governmental Rationality* (Hemel Hempstead: Harvester Wheatsheaf), pp. 281–98.

CBS America (2006) *60 Minutes*, http://www.cbsnews.com/stories/2006/04/12/60minutes/main1494021_page3.shtml (accessed 4 June 2007).

Channel 4 (2006) *Jamie's School Dinners: The Campaign*, http://www.channel4.com/life/microsites/J/jamies_school_dinners/campaign/index.html (accessed 6 March 2007).

Channel 4 (2007) *Return to Jamie's Kitchen: Meet the Trainees*, http://www.channel4.com/life/microsites/J/jamie/trainees (accessed 6 March 2007).

Chappell, C. (2001) 'Issues of Teacher Identity in a Restructuring VET System', Working Paper 99-42, *Australia and New Zealand Journal of Vocational Education*, pp. 2–13.

Chappell, C. (2003) 'Researching Vocational Education and Training', *Journal of Vocational Education and Training*, 55 (1), pp. 21–31.

Chater, A. (2007) 'Junior Gourmet', *The Age Sunday Life*, 1 April p. 8.

Cilliers, P. (1999) 'Complexity and Postmodernism: Understanding Complex Systems', Reply to David Sparrett, *South African Journal of Philosophy*, 18 (2), pp. 275–8.

Cincotta, L. (2007) 'Small Fry', *Epicure*, in *The Age*, 27 March, p. 4.

Clegg, S. (2000) 'Foucault, Power and Organizations', in A. McKinlay and K. Starkey (eds), *Foucault, Management and Organization Theory* (London: Sage), pp. 29–48.

Connell, R.W., Ashenden, D.J., Kessler, S. and Dowsett, G.W. (1982) *Making the Difference: Schools, Families and Social Division* (Sydney: George Allen & Unwin).

Connell, R.W. and Messerschmidt, J.W. (2005) 'Hegemonic Masculinity: Rethinking the Concept', *Gender & Society*, 19 (6), December, pp. 829–54.

Connolly, E. (2003) *Hollywood Knives*, http://www.theage.com.au/articles/2003/12/06/1070625578560.html (accessed 23 March 2007).

Conrad, J. (1899 [2005]) *Heart of Darkness* (RIA Press), www.riapress.com (accessed 8 June 2007).

Couldry, N. (2006a) *Inside Culture: Re-imagining the Method of Cultural Studies* (London: Sage Publications).

Couldry, N. (2006b) *Listening beyond the Echoes: Media, Ethics, and Agency in an Uncertain World* (Boulder, CO: Paradigm Publishers).

Dean, M. (1994) *Critical and Effective Histories* (London: Routledge).

Dean, M. (1995) 'Governing the Unemployed Self in an Active Society', *Economy and Society*, 24 (4), pp. 559–83.

Dean, M. (1999a) 'Risk, Calculable and Incalculable', in D. Lupton (ed.), *Risk and Sociocultural Theory* (Cambridge: Cambridge University Press).

Dean, M. (1999b) *Governmentality: Power and Rule in Modern Society* (London: Sage Publications).

Defert, D. (1991) 'Popular Life and Insurance Technology', in G. Burchell, C. Gordon and P. Miller (eds), *The Foucault Effect: Studies in Governmental Rationality* (Hemel Hempstead: Harvester Wheatsheaf), pp. 211–34.

Defourny, J. (2001) 'Introduction: From Third Sector to Social Enterprise', in C. Borzaga and J. Defourny (eds), *The Emergence of Social Enterprise* (London: Routledge), pp. 1–28.

Eckersley, R. (1988) *Casualties of Change: The Predicament of Youth in Australia* (Carlton South: Australia's Commission for the Future).

Eckersley, R. (1992) *Youth and the Challenge to Change* (Carlton South: Australia's Commission for the Future).

Eckersley, R. (1995) 'Values and Visions', *Youth Studies Australia*, 14 (1), pp. 13–21.

Ehrenreich, B. (2001) *Nickel and Dimed: Undercover in Low-Wage USA* (London: Granta Books).

Ewald, R. (1991) 'Insurance and Risk', in G. Burchell, C. Gordon and P. Miller (eds), *The Foucault Effect: Studies in Governmental Rationality* (Hemel Hempstead: Harvester Wheatsheaf), pp. 197–211.

EyesOnSales (2007) *About us*, http://www.eyesonsales.com/ (accessed 6 June 2007).

Faye, E. (1991) 'Producing the Australian Adolescent as Schoolchild in the 1950s: The Fantasised Object of Desire', *History of Education Review*, 20 (2), pp. 66–77.

Fifteen Foundation (2005) *What's Right with these Young People*, (London: Fifteen Foundation).

Fifteen Foundation (2007) http://www.fifteenrestaurant.com (accessed 6 March 2007).

Foster, S. (2001) 'Pragmatic, Problem-Solving Approaches to Curriculum and Assessment Policy', *Journal of Education Policy*, 16 (1), pp. 53–66.

Foucault, M. (1977) *Discipline and Punish* (London: Penguin Press).

Foucault, M. (1978) *The History of Sexuality: Volume 1 an Introduction* (London: Penguin).

Foucault, M. (1983) 'The Subject and Power', in H.L. Dreyfus and P. Rabinow (eds), *Michel Foucault: Beyond Structuralism and Hermeneutics* (Chicago: University of Chicago Press), pp. 208–26.

Foucault, M. (1985) *The Use of Pleasure* (New York: Pantheon).

Foucault, M. (1986) *The Care of the Self* (New York: Pantheon).

Foucault, M. (1988) 'Technologies of the Self', in L. H. Martin, H. Gutman and P. H. Hutton (eds), *Technologies of the Self: A Seminar with Michel Foucault* (London: Tavistock), pp. 16–49.

Foucault, M. (1991) 'Governmentality', in G. Burchell, C. Gordon and P. Miller, *The Foucault Effect: Studies in Governmental Rationality* (Hemel Hempstead: Harvester Wheatsheaf), pp. 87–104.

Foucault, M. (1994) *The Order of Things: An Archaeology of the Human Sciences* (New York: Vintage Books).

Foucault, M. (2000a) 'The Ethics of the Concern of the Self as a Practice of Freedom', in Paul Rabinow (ed.), *Michel Foucault Ethics, Subjectivity and Truth* (London: Penguin), pp. 281–302.

Foucault, M. (2000b) 'Technologies of the Self', in Paul Rabinow (ed.), *Michel Foucault Ethics, Subjectivity and Truth* (London: Penguin), pp. 223–52.

Foucault, M. (2000c) 'What is Enlightenment?', in Paul Rabinow (ed.), *Michel Foucault Ethics, Subjectivity and Truth* (London: Penguin), pp. 303–20.

Foucault, M. (2000d) 'Subjectivity and Truth', in Paul Rabinow (ed.), *Michel Foucault Ethics, Subjectivity and Truth* (London: Penguin), pp. 87–92.

Foucault, M. (2007) *The Politics of Truth* (Los Angeles: Semiotext(e)).

Fournier, V. and Grey, C (2000) At the Critical Moment: Conditions and Prospects for Critical Management Studies, *Human Relations*, 53 (1), pp. 7–32.

Fraser, N. (1989) *Unruly Practices: Power, Discourse and Gender in Contemporary Social Theory* (Cambridge: Polity Press).

Fraser, N. and Gordon, L. (1994) 'A Genealogy of Dependency: Tracing a Keyword of the U.S. Welfare State', *Signs*, 19 (2), pp. 309–36.

Freeland, J. (1996) 'The Teenage Labour Market and Post-Compulsory Curriculum Reform', Paper presented at 'Making it Work: Vocational Education in Schools Conference', March, (Melbourne Victoria).

Furlong, A., Cartmel, F., Biggart, A., Sweeting, H. and West, P. (2003) *Youth Transitions: Patterns of Vulnerability and Processes of Social Inclusion* (Edinburgh: Central Research Unit, Scottish Executive).

Furlong, A. and Kelly, P. (2005) 'The Brazilianisation of Youth Transitions in Australia and the UK?', *Australian Journal of Social Issues*, 40 (2), pp. 207–25.

Gallagher, J. (1996) 'Workers United? Not Us', *New Statesman,* 30 August pp. 30–1.

Gee, J., Hull, G. and Lankshear, C. (1996) *The New Work Order: Behind the Language of the New Capitalism* (St Leonards, NSW: Allen & Unwin).

Giddens, A. (1990) *The Consequences of Modernity* (Stanford: Stanford University Press).

Giddens, A. (1991) *Modernity and Self Identity: Self and Society in the Late Modern Age* (Cambridge: Polity Press).

Giddens, A. (1994a) *Beyond Left and Right* (Cambridge: Polity Press).

Giddens, A. (1994b) 'Living in a Post-traditional Society', in U. Beck, A. Giddens and S. Lash, *Reflexive Modernization: Politics, Tradition and Aesthetics in the Modern Social Order* (Cambridge UK: Polity Press), pp. 56–109.

Giddens, A. (1994c) 'Risk, Trust, Reflexivity' in U. Beck, A. Giddens and S. Lash, *Reflexive Modernization: Politics, Tradition and Aesthetics in the Modern Social Order* (Cambridge UK: Polity Press), pp. 184–97.

Giddens, A. (1999) *BBC Reith Lectures: Runaway World,* http://news.bbc.co.auk/ (accessed 30 August 2007).

Gordon, C. (1991) 'Governmental Rationality: An Introduction', in G. Burchell, C. Gordon and P. Miller (eds), *The Foucault Effect: Studies in Governmental Rationality* (Hemel Hempstead: Harvester Wheatsheaf), pp. 1–52.

Grey, C. and Willmott, H. (eds) (2005a) *Critical Management Studies: A Reader* (Oxford: Oxford University Press).

Grey, C. and Willmott, H. (2005b) 'Introduction', in C. Grey and H. Willmott (eds), *Critical Management Studies: A Reader* (Oxford: Oxford University Press), pp. 1–20.

Hage, G. (2003) 'A Viable Ethics: Journalists and the "Ethnic Question"', in C. Lumby and E. Probyn (eds), *Remote Control: New Media, New Ethics* (Cambridge: Cambridge University Press).

Hager, P. and Smith, E. (2004) 'The Inescapability of Significant Contextual Learning in Work Performance', *London Review of Education*, 2 (1), pp. 33–46.

Hall, S. (1988) *The Hard Road to Renewal* (London: Verso).

Hayek, F.A. (1944) *The Road to Serfdom* (London: Routledge & Kegan Paul).

Hayek, F.A. (1988) *The Fatal Conceit: The Errors of Socialism* (Chicago: University of Chicago Press).

Heilbroner, R.L. (1969) *The Worldly Philosophers: The Great Economic Thinkers* (London: Penguin Press).

Hinkson, J. (1995) 'Governmentality: The Specific Intellectual and the Postmodern State', *Arena Journal*, 5, pp. 153–84.

House of Representatives Standing Committee on Employment, Education and Training (HRSCEET) (1997) *Youth Employment. A Working Solution* (Canberra, Australian Capital Territory: AGPS).

Houston, M. (2006) 'Top Pick, Jamie's Kitchen: Final,' *The Age Critic's Choice*, 12 November, p. 58.

Howard, J. (2005) 'Workplace Relations Reform: The Next Logical Step', Address to the Sydney Institute, 11 July, http://www.pm.gov.au/news/speeches/speech1455.html (accessed 14 July 2005).

Hunter, I. (1993) 'Subjectivity and Government', *Economy and Society*, 22, pp. 121–34.

Hunter, I. (1994) *Rethinking the School* (New York: St Martin's Press).

Huntley, R. (2006) *The World According to Y: Inside the New Adult Generation* (Sydney: Allen & Unwin).

International Labour Office (ILO) (2006) *Global Employment Trends for Youth* (Geneva: International Labour Office).

James, P. (2001) 'The Double Edge of Competency Training: Contradictory Discourses and Lived Experience', *Journal of Vocational Education and Training*, 53 (2), pp. 301–24.

James, P. (2002) 'Discourses and Practices of Competency-Based Training: Implications for Worker and Practitioner Identities', *International Journal of Lifelong Education*, 21 (4), July/August, pp. 369–91.

Johnstone, B. (2002) *Discourse Analysis* (Oxford: Blackwell).

Kelly, D. (2000) *Pregnant with Meaning: Teen Mothers and the Politics of Inclusive Schooling* (New York: Peter Lang).

Kelly, I. (2003) Crème du Carême, *The Observer*, Sunday 12 October, http://lifeandhealth.guardian.co.uk/food/story/0,,1614002,00.html (accessed 13 March 2007).

Kelly, P. (1999) 'Wild and Tame Zones: Regulating the Transitions of Youth at Risk', *Journal of Youth Studies*, 2 (2), pp. 193–211.

Kelly, P. (2000a) 'Youth as an Artefact of Expertise', in J. McLeod and K. Malone (eds), *Researching Youth* (Hobart: Australian Clearing House for Youth Studies), pp. 83–94.

Kelly, P. (2000b) 'The Dangerousness of Youth at Risk: The Possibilities of Surveillance and Intervention in Uncertain Times', *Journal of Adolescence*, Special Issue; Adolescents and Risk-Taking, 23, pp. 463–76.

Kelly, P. (2000c) 'Youth as an Artefact of Expertise: Problematising the Practise of Youth Studies', *Journal of Youth Studies*, 3 (3), pp. 301–15.

Kelly, P. (2001a) 'Youth at Risk: Processes of Responsibilization and Individualization in the Risk Society', *Discourse*, 22 (1), pp. 23–34.

Kelly, P. (2001b) 'The Post Welfare State and the Government of Youth at-Risk', *Social Justice*, Special Issue, 'In the Aftermath of Welfare Reform', 28 (4), pp. 96–113.

Kelly, P. (2003) 'Growing Up as Risky Business? Risks, Surveillance and the Institutionalised Mistrust of Youth', *Journal of Youth Studies*, 6 (2), 165–80.

Kelly, P. (2006) 'The Entrepreneurial Self and Youth at-Risk: Exploring the Horizons of Identity in the 21st Century', *Journal of Youth Studies*, 9 (1), pp. 17–32.

Kelly, P. and Kenway, J. (2001) 'Youth Transitions in the Network Society', *British Journal of Sociology of Education*, 22 (1), pp. 19–34.

Kelly, R. and Lewis, P. (2000) *Neighbourhoods, Families and Youth Employment Outcomes* (CLMR Discussion Paper Series, 00/4).

Kenway, J. and Kelly, P. (2000) 'Local/Global Labour Markets and the Restructuring of Gender, Schooling and Work', in N. Stromquist and K. Monkman (eds), *Globalisation and Education: Integration and Contestation across Cultures* (Lanham, MD: Rowman & Littlefield), pp. 173–97.

Kenway, J., Kraack, A. and Hickey-Moody, A. (2006) *Masculinity Beyond the Metropolis* (Basingstoke: Palgrave Macmillan).

King, D. (2005) 'In Pursuit of Passion: A Frame Analysis of the Popular Management Literature', paper presented at The Australian Sociology Association, Annual Conference, 5–8 December (Hobart: TASA).

King, D. (2006) 'Conceptualising Passion: Problematising "Positive" Emotions', paper presented at The Australian Sociology Association, Annual Conference, 4–7 December (Perth: TASA).

Kirk, D. and Spiller, B. (1993) 'Schooling for Docility-Utility: Drill, Gymnastics and the Problem of the Body in Victorian Elementary Schools', in D. Meredyth and D. Tyler (eds), *Child and Citizen: Genealogies of Schooling and Subjectivity* (Brisbane: Institute for Cultural Policy Studies, Griffith University).

Lallo, M. (2007) 'Making the Cut', *The Age Metro*, 18 March, pp. 8–10.

Lethlean, J. (2006) 'Jamie's First Course: 20 for Fifteen', http://www.theage.com.au/articles/2006/05/16/1147545327260.html (accessed 17 May 2006).

Lewis, P. and McLean, B. (1999) *The Youth Labour Market in Australia* (Centre for Labour Market Research (CLMR) Discussion Paper Series 99/1, Perth, Western Australia: CLMR).

Lichtenstein, B. (2000) 'Emergence as a Process of Self-Organizing: New Assumptions and Insights from the Study of Non-linear Dynamic Systems', *Journal of Organizational Change Management*, 13 (6), pp. 526–44.

Lifeofbob (2007) http://www.lifeofbob.com/jamieoliver.html (accessed 6 February 2007).

Lowe, G. and Rastin, S. (2000) 'Organizing the Next Generation: Influences on Young Workers', Willingness to Join Unions in Canada, *British Journal of Industrial Relations*, 38 (2), pp. 203–22.

Lumby, C. (2003) 'Real Appeal: The Ethics of Reality TV', in C. Lumby and E. Probyn, *Remote Control: New Media, New Ethics* (Cambridge: Cambridge University Press), pp. 11–24.

Lumby, C. and Probyn, E. (2003a) 'Beyond Food Porn: Interview with Cherry Ripe', in C. Lumby and E. Probyn (eds), *Remote Control: New Media, New Ethics* (Cambridge: Cambridge University Press), pp. 124–32.

Lumby, C. and Probyn, E. (eds) (2003b) *Remote Control: New Media, New Ethics* (Cambridge: Cambridge University Press).

Lupton, D. (1996) *Food, the Body and the Self* (London: Sage Publications).

Lyall, S. (2003) 'The Naked Chef's Wicked Act', *New York Times*, 29 January http://query.nytimes.com/gst/fullpage.html?sec = travel&res = 9B07EFDC1039F93AA15752C0A9659C8B63 (accessed 14 March 2007).

Lyotard, J.F. (1984) *The Postmodern Condition* (Minneapolis: University of Minnesota Press).

Marles, R. (2002) 'Young and Union', http://www.actu.asn.au/news/1034301276_11364.html (accessed 15 July 2003).

Marx, K. (1852) *The Eighteenth Brumaire of Louis Bonaparte*, available online at http://www.marxists.org/archive/marx/works/1852/18th-brumaire/ch01.htm (accessed May 2009).

McDowell, L. (2000) 'Learning to Serve? Employment Aspirations and Attitudes of Young Working-Class Men in an Era of Labour Market Restructuring', *Gender, Place and Culture*, 7 (4), pp. 389–416.

McKinlay, A. and Starkey, K. (2000a) *Foucault, Management and Organization Theory* (London: Sage).

McKinlay, A. and Starkey, K. (2000b) 'Managing Foucault: Foucault, Management and Organization Theory', in A. McKinlay and K. Starkey (eds), *Foucault, Management and Organization Theory* (London: Sage), pp. 1–13.

McLeod, J. and Malone, K. (eds) (2000) *Researching Youth* (Hobart: Australian Clearing House for Youth Studies).

McLeod, J. and Yates, L. (2006) *Making Modern Lives: Subjectivity, Schooling and Social Change* (Albany: State University of New York Press).

McNeil, R. (2002) 'Chef who Couldn't Stand the Heat in Jamie's Kitchen', *Evening Standard* (London), 19 November, http://www.findarticles.com/p/articles/mi_qn4153/is_20021119/ai_n12031334 (accessed 10 May 2007).

McWilliam, E. (1999) *Pedagogical Pleasures* (New York: Peter Lang Publishing).

McWilliam, E. and Brannock, J. (2001) 'The Way to a Boy's Heart? New Mechanisms for Making Boys Better', *Asia-Pacific Journal of Teacher Education*, 29 (1), pp. 7–17.

Miller, P. and Rose, N. (1990) 'Governing Economic Life', *Economy and Society*, 19 (1), pp. 1–31.

Miller, P. and Rose, N. (1995) 'Production, Identity and Democracy', *Theory and Society*, 24, 427–67.

Miller, T. (2001) *Sportsex* (Philadelphia: Temple University Press).

Mol, A. and Law, J. (2002) 'Complexities: An Introduction', in J. Law and A. Mol (eds), *Complexities: Social Studies of Knowledge Practices* (Durham, NC: Duke University Press), pp. 1–22.

Mythen, G. (2005) 'Employment, individualization and insecurity: rethinking the risk society perspective', *The Sociological Review*, pp. 129–49.

Nehamas, A. (2000) *The Art of Living: Socratic Reflections from Plato to Foucault* (Berkeley, CA: University of California Press)

Neusner, N., Basso, P., Brenna, S. and Lobet, I. (2001) 'The Boomers' Kids get a Job', *US News & World Report*, 131 (8), p. 28.

O'Leary, T. (2002) *Foucault and the Art of Ethics* (London: Continuum)

Oliver, J. (1999) *Jamie Oliver: The Naked Chef* (Harmondsworth, UK: Penguin Books Ltd).

Oliver, J. (2002) *Jamie's Kitchen* (London: Michael Joseph).

Oliver, J. (2005) *Jamie Oliver: Jamie's Italy* (London: Penguin Books).

Palmer, D. (1991) 'It All Just Feels Above Me', *Youth Studies*, 10 (3), pp. 19–23.

Pati, A. (2007) 'Loan Voices', *The Big Issue (UK)*, 9–15 April, pp. 7–8.

Paton, R. (2005) *Managing and Measuring Social Enterprises* (London: Sage Publications).

Probyn, E. (2003) 'Eating into Ethics: Passion, Food and Journalism', in C. Lumby and E. Probyn (eds),*Remote Control: New Media, New Ethics* (Cambridge: Cambridge University Press).

Quinlivan, K. (2004) 'So Far So Queer', in L. Alice and L. Star (eds), *Queer in Aotearoa New Zealand* (Palmerston, North NZ: Dunmore Press), pp. 87–102.

Quintini, G. and Martin, S. (2006) *Starting Well or Losing their Way? The Position of Youth in the Labour Market in the OECD Countries*, OECD Social, Employment and Migration Working papers, No 39 (Paris: Organisation for Economic Co-operation and Development).

Real World Training and Consulting, (2002) *The Generation Gap*, www.rwtraining.com/Issue20.html (accessed 15 July 2003).

Reay, D. (2001) 'Finding or Losing Yourself?: Working-Class Relationships to Education', *Journal of Education Policy*, 16 (4), pp. 333–46.

Reay, D. (2002) 'Shaun's Story: Troubling Discourses of White Masculinities', *Gender and Education*, 14 (3), pp. 221–34.

Reay, D. (2004) 'Gendering Bourdieu's Concepts of Capitals? Emotional Capital, Women and Social Class', *Sociological Review*, pp. 57–72.

Reh, F.J. (2007) *Passion Pays*, http://management.about.com/cs/yourself/a/PassionPays.htm (accessed 6 June 2007).

Reimer, S. (1998) 'Working in a Risk Society', *Transactions of the Institute of British Geographers*, 23, pp. 116–27.

Restaurant and Catering Australia (2007) *Submission to the Joint Standing Committee on Migration Inquiry into Eligibility Requirements and Monitoring, Enforcement and Reporting Arrangements for Temporary Business Visas*, 16 February, http://www.restaurantKater.asn.au/rc/content.arpx?id+1 (accessed 24 May 2007).

Reynolds, J. (2007) 'The Business of Progress', *The Big Issue (UK)*, 9–15 April, pp. 4–5.

Rich, A. (1994) 'Compulsory Heterosexuality and Lesbian Existence', *Blood, Bread and Poetry* (New York: Norton Paperback).

Rifkin, J. (1995) *The End of Work* (New York: G. P. Putnam).

Roscoe, J. (2001) 'Big Brother Australia: Performing the "Real" Twenty-Four-Seven', *International Journal of Cultural Studies*, 4 (4), pp. 473–88.

Rose, N. (1990) *Governing the Soul* (London: Routledge).

Rose, N. (1992) 'Towards a Critical Sociology of Freedom, Inaugural Lecture', 5 May (London: Goldsmiths College, University of London).

Rose, N. (1996a) 'Governing 'Advanced' Liberal Democracies', in A. Barry, T. Osborne and N. Rose (eds), *Foucault and Political Reason: Liberalism, Neo-liberalism and Rationalities of Government* (London: UCL Press), pp. 37–64.

Rose, N. (1996b) 'The Death of the Social? Re-figuring the Territory of Government', *Economy and Society*, 25 (3), pp. 327–56.

Rose, N. (1999a) 'Inventiveness in Politics', *Economy and Society*, 28 (3), pp. 467–93.

Rose, N. (1999b) *Powers of Freedom: Reframing Political Thought* (Cambridge: Cambridge University).

Rose, N. and Miller, P. (1992) 'Political Power beyond the State: Problematics of Government', *British Journal of Sociology*, 43 (2), pp. 173–205.

Russell, J. (2002) *Review of Sweet Sixteen*, BBCi/Films/Reviews, http://www.bbc.co.uk/films/2002/09/18/sweet_sixteen_2002_review.shtml (accessed January 2004).

Scanlon, C. (2006) 'Gen X, Gen Y – It's Generation Con, Actually', *The Age*, 24 July.

Sennett, R. (1998) *The Corrosion of Character: The Personal Consequences of Work in the New Capitalism* (New York: Norton & Co).

Sennett, R. (2006) *The Culture of the New Capitalism* (New Haven: Yale University Press).

Sheahan, P. (2005) *Generation Y: Thriving and Surviving with Generation Y at Work* (Prahran: Hardie Grant Books).

Sincevich, M. (2007) *5 Ways to Keep Your Passion at Work*, http://www.eyesonsales.com/archives/article/5_ways_to_keep_your_passion_at_work, (accessed 6 June 2007).

Smart, B. (2005) *The Sport Star: Modern Sport and the Cultural Economy of Sporting Celebrity* (London: Sage Publications).

Smith Family (2007) 'Australian Young People: Their Stories, their Families and Post-school Plans', *ACER* (Sydney: Australian Council for Educational Research).

Smith, G. (2006) *Jamie Oliver: Turning Up the Heat* (Sydney: Pan Macmillan Australia).

Stenson, K. (1996) 'Governmentality and the Youth Service', Paper given at a History of the Present seminar, 10 January (London School of Economics).

Stenson, K. (1999) 'Crime Control, Governmentality and Sovereignty', in R. Smandych (ed.), *Governable Places: Readings in Government and Crime Control* (Aldershot: Dartmouth Press).

Sweet, R. (1995) *All of their Talents? Policies and Programs for Fragmented and Interrupted Transitions* (Melbourne: Dusseldorp Skills Forum).

Tait, G. (1995) 'Shaping the 'At-Risk Youth': Risk, Governmentality and the Finn Report', *Discou.rse*, 16 (1), pp. 123–34.

Takahashi, H. and Voss, J. (2000) 'Parasite Singles: A Uniquely Japanese Phenomenon?', *Japan Economic Institute Report*, 31.

Teese, R. and Polesel, J. (2003) *Undemocratic Schooling: Equity and Quality in Mass Secondary Education in Australia* (Melbourne: Melbourne University Press).

The Richardson Company (2006) *Jamie's Kitchen: Fifteen Lessons on Leadership*, http://www.rctm.com//8241.htm?pcategory=22160 (accessed 6 February 2007).

Thompson, P. (2005) 'Brands, Boundaries, and Bandwagons: A Critical Reflection on Critical Management Studies', in C. Grey and H. Willmott (eds), *Critical Management Studies: A Reader* (Oxford: Oxford University Press), pp. 364–82.

Townley, B. (2000) 'Beyond Good and Evil: Depth and Division in the management of Human Resources', in A. McKinlay and K. Starkey (eds), *Foucault, Management and Organization Theory* (London: Sage), pp. 191–211.

Trinca, H. and Fox, C. (2005) *Better than Sex: How a Whole Generation got Hooked on Work* (Sydney: Random House).

Turner, G. (2005) 'Cultural Identity, Soap Narrative, and Reality TV', *Television and New Media*, 6 (4), November, pp. 415–22.

Usher, R. and Edwards, R. (1994) *Postmodernism and Education* (London: Routledge).

Wacjman, J. (1999) *Managing Like a Man: Women and Men in Corporate Management* (St Leonards NSW: Allen & Unwin).

Walkerdine, V. (1997) *Daddy's Girl: Young Girls and Popular Culture* (Basingstoke: Macmillan Press).

White, M.P. (2006) *White Slave: The Autobiography* (London: Orion Books).

White, R. (1993) 'Youth Studies: Debate and Diversity', in R. White (ed.), *Youth Subcultures: Theory, History and the Australian Experience* (Hobart: National Clearinghouse for Youth Studies), pp. viii–ix.

Williams, C. (2005) 'The Discursive Construction of the "Competent" Learner-Worker: From Key Competencies to Employability Skills', *Studies in Continuing Education*, 27 (1), pp. 33–49.

Willis, P. (2000) *The Ethnographic Imagination* (Cambridge: Polity Press).

Wood, B. (1991) 'Yes, Unions Can Survive', *Youth Studies*, 10 (3), pp. 12–18.

Woolworths Ltd (2002) *Our People*, http://www.woolworthslimited.com.au/aboutus/ourpeople/index.asp (accessed 23 June 2002).

Workplace Relations Act (1996) Work Place Relations and Other Legislation Amendment Act 1996, Australian Government Printing Service, Canberra.

Wyn, J. (2004) 'Youth Transitions to Work and Further Education in Australia', paper presented to the *American Educational Research Association Annual conference*, April (San Diego).

Wyn, J. and White, R. (1997) *Rethinking Youth* (Sydney: Allen & Unwin).

Wyn, J. and Woodman, D. (2006) 'Generation, Youth and Social Change in Australia', *Journal of Youth Studies*, 9 (5), pp. 495–514.

Your Business Network (2000) *Are You a Career Entrepreneur?*, http://eriepa.ybn.com/print_this_article/1,3215,263,00.html (accessed 4 February 2004).

# Index